Praise for

GODDESSES IN
OLDER WOMEN

"Wow! This is an empowering book. It helped me better understand the energy of my mature years, how to use it with compassion and humor, and where to get it when it seems to fail."

—Isabel Allende,
author of *Daughter of Fortune*

"*Goddesses in Older Women* will inspire now older and wiser women's movement women to once again transform society."

—Marianne Williamson, editor of
Imagine: What America Could Be in the 21st Century

"*Goddesses in Older Women* offers a brilliant and exhilarating perspective that will revolutionize every woman's thinking about aging and free her to see the face in her mirror in a completely different way."

—Rachel Naomi Remen, M.D.,
author of *My Grandfather's Blessings and Kitchen Table Wisdom*

"Bolen sees the aging woman as not only a font of wisdom but also a vibrant creative force whose energies are free to move beyond the personal into the interpersonal and the transpersonal. Whether laughing like the mirthful Uzume or meditating with Hestia at the hearth, this 'juicy crone' models power and passion in these pages."

—*Booklist*

Willie C. Gordon

About the Author

JEAN SHINODA BOLEN, M.D., is an
internationally known Jungian analyst,
clinical professor of psychiatry at the University of California at San Francisco, and a
former member of the board of the Ms.
Foundation for Women. She is also the
author of *The Tao of Psychology, Goddesses
in Everywoman, Gods in Everyman, Ring of
Power, Crossing to Avalon, Close to the
Bone,* and *The Millionth Circle.* She lives
in Mill Valley, California. Contact Jean
Bolen at www.jeanbolen.com.

GODDESSES IN OLDER WOMEN

ARCHETYPES IN WOMEN OVER FIFTY

JEAN SHINODA BOLEN, M.D.

HARPER
PERENNIAL

HARPER ●① PERENNIAL

ACKNOWLEDGMENTS

Gail Winston, my editor at HarperCollins,
and Katinka Matson, my literary agent at Brockman, Inc.

This work is grounded in
C. G. Jung's archetypes of the collective unconscious,
concepts of psychological types, synchronicity, stages of life,
and my decades in practice as a Jungian analyst.

A hardcover edition of this book was published in 2001 by HarperCollins
Publishers.

First Quill edition published 2002.

Designed by Nancy Field

The Library of Congress has catalogued the hardcover edition as follows:

Bolen, Jean Shinoda.
    Goddesses in older women : archetypes in women over fifty / Jean
  Shinoda Bolen.—1st ed.
      p.   cm.
    Includes bibliographical references.
    ISBN 0-06-019152-X
    1. Goddesses.   2. Aged women—Religious life.   I. Title.
  BL473.5 .B64 2001
  155.67'082—dc21   00-058156

ISBN 0-06-092923-5 (pbk.)   ISBN 978-0-06-092923-7

    05 06 ❖/RRD 10 9 8

DEDICATION

GLORIA STEINEM
*archetypal big sister, visionary, supportive activist, vulnerable woman,
consciousness-raiser, inspiration, role model, friend.
For all you have done for women.*

Thank you.

CONTENTS

PART 3 She Is a Goddess Growing Older: *Goddesses in Everywoman*, Revisited

PART 4 She Is a Circle

INTRODUCTION

How to Be a Juicy Crone

On becoming fifty, most of the women I know are celebrating instead of denying their age. Turning fifty may have been an over-the-hill marker for their mothers, but it's a day to break out the champagne for them. Becoming fifty is inspiring reunions of girlfriends who have reached this passage year together. It's party time for some, and a time for rituals or retreats for others. Most women at fifty are also celebrating how young they still feel and look. Even so, there is a certain unease at growing older. Women reaching fifty do not have many clues about who they might become, or know of the potential energies that menopause can bring, or understand that they are on the threshold of a phase of their lives in which they may become more themselves than at any other time before.

I have written *Goddesses in Older Women* so women may recognize and name what is stirring inside of them. The wellsprings for these feelings are the goddess archetypes within us, the patterns and energies in our psyches. By knowing who the goddesses are, women can become more conscious than they would otherwise be of the potentials within them that, once tapped, are sources of spirituality, wisdom, compassion, and action. When archetypes are activated, they energize us and give us a sense of meaning and authenticity.

At some point after fifty, or postmenopausally, every woman crosses a threshold into the third phase of her life, thereby entering uncharted territory. In a youth-oriented patriarchy, especially, to become an older woman is to become invisible; a nonentity. From the archetypal perspective that I elucidate, however, it is possible for this third trimester to be a time of personal wholeness and integration; when what you do is an expression of who you deeply are. In the active years after fifty, you may become more visible in the world than ever before, or you may develop your inner life and pursue creative interests, or you may be the centering influence in a family constellation. Far from being a nonentity, it is in the third trimester that it is possible to be more defined and substantial a person than ever. In the Native American tradition, a woman becomes fully grown at the age of fifty-two.[1]

Women who came of age during the feminist movement in the late sixties and seventies have been rejecting stereotypes, exploring new possibilities, challenging old limitations and insisting on defining themselves anew each decade. As the baby-boomer generation of women pass into this third crone phase, I anticipate that the connotation of the word "crone" itself will shift. It is my intention in writing *Goddesses in Older Women* to help to redeem the crone word, the third stage of life, and, most of all, to help women recognize the archetypes that become accessible as sources of energy and direction at this time.

MENOPAUSE

Unlike turning fifty, becoming postmenopausal is a very private affair. For most women, menopause occurs at fifty, plus or minus five years, or between ages forty-five and fifty-five. Usually a woman decides she has passed through menopause and is on the other side only after she has ceased menstruating for a year. But most women experience irregularities that make it difficult to be exact. There are stops and starts to regular periods, and often a question of spotting versus a scanty period. To further confuse the issue, replacement hormone therapy regimes may induce menstrual periods, while removal of the uterus or chemotherapy brings menstrual periods to an end artificially. Some perimenopausal women may mourn the ending of their childbearing years, others are relieved. Some may worry about the possibility of having a change-of-life baby, others hope they will. Physical and psychological discomfort may occur, and the reaction of others, especially men, makes menopause a confusing physiological event that most women do not celebrate.

This does not necessarily have to be the case. There have been and still are cultures with women elders or wisewomen in which menopause is acknowledged as marking the transition into a new and honored status. This happens when women and nature are seen as positive reflections of each other. As in many Native American tribal traditions, menarche (the onset of menstruation) and menopause mark major transitions in the awesome cycle—the *blood mysteries*—in which women, the moon, and the divine feminine are related.

Whether it is a crescent sliver or gloriously full, we know we are only observing a facet of the same spherical moon. In the same way, ancient people saw the goddess as one, yet triple in her three phases of maiden-mother-crone. Cycles were observed in the moon, in the seasons and fertility of the earth, and in women's bodies, which shared qualities with both.

In ancient times and in indigenous traditions, when a girl began to bleed, she became a woman in the maiden phase of her life, the metaphoric equivalent of the waxing moon. A ritual marked her new status. After the onset of menstruation, her menstrual periods would come into synchrony with other menstruating women (as happens with women who live together in dormitories or sororities) and with the moon. Then, once a month, she would bleed during her menses, or "moon time," until she became pregnant. Her first pregnancy was an initiation into the second phase of her life, corresponding to the full moon and the second phase of the triple goddess. When she became pregnant, it was said that she retained the blood in her body to make a baby. Only after she gave birth and stopped lactating would she begin her monthly bleeding again. She would then continue to do so until she became pregnant once more, or until she entered menopause. The cessation of menstruation now marked another awesome change. Once again, it was said that a woman retained blood in her body; only this time, it was not to make a baby but to make wisdom. Menopause marked the transition into the third phase of a woman's life, corresponded to the waning moon, and was the initiation into the wisewoman or elder phase of a woman's life.

Native American traditions, once a woman ceased to men-
e was eligible to become a clan mother or member of the
er lodge. Her acquired wisdom was an asset and her concern now extended beyond her personal family to all the children and
the well-being of the tribe. In such societies, there was clearly a place
and honored role for a postmenopausal woman.

THE THREE PHASES OF WOMEN'S LIVES

I think of maiden-mother-crone, the three phases of the triple goddess, as stages in a woman's life regardless of whether she has borne
children. Most women move through a maiden phase in which they
are uncommitted and are sampling life; changing jobs and educational
goals, trying out relationships. The archetype is the *puella eterna*, the
eternal girl. With birth control and the autonomy that most young
women have, the maiden phase can now be extended decades into the
usual age when women formerly became mothers. They can also stay
in the maiden phase even when they become biological mothers, if
they are not maternal, responsible, or mature.

I sometimes speak of the three phases as "maiden, mother (or
matron), and crone" or "young woman, mature woman, and wisewoman" in order to make the point that a woman does not have to be
a biological mother in the second phase, though "mother" is an appropriate metaphor for what the second phase usually involves. Women in
the second phase make commitments and grow in maturity through
nourishing them. The commitment could be to a person, a career, a
cause, a talent—to anything that is personally significant. Children—
and any meaningful commitment—take more effort and devotion than
most women anticipate, at the same time that they are a source of joy
and pain, and an impetus to growth and creativity. The second phase is
one of involvement and active effort.

Most women enter the third phase of the wisewoman or crone only
after they pull back from the concerns of the second phase and shift
gears inwardly. The hormonal changes and symptoms of menopause
usually make us cope with the reality of entering this third phase phys-
iologically—though the cessation of menses is not the same as becom-

ing a wisewoman, or of even having the life of a woman in the third phase. The psychological stages of maiden-mother-crone are no longer closely tied to age. Women who have had their children late in their childbearing years or adopted them late, are still very much involved in second-phase commitments. They are entering menopause with children in elementary school or as a child is entering adolescence, and may want to go inward just as more demands are made on them by others. Women who returned to college and graduate schools at midlife or made career shifts may be involved in new careers and menopausal at the same time. Usually menopause coincides with winding down: the last child leaves home, and early retirement is not very far away. In any event, with the onset of menopause, there will be below-the-surface shifts occurring in the psyche as well as the body.

It is in this third phase of a woman's life that the crone goddess archetypes most naturally make themselves known. When archetypes are activated by a new stage in life, there is vitality and energy in them. The more you know about yourself at this stage of life, the easier they will be to activate. The more interest you have in them, and the more they represent the growing edge of your own independent thinking and purpose, the larger their presence can become within you. Their names, images, qualities, and stories—which I describe in the chapters to follow—are important to know, because this knowledge brings them alive in your imagination and gives you a vocabulary for what you are already experiencing.

When I hear women call their hot flashes "power surges," it strikes me that our humor is a step ahead of the vaguely apprehensive attitude we have toward menopause. What if each time a woman had a hot flash, she really felt it was a power surge—as if her archetypes of wisdom and inner authority were being energized?

How to Be a Green and Juicy Crone

There is something delightfully outrageous about the phrase "green and juicy crone." The descriptive adjectives *green* and *juicy*, used together with *crone*, boggle the mind before they grab hold. Several years ago, I gave a talk on the wisewoman archetype,[2] and out came this phrase, which was immediately embraced by the almost all-women audience. I think this aptly describes a woman in her crone years, who has integrated the archetypes and tasks of maiden and mother as aspects of her personality. Her attitude and spirit are like the fresh green of spring; she welcomes new growth and possibilities in herself and in others. There is something solid about her being an adult whose life has borne fruit through cultivation and pruning, as well as tempering and work; she knows from experience that it takes commitment and love for budding possibilities in herself or in others to grow into reality. There is also something about her passion for life that is like the juiciness of summer's ripe fruit. Now, at menopause, she enters a new phase and is alive to new possibilities.

To be a green and juicy crone comes from having lived long enough to be deeply rooted in wholehearted involvements, of living a personally meaningful life, however unique, feminist, or traditional it may appear to others. It has to do with knowing who we are inside and believing that what we are doing is a true reflection or expression of our genuine self. It is having what Margaret Mead called PMZ, or *postmenopausal zest* for the life you have.

My inspiration for "green and juicy" was the *viriditas* ("greening power") theology of Hildegard of Bingen, a remarkable woman who lived eight hundred years ago. Hildegard was a Renaissance woman before there was Renaissance and a feminist before there was feminism. In *Illuminations of Hildegard of Bingen,* theologian Matthew Fox introduced Hildegard to a reading audience. Hildegard (1098–1179 C.E.) was a woman of considerable influence, a Benedictine abbess, a mystic, a physician, a theologian, a musician, a botanist, and a painter. At a time when few women could write and most were denied a formal education, she corresponded with emperors, popes, archbishops, nobility, and nuns. She traveled, preached widely, established monasteries, and was politically astute and outspoken. At key junctures in her life, she defied the authority of her church superiors and prevailed.

Hildegard's authority and creativity grew as she grew older. She had an exceptionally long life for her time (eighty-one years), which will not be at all unusual for women entering their crone years now. To achieve what she did and be the person she was, Hildegard had to develop her intellect and talents. This was possible then only because she lived in a religious community of women, which allowed her to pursue her interests. She was able to take herself seriously, to draw spiritual support from meditation and prayer, and over and over again, to react to external events. Hildegard, as an exemplar of a green and juicy crone, was what I call a choicemaker.

CHOICEMAKER

To be a *choicemaker* in the third phase means that what you choose to do or be must correspond with what is true for you at a soul level. What you do with your life is then *meaningful;* it is something you know in your bones, at your core, in your soul. It is impossible for anyone else to know your truth or judge it, particularly since the same role and set of circumstances can fulfill one woman and constrict another. Why this is so can be understood through the archetypes of the collective unconscious, which C. G. Jung, the Swiss psychologist, saw as inherent potentials in the psyche. When an active archetype rather than an external expectation is the basis for a role we take, there is depth to the choice. When we find meaning as well, then the archetype which Jung called the Self is also engaged. I think of the Self as a generic term for whatever we experience as sacred, divine, or spiritual. It has to do with personal values and integrity, and what is deeply right for each of us in particular. There are significant choice points in everyone's life, when what we choose and who we become are linked. At these moments of truth, we find ourselves at a fork in the road and have to choose which path to take. There is always a cost to such choices. The price we pay is the path not taken, that which we give up.

A green and juicy crone has a life that is soul-satisfying. Maybe you can fall into such a life with the help of serendipity and grace. But for a contemporary crone-aged woman, a soul-satisfying life usually involves making choices, as well as taking risks. For so many of us, the obligations and demands made on our time and energy have a way of expanding to take up our whole life. There are conflicting loyalties to sort out and unchosen circumstances and limitations, including the reactions of others who may be angry at us for not fulfilling their expectations.

Think of yourself as the main character in a novel or motion picture that is being written by the choices you make or the roles you play, and by whether you are committed to your own story. Your parents' positive aspirations for you, or their negative expectations, or the examples they set, may have provided you with a ready-made script to follow. That prescribed path may have helped you to develop in ways that were positive, or may have done you great harm if there was a major discrepancy between who you were supposed to be and your own potential and needs. Others in your life, especially any that you gave authority to, or loved, further defined you. As a result, you may see yourself in a perennial supporting role, or as a victim, instead of as the protagonist in your own story. There are, as fiction writers often note, only so many basic plots, and only so many typical or archetypical characters—which is true in life, as well.

It may be that the past is but the prelude to the most authentic period of your life. Even if until now you more or less went along with the expectations of others, you can now choose to be yourself. As Jenny Joseph says in the first line of *Warning*: "When I Grow Old, I Shall Wear Purple." By this she means that she will finally wear what pleases her and do what delights her, thereby becoming authentically herself.

Women become truer to themselves after menopause not only because they grow older but because their circumstances change. Children grow up and leave home. Marriages often become more companionable with age. The death of a parent may bring freedom from guilt or caretaking, or provide you with an inheritance. You may become a widow. Your spouse may leave you, or you him, forcing a change in circumstances. You may fall in love and change your life or even your lifestyle. Your career may be winding down. You may begin a meditative spiritual practice, or find that one has now taken hold. Psychotherapy may cause you to reassess your life. Or, as I wrote in *Close to the Bone*, a life-threatening illness may be a turning point that liberates you to find what does have meaning and nourishes your soul.

When you see yourself as a choicemaker, you take on the role of protagonist in your life story. You know that what you choose to do, or not do, has an effect. You learn that when circumstances are unavoidable or even terrible, then how you respond inwardly is a choice that may make all the difference.

The choices that shape your life and give it meaning may also depend on the possibility of imagining what you could do or having a name or image for what is stirring in your psyche. This is where stories and role models may make the difference. This is also when you need spiritual resources, especially if others do not support the changes that you are making. The crone phase is associated with the archetype of the wisewoman, which, as you will see in subsequent chapters, has been cross-culturally expressed through mythology and religion.

FROM PENIS ENVY TO *GODDESSES IN EVERYWOMAN*

My perspective comes from being a Jungian analyst and a feminist, an observer and an activist. I was in a psychiatric residency in the mid-sixties when the women's movement began. Betty Friedan's *The Feminine Mystique* struck a chord when she described "the problem with no name": Women were supposed to be fulfilled by being wives and mothers and blamed themselves when they were not. *Life* magazine and other publications were wondering, "What's wrong with women?" Meanwhile, I was seeing women in therapy who were depressed and anxious. They were said to be suffering from "suburban housewife syndrome," an unofficial and pejorative diagnosis, meaning that they had only trivial concerns to be unhappy about. I was being taught the psychology of women by male Freudian analysts who believed that all women were inherently inferior because they lacked a penis. Their penis envy was supposedly helped temporarily by becoming pregnant and having a son. Men didn't challenge this theory and women were put into a bind if they did—since in Freud's psychology, a woman who protested suffered from a masculinity complex.

That same year, 1963, President John F. Kennedy's Commission on the Status of Women published *The American Woman*, a report revealing that women were paid less for doing the same work as men, were not promoted, and were not allowed entry into many occupations and professions. The discrimination against women documented in this report and the publication of *The Feminine Mystique*, in which Friedan analyzed the stereotypical roles that society expected women to fill (and included a strong critique of Freudian theory), were the beginning of a growing torrent of information, women's meetings, and protests, which led to the women's movement.

Beginning in the mid-1960s, consciousness-raising groups were formed. Women met in small groups and told about the sexism they had experienced personally. With group support, women wrote articles that were collected in anthologies; court cases focusing on discrimination against women were initiated; the National Organization for Women (NOW) was formed; and affirmative action was extended to women. These events and their effects resulted in the 1970s becoming the decade of the women's movement. Meanwhile, I married, finished my residency, started a private practice, and began my analytic training at the C. G. Jung Institute in San Francisco.

In the 1970s, while I was immersed in a busy life that included two children and a profession, the issues raised by the women's movement were vividly brought to me by my women patients. In the early 1980s, when the American Psychiatric Association would not support the Equal Rights Amendment and held its conventions in nonratified states, I became an activist, cofounded an organization, led a boycott, and enlisted Gloria Steinem's help. Later I became a member of the board of the Ms. Foundation for Women, which further broadened my awareness of how strong and how oppressed women could be.

Goddesses in Everywoman: A New Psychology of Women was published in 1984. In it I described how women were acted upon by two powerful forces: the archetypes of the collective unconscious and the stereotypes of the culture. This Jungian-feminist perspective gave me "binocular vision" into the psychology of women. Just as each eye sees the same thing from a different angle and the merging of the two visual fields results in depth perception, identifying the archetypes and noticing what culture rewarded or punished provided a depth of insight that had not been afforded earlier. Others came to the same conclusion.

Goddesses in Everywoman had a powerful effect on readers who recognized themselves in the archetypal patterns described there. I had based them on Greek goddesses who resided in the patriarchal Olympian world where they related, adapted, or were dominated in ways that women of today could identify with. Some of these goddesses had qualities that fit traditional roles for women, such as Hera, the archetype of the wife; Demeter the mother; Persephone the maiden; and Aphrodite the lover, but others had attributes that society and psychology said belonged to men—Artemis the huntress could protect women from male violators and seek her own goals, while Athena was entrusted with power and had the clearest mind of any Olympian. It was a perspective that broadened Jung's psychology of women and had exceptions to his theory,* but it drew from the archetypal structure of the psyche that he discerned and described.

The archetypes are inherent patterns or predispositions in the human psyche. The formation of crystals in a solution was an analogy Jung used to help explain the difference between archetypal patterns and activated archetypes: an archetype is like the invisible pattern that determines what shape and structure a crystal will take when it does form—something it can do only if conditions exist where this can happen. Once the crystal forms, it is recognizable. Archetypes might also be compared to the "blueprints" in seeds. Growth from seeds depends on soil and climate conditions, the presence or absence of certain nutrients, loving care or neglect on the part of the gardener, the size and depth of the container, and the hardiness of the variety itself. Under optimal conditions, the full potential in the seed is realized. While the psyche is considerably more complex, archetypes in women are also activated by a variety of interacting elements—inherited predisposition, family and culture, hormones, circumstances, and the stages of life.

Goddesses in Everywoman was a psychology of women that accounted for the diversity among women and complexity in them. It was truer to the female experience than any psychology that had a single, limited model for a normal woman. It was especially helpful for women in the first and second phases of adulthood. I also described

---

*Jung postulated that there was a contrasexual archetype in everyone; this was the *animus* in women and the *anima* in men. According to this theory, woman's thinking, assertiveness, and spirituality were attributes of her animus, a less conscious part of her psyche than her feminine ego. Animus thinking, by definition, is inherently inferior, which did not describe Athena or women whose superior function is thinking. Jung's anima-animus theory attributes feeling and relatedness in men to their correspondingly less conscious anima. Again, the exception is a man whose superior function is feeling.

how each particular goddess archetype might be expressed in later years, but that was not at all the focus of the book. These archetypes often do continue to be recognizable in us in our later years. In part 3 of this book, I provide a thumbnail sketch of each one, describe their positive qualities and characteristic problems, and tell how they may continue to shape the crone years or even appear as a "late-blooming" archetype in the third phase of our lives.

FROM *GODDESSES IN EVERYWOMAN* TO *GODDESSES IN OLDER WOMEN*

One of the major effects of *Goddesses in Everywoman* was entirely unexpected. Although I had written the book as a psychology text, I saw it become one of the foundations of the women's spirituality movement. It contributed to bringing the word "goddess" back into the vocabulary as other than a Hollywood label for a beautiful movie star. The goddess as feminine divinity is returning in stages, beginning with the usage and familiarity of the word itself. In the 1980s, the word "goddess" had a forbidden aura about it—as it still does in many minds—but the Jungian psychological term "goddess archetype" was acceptable. Discomfort with the word "goddess" was felt by many women for no reason that they knew of; much the same way that very young children seem to know that four-letter words are secret and forbidden, even before they say them out loud and observe the reactions of adults.

Interest in goddess archetypes led women to create art and rituals, to focus on goddess images in meditation and make home altars upon which personal symbols were placed, actions that evoked long-buried yearnings in women for the sacred feminine. Or, conversely, women made the connection between a particular goddess and themselves after reading *Goddesses in Everywoman* and were awed to realize that a cherished object, a dream image, or the art they had on their walls were symbols of the goddess archetype that was most important to them. When a connection is made between a goddess archetype and a symbol or image, a depth of feeling and a sense of meaning accompanies that connection, which was the case. Of further subjective significance, women felt that what they were doing had a sacred dimension when a particular role was also an active archetype in them. Once a connection was *felt* between the psychological and the spiritual meaning of a goddess archetype, it was the beginning awareness that there could be a goddess-centered or goddess-connected spirituality—which is unthinkable in the religious context of monotheism.

When I wrote *Goddesses in Everywoman*, I was not familiar with goddess spirituality myself but as I related in *Crossing to Avalon* (1994), this changed when I went on a pilgrimage to sacred sites in Europe in the mid-1980s. At Chartres Cathedral, which had been built over an ancient goddess site, I felt a sense of warmth and pressure in the center of my chest, the heart chakra area. I came to think of this as my "tuning fork" response, a bodily sensation that guided me to where the energy was at other sacred sites and places. It was an initiation into a dimension of the sacred that was of the earth and of the body, and it was like the first wondrous experience of quickening in pregnancy. It led me to recall other events in my own life that were mystical and timeless, though I had never defined them as sacred. One reason is because in monotheism the body, especially a woman's body, is not considered holy. I came to see these events as archetypal goddess experiences, in which a feminine archetype imbues the moment with depth and meaning. My experience was far from unique, for people have always had such holy moments, but Judeo-Christianity made it heretical to say so.

Since the publication of *Goddesses in Everywoman*, I've led women's workshops and spoken at women's spirituality conferences. I often tell the story of Demeter and Persephone, and am asked—usually by an older woman—"What about Hecate?" Hecate is the third goddess in the story, the little-known, mysterious one. As goddess of the crossroad, whose time was twilight, Hecate was an older woman who supported Demeter in her grief after she searched futilely for her abducted daughter, Persephone. Hecate suggested that Demeter seek the truth and accompanied her to find out what had happened and why. At the end of the myth, when Persephone returned from the underworld, Hecate became an invisible presence who would accompany her from that time forth. In this myth, the triple goddess of prepatriarchal classical Greece was now three separate and diminished goddesses: Persephone the maiden, Demeter the mother, and Hecate the crone.

I had not included Hecate in *Goddesses in Everywoman* because I wasn't old enough when I wrote that book. I needed to live longer, to become postmenopausal, to mature—in much the same way as a full-bodied red wine needs time to age, acquire clarity, and soften its bite. Only when I came to know Hecate as an archetype in myself, and became part of a generation of crone-aged women who were reinventing what this stage of life could be, was I able to give Hecate her due. With that shift, *Goddesses in Older Women* was born.

THE COMMITTEE

As I explained in *Goddesses in Everywoman*, one way of understanding how deeply committed you are to a particular course at any stage of life is through an understanding of archetypes. To stay a course that is very difficult but feels right no matter how others may see it, means that you have within your psyche an archetype or archetypes to go in this particular direction. When you do so, you experience the joy of self-recognition, a deep feeling of becoming who you are, of "coming home to yourself."

Most of us are familiar with the notion of having an "inner child," so it isn't much of a stretch to think of yourself as having an inner collection of archetypes or subpersonalities. In Jungian psychology, archetypes are potential human patterns that, once activated, are expressed through our attitudes and actions, or projected by us onto others. We inherit the whole lot of them, male and female, young and old.

Archetypes are not simple images but patterns with a range of expression. Each woman who lives out an underlying archetype in her own true way is like a unique variation on a theme. However, most women of any complexity have more than one active archetype within her competing for expression. Even when we are able to develop along archetypally true for us lines, there are shifts as we grow older. Archetypes that provided meaning and energized us during one phase of our life may continue to be important to us throughout the entire course of our lives if the depth and breadth of their expression allows us to keep growing. However, often an archetype will be a ruling influence and impetus for us during a particular phase of life, but when we complete the phase, that archetype may lose its importance and its psychic energy. When that happens, a role that once was alive becomes rote.

In *Goddesses in Everywoman*, I suggested imagining the goddess archetypes as committee members, each speaking for her particular values.[3] Ideally, you should have a well-functioning ego chairing the committee, so that order is maintained, and all perspectives are heard. Knowing which archetypes are active means knowing what is important to you at a given time in your life. It is a way of seeing inner complexity that can lead to understanding inner alliances and conflicts that arise with changing circumstances. These archetypes are not all female. Most women have at least one strong male archetype—in *Gods in Everyman*, I used the Greek gods as patterns for these archetypes and encouraged women to find this aspect of themselves as a source of meaning.

The committee metaphor serves as a shorthand. To call a "committee meeting" means going inward and "listening" to the particular archetypes that are active in you. It is a way to make a decision, or find a solution that depends on which archetypes are most important at a given time and resolving inner conflicts and loyalties, before you act. When you pay careful attention and wait for clarity, a choice will emerge that will be right for you. What you do and who you are then coincide.

MENOPAUSE AS A TRANSITION

When women enter menopause, there is usually less psychic energy going where it once went. The primary goddess archetypes in one stage of life may change or shift in importance, making room for other aspects in a woman to emerge. When archetypes shift in importance, it means your priorities also will. There may now be energy for an artisan or writer, a political activist or traveler to far-off places, an aspect of yourself that has been waiting in the wings until now. Or you may feel new archetypal stirrings that are not clearly recognizable, and instead of being drawn toward whatever you know you deferred doing earlier in your life, you seem "pregnant" with something else. It may be that what you most desire is to be left alone so you can meditate, putter around, and see what comes up in you. To do "nothing" (for others or for work) is a most attractive idea when your attention is drawn inward—quite possibly by the crone archetypes.

Entering menopause has some similarities to adolescence and puberty: it's a time when hormone shifts affect moods, when changes in your body are often accompanied by self-consciousness, when worries about being attractive and concerns about the next stage of life begin to surface. Insomnia and vivid dreams are common. For the first time since adolescence, women tell of having the urge to gaze at the moon and write poetry, and of having the time for it due to the extra hours of wakefulness brought on by insomnia or awakening before dawn. Restlessness, irritability, and hot flashes may also be discomforting symptoms.

Restlessness amidst your usual activities may be a sign that what used to occupy your mind and time no longer holds as much interest or is as important to you. Irritability may indicate that you are out of harmony with what you are doing. Or it may be a sign that you cannot keep the lid on what bothers you. Or it may signal an impatience in yourself with yourself. Or it may be that irritability is simply an expression of a wish you yourself are ignoring: namely, the need to spend time alone.

If you consider menopausal symptoms as body metaphors, there are other possibilities. Restlessness can be equated with the stirrings of any one of the crone-goddess archetypes. Irritability and hot flashes, as you will see, may portend the energies of the goddesses of transformative wrath. As if sensing these stirrings, men tend to fear menopausal women. They worry that you will make life difficult, be out of control, irrational, or withholding. It's as if underneath their vague apprehensions, men are afraid that a menopausal woman will turn into a powerful witch or crone goddess. Maybe they are vaguely afraid that it will be a time of retribution.

Many women go through menopause smoothly; for others it is a turbulent passage. You may miss the opportunity to know how you feel about yourself and your life if you attribute your symptoms only to hormones. Hormone replacement therapy is prescribed to avoid uncomfortable physical symptoms. However, I can't help but note that everybody else is more comfortable when menopausal symptoms—and therefore, menopausal women—*are under control.*

Puberty and menopause are transitional states between one phase and the next. You are no longer in the stage you are leaving and not yet established in the next. However, unlike most adolescents, women entering menopause do not look forward to the next stage that until now has been one of uncertainty and invisibility.

POSTMENOPAUSAL GODDESSES

Greek mythology offers us no distinct images of crone-aged goddesses in their pantheon. When they exist at all, they are invisible or dimly perceived. The major Olympian goddesses were mostly portrayed as maiden goddesses (Persephone, Artemis, and Athena the archetypal father's daughter) or as mature women (married Hera, maternal Demeter, and sexual Aphrodite who had several children). Notably absent were goddesses that embodied qualities associated with older women. Hestia, the goddess of the hearth and temple, the eldest and least known of the Olympians, began as one of the original twelve Olympians but was replaced on this pantheon by Dionysus. Hestia was considered to be the fire at the center of a round hearth, whose presence made home or temple sacred. She is ageless and does not have a persona. Hestia is the only goddess that is a major archetype in both *Goddesses in Everywoman* and in *Goddesses in Older Women*.

There are traces in Greek mythology of goddesses with crone attributes who were dimly seen, had disappeared, or lost their divinity. Besides the invisible presence of Hestia, there was Metis, a goddess of wisdom who was tricked into becoming small and swallowed by Zeus; mysterious Hecate; and Baubo, once a pre-Olympian goddess whose status was reduced to being a servant. Since there was such a lack of crone-aged feminine archetypes in Greek mythology, probably because their qualities were so feared and therefore denied until they no longer could be imagined, I had to look to other mythologies to find them.

Other mythologies from patriarchal cultures retained powerful and angry female figures such as the Hindu goddess Kali or the ancient Egyptian lion-headed goddess Sekhmet. These are archetypes of transformative wrath who took action when good men or male divinities could not banish evil-doers. Greek mythology also lacked a goddess of compassion, and for this crone-age attribute I had to turn to the Chinese goddess Kuan Yin or her Japanese equivalent, Kannon. (Aphrodite, the Greek goddess of love, was a goddess of erotic, sexual love.) Notably absent from classical Greek mythology was a goddess of humor, which is not surprising, considering how much men fear being laughed at by women. She can be found in Japanese mythology as Uzume the goddess of mirth whose earthy humor and laughter brought light and warmth back to the world.

However, *Goddesses in Older Women* is not meant to be a comprehensive study of the crone in world mythologies. I turned to nonwestern mythologies when I couldn't find goddess archetypes to correspond to the archetypal energies that I was seeing and appreciating in older women—wisdom, spirituality, sexuality, compassion, restorative humor, and capacity to act decisively. My familiarity with women's psyches was the starting point for my research. It was a search that is similar to seeing a particular symbol arise in a dream and then seeking references and images to understand its meaning. The presence or absence of goddesses with particular qualities in a culture's mythology are reflections of the range of power and the awe or its lack that is held for a sacred feminine.

As I sought and found these goddesses, I also became increasingly aware of how badly goddesses fared in western civilization—which is the history of patriarchy—and how the status of women and the fate of goddesses declined together. While *Goddesses in Older Women* is also not a comprehensive study of the historical treatment of older women, to understand the shared fate of both helps us understand the significance of how each individual woman and women together are bringing suppressed goddess archetypes back into western culture. In the collective unconscious there are archetypal patterns that exist even when they are not allowed expression. These archetypes can remain dormant during most of a woman's life and emerge in the third phase. They can also be suppressed for millennia and reemerge when the cultural climate changes. Morphic resonance theory suggests that we may be able to access collective memories of prepatriarchal times when older women had authority, as well as those derived from centuries of the Inquisition, when any woman of crone age was at risk of being denounced, tortured, and burnt at the stake—especially women most like us. History has shaped the attitudes and inhibitions that we hold about ourselves, to learn of this is part of growing beyond them; just as remembering past traumatic events and seeing family patterns begins the process of individual psychological growth.

Over twenty million baby-boomer generation women will turn fifty in the few years before and after the beginning of the twenty-first century, which will more than double the number of women already in their active crone years. There will soon be over forty-five million women on the far side of fifty, whose lives and attitude have been shaped by the women's movement. Never before in recorded history have there been so many such women with so much competence, experience, independence, and resources. At fifty, most women can look forward to several decades of prime time. For them, seventy is what fifty used to be. And as each woman turns fifty, she joins a growing tide of crone-aged women now in their sixties and many in their seventies and older who have learned to trust themselves and each other. Now, as the goddess, goddess spirituality, and goddess archetypes increasingly become part of language and experience, women of crone age are also becoming visible, influential, and numerous. *Goddesses in Older Women* is a guide to the interior terrain and a handbook on how to be a green and juicy crone.

PART 1

HER NAME
IS WISDOM

What does it mean to be an elder in this culture? What are my new responsibilities? What has to be let go to make room for the transformations of energy that are ready to pour through the body-soul?

—Marion Woodman

Wisdom is a woman, a crone, a goddess, and a feminine archetype. In Greek mythology, she is a barely personified Metis, swallowed by Zeus. In the Bible, she is a hidden Sophia, the goddess who became an abstract and ungendered concept. Wisdom may be found at twilight where the three roads meet as Hecate, or in the hearth fire as Hestia. She may be the invisible Shekinah who enters the Jewish home for the meal that begins the Sabbath. She was once the Celtic goddess Cerridwen. She is Saraswati, the Hindu goddess of wisdom, and Erda in Richard Wagner's *Ring of the Nibelung*. In the world's mythologies and in the collective unconscious, which are mirrors of each other, wisdom is feminine. Wisdom is usually an attribute of a goddess who is often not seen or personified, and an attribute of a woman in whom wisdom has become a conscious part of her psyche.

The archetype of the wisewoman or wise crone is a generic description for the inner development of soul qualities most associated with the third phase of women's lives. Because she is a human archetype, she is not exclusively in the psyche of women, but her development is stifled in men and, in general, in patriarchy. Nor does this archetype develop only in adults. In my practice, I hear how children who were neglected or suffered abuse drew solace and wisdom from an inner source. As a result, they did not identify with their oppressors and so did not grow up to become like the adults who neglected or abused them. Drawing from wisdom beyond their years, they could survive such childhoods without a loss of soul. In fairy tales, such solace and wisdom is personified; often by an old woman, either a fairy god-mother with a magic wand and wisdom, or a crone who helps a young person interpret a riddle or make the right choice.

More commonly, we become wiser as we grow older, but as we all have observed, a long life itself is no guarantee of wisdom.

There are different kinds of wisdom and therefore different kinds of archetypal wisewomen. Metis's wisdom is practical, applied wisdom that utilizes intelligence and mastery of a skill, usually with tangible results made evident through her work. I think that this wisdom is what the Japanese are recognizing when they designate artists and craftspersons as "national treasures." Sophia's wisdom comes from her quest for spiritual meaning and experiences of mystical insight. Hecate's intuitive wisdom is honed by observation and enhanced by psychic awareness. Hestia is a wise presence, the inner serenity that translates into outer harmony. Hestia makes a house a home, creates sanctuaries, and quietly aids in transforming a group of strangers into a community.

In this section, "Her Name is Wisdom," I focus on four god-desses—Metis, Sophia, Hecate, and Hestia—as archetypes of wis-dom. None of them are visually familiar to us, their qualities are intangible, and they were either rendered invisible or dimly seen in their mythologies or theology. These goddesses were once part of myth and religion. They are now latent patterns in the collective uncon-scious that are waiting to be reimagined and made a conscious part of ourselves. I have differentiated one from another and described their attributes, using the research and writing of others in mythology, archeology, theology, and history. I note my main sources in the end-notes. My own expertise as a Jungian analyst guided my selection of these four goddesses as archetypal figures because they correspond to qualities of wisdom that I see emerging in the psyches of older women.

I begin by describing each of these goddesses and what we know of them. You may recognize qualities in yourself in one or more of these, or have an *Aha!* flash of insight, and intuitively know that a particular "goddess" is part of your psyche. The goddesses of wisdom may represent your growing edge—the direction of your own development after fifty. Or the description may fit a woman you particularly admire, and if so, she might represent the archetype that you are growing toward yourself. If you have a woman companion—a sister traveler—in your dreams, she may represent this growing edge, and be a symbol of your inner wisewoman (or another emerging archetype) who joins you in dreams in which you are on a journey to unfamiliar places.

If you meditate upon a goddess or imagine a dialogue with her, this wise part of yourself becomes more conscious and accessible in ordinary life. What we focus on, we energize. What we imagine becoming precedes our development. The more we want to know a wisewoman archetype, the more likely that archetype will emerge in ourselves; and the more of us who engage in this process, the more certain it will be that the goddess archetype will come back into the culture.

As I write this, I think of the "We're Back" issue of *Ms.* magazine, which celebrated its repossession from corporate ownership by feminist women in 1999 with the cover question, "Need Wisdom?" This association of women and wisdom is at once new, due to the aging of the post–women's movement generation, and very old, that is, prepatriarchal. Even if the wisewoman archetypes and the crone goddesses have been largely forgotten for five or six thousand years, when we awaken to our own wisdom, they return to life through us. As Jung wrote: "Archetypes are like riverbeds, which dry up when the water deserts them, but which it can find again at any time. An archetype is like an old watercourse along which the water of life flowed for centuries, digging a deep channel for itself. The longer it has flowed in this channel the more likely it is that sooner or later the water will return to its old bed."[1]

When the goddesses and their attributes were assimilated, trivialized, and demonized, women had nothing to identify with. We need to usher in another round of consciousness-raising, this time to challenge negative stereotypes of older women and understand the relationship between the fate of goddesses and the treatment of women, the effect of the absence of a sacred feminine on women's spirituality, and the theological basis of patriarchy.

Goddess of Practical and Intellectual Wisdom

Metis in the Belly of Zeus

Each of the goddess archetypes of wisdom has her particular distinctive wisdom. Metis's is centered in the experiential and tangible world. For a woman in whom the wisewoman is Metis, what she does with her mind or with her mind and her hands engages her soul. She brings the wisdom she has learned from life to her craft. Metis is a personification of applied ways of knowing and doing. It is an expertise that goes beyond technically mastering a skill or a practice. Metis connotes the ability to intellectually grasp the situation and act wisely and skillfully. When a woman's work and her deeper wisdom come together, then Metis is the archetype of the wisewoman that she exemplifies. Metis was a pre-Olympian goddess of wisdom, who was pursued by Zeus and became his first wife. She provided Zeus with the means through which he could become the chief god atop Mount Olympus.

In Greek, the word *metis,* which was derived from the name of the goddess Metis, came to mean "wise counsel" or "practical wisdom."[1] You may call upon *metis* in running a household easily and well, knowing that what appears to others as mere efficiency is actually creating harmony. In the studio, *metis* is more than the sum of the skills you have acquired and made your own; it becomes an alchemical process through which inspired work can come. If you are a physician, *metis* becomes part of your clinical acumen. If you are in business, politics, or law and have *metis,* your wisdom helps to steer a wise course, to get to the heart of a matter, to settle conflicts through mediation and dia-logue, to work out mutually satisfactory outcomes rather than winning at the other's expense. *Metis* in this sense is a form of diplomacy that takes a long-range view as to what the best outcome is for all. For a scholar, the wisdom of *metis* is a discerning and creative way of think-ing that makes it possible to see a pattern to the research or find an explanation for the evidence. If the wisdom of Metis grows or deepens in the course of your life, then *metis* will be a crone-age attribute.

I think of *metis* in the creative or artistic realm as that quintessen-tial and mysterious divine inspiration that transforms a technically skilled performer into an artist, or the work into art. This is most likely to happen to a craftsperson, artist, actor, or musician who has mas-tered the medium, the instrument, or craft and draws from an arche-typal depth of feeling that touches others. The work or performance then has the power to move people to respond from a corresponding depth in themselves.

METIS THE GODDESS

Metis was the daughter of two Titans: Tethys, the goddess of the moon, and Oceanus, the god whose realm was a vast body of water that encircled the earth. As a Titan, she was part of the ruling older order of divinities that Zeus intended to overthrow. He pursued her and she fled, turning into many shapes in order to escape him. Finally, Zeus caught her and she became his first wife.

For Zeus to defeat Cronus and the mighty Titans, he needed to free his brothers whom Cronus had swallowed. Cronus had previously deposed his own father, Uranus, who had ruled before him, by castrat-ing him and taking his power. Cronus feared that his wife Rhea would bear a son that would do to him what he had done to his father, and to avert this, he had swallowed each of their children as soon as they were born. After he had swallowed their first five newborn infants, and she was pregnant with Zeus, Rhea was determined to save this last child. She hid him in a cave as soon as he was born and, in his place, put a stone wrapped in swaddling clothes. This fooled Cronus, who, in his haste, swallowed the stone instead of Zeus.

Years later, it was Metis's counsel that made it possible for Zeus to succeed. She devised a plan to put an emetic into a honeyed drink for Cronus, who then regurgitated one stone, two sons, and three daughters. They were now full grown, and grateful to Zeus. His brothers Poseidon and Hades were ready to fight with Zeus against the Titans, and after gaining other allies, Zeus defeated the Titans and overthrew Cronus in a ten-year war. Zeus killed his father with a thunderbolt.

When Metis was pregnant with Zeus's child, an earth oracle told him that this child was a daughter and that if she conceived again, Metis would bear a son with a loving heart who would supplant him. To rid himself of this possibility, he approached Metis with clever words and guile. Metis was charmed and distracted by Zeus, who coaxed her to a couch, tricked her into becoming small, and swallowed her. This was the end of Metis in classical mythology, though Zeus claimed afterward that she could counsel him from his belly. He incorporated her into himself and took her attributes and power as his own, including childbirth. Zeus birthed Athena out of his head, as an adult with no memory of having a mother.

My capsule synopsis of the goddess Metis was told by Hesiod, who lived between the second half of the eighth century B.C.E. and the first quarter of the seventh, in the *Theogony,* an epic poem about the birth of the gods and a cosmology that tells of the origins of the universe. The overall theme of the *Theogony* is the establishment of Zeus as supreme god, and yet for most of the poem it is the mother goddesses who matter. Given the fiercely patriarchal character of Hesiod's own society, the *Theogony* was a remarkable testimony to the tenacity of myths that persist when earlier history or prior religions are forgotten.

SWALLOWED METIS AS PERSONAL METAPHOR

The story of Zeus and Metis is a recapitulation of the lives of many first wives of successful men. These women provided the means and the strategy through which their particular Zeus reached the top, only to find themselves treated like Metis. In this archetypal situation, the woman is metaphorically a daughter of Titans; socially and economically, a member of the class to which her husband aspires, or even aspires to supplant, if like Zeus, he has dynastic ambitions. She may be better educated, even brighter than he. She may have more money or access to it. She may provide introductions, ideas, and strategy to further his goals. Once his ambitions are realized with her help, and she becomes involved in home and children, her role in his success and her importance to him diminishes considerably. She is thus made small, "tricked" into insignificance, and "swallowed," as her attributes, ideas, and resources become his. After a divorce and his remarriage, like Metis the goddess, she disappears from sight socially. The invisibility that results is vividly described in the novel *A Man in Full* by Tom Wolfe through his portrayal of Martha, who became "the superfluous woman" once Charlie Croker divorced her after twenty-nine years to marry a woman half his age.

When a wife's ideas or creative work are attributed to her husband, it is another version of swallowed Metis. Usually she is given no public credit. Whatever the contribution Albert Einstein's wife made to his theories remains unknown, yet she was a brilliant physics student when they met. Will and Ariel Durant worked together on *The History of Civilization*, yet her name did not appear as a coauthor until the seventh volume. When it was impossible for women to have their intellect taken seriously, their ideas had to be attributed to a man, or bear a man's name.

The same pattern occurs in work environments of all kinds, when a Zeus co-opts the work or ideas of women who are seen as helpmates to the important man. In *Molecules of Emotion*, Dr. Candace Pert describes how this happened to her.[2] Pert had a pivotal role in the discovery of opiate receptors and endorphins for which her mentor and two male researchers received the Lasker Award, second only to the Nobel Prize in prestige. A large percentage of Lasker recipients do go on to win the Nobel, and this might have happened, except that Pert did not remain silent about her crucial contribution and subsequently was also nominated for the Nobel Prize; after a long and heated debate, the award was conferred for another discovery. Pert's decision was influenced by the experience of Rosalind Franklin, a brilliant scientist who provided the critical link in the chain of reasoning that allowed Francis Crick and John Watson to show that the DNA structure was a double helix, for which they received the Nobel Prize in

1962. Rosalind Franklin remained silent and died of cancer a few years later. Pert's research on the connection between emotions and disease gives her grounds for her comment: "I felt that by not speaking up, I would be sacrificing my self-esteem and self-respect, not to mention possibly setting myself up for a nice case of depression and maybe a cancer or two down the line."[3]

Yet another instance of Metis-swallowing occurs when an organization that was conceived and nurtured by a woman, who struggled body and soul to keep it going, is taken over for its prestige or profitability by men, once it has gained status. A noted example of this was Physicians for Social Responsibility, founded by Helen Caldicott, M.D. When it won the Nobel Peace Prize, Caldicott was not on stage to receive the honor she so well deserved because she had been made insignificant by internal politics and was not even invited to be in the audience. The male officers of this now huge group accepted the prize.

ATHENA'S IDENTIFICATION WITH THE PATRIARCHY

With the swallowing of Metis and the unusual birth of Athena, Zeus set a standard that Apollo would cite in the first courtroom scene in Western literature. In Aeschylus's *Oresteia*, Orestes has killed his mother to avenge the murder of his father. Apollo, speaking in his defense, denies the primacy of maternal blood ties, arguing that the mother is only the nourisher of the seed planted by the father. As proof that a mother is unimportant, he points to Athena, explaining that she was not even born from the womb of a woman. Arguing on the other side are the avenging Furies who see matricide as the most heinous of crimes. The Furies contend that the younger gods have ruthlessly abrogated the rights of the older generation of divinities by permitting a matricide to escape.

Twelve Athenians hear the arguments, deliberate, and the vote is tied. Athena then casts the decisive vote. Since Athens is her city, this is her prerogative. She sides with Apollo's male Olympian point of view, and frees Orestes. Prior to patriarchy, the mother rather than the father was the significant parent; after patriarchy, father-right dominated. In the play, this trial symbolizes the establishment of male superiority. The Furies are portrayed as black-robed enraged hags, who are transformed after the trial into the purple-robed Eumenides, the "Kindly Ones," by Athena. The trilogy ends in a triumphant procession in which the now venerable goddesses are led to their new home, transformed from furies into sweet old ladies.

The goddess Athena was the Greek goddess of wisdom and the archetypal father's daughter. Though she was given her mother Metis's title as Goddess of Wisdom, she had no memory of ever having had a mother. Athena was an armored warrior and strategist, who championed heroes and never lost her head in the heat of battle. She favored Greek heroes, such as Achilles and Perseus, as well as Odysseus, gave them advice or weapons or aided them by deceptions that gave them a strategic advantage.

When Zeus gave birth to Athena, his labor pains took the form of terrible headaches; Hephaestus, the god of the forge, used a double-edged axe to open a way for Athena to emerge out of her father's head. She was born as a fully grown woman in golden armor, carrying a spear, and announced her arrival with a mighty war cry. Mount Olympus shook when her feet hit the ground. She immediately took her place at the right hand of her father and was his favorite and the only Olympian he trusted with his symbols of power.

Zeus as an archetypal chief executive may "birth" or bring women into an organization. Her war cry may not be audible in contemporary Olympian heights and the golden armor may be her reputation and résumé, but the message is the same: Athena has arrived and Zeus is her mentor.

The last three decades of the twentieth century have provided golden opportunities for women to enter the bastions of corporate, political, academic, or professional power. Women like the goddess Athena, who have an affinity for male mentors in fields where a strategic mind is an advantage, have been the greatest beneficiaries of the women's movement. Without the women's movement, there wouldn't be two women Supreme Court justices or a woman secretary of state. And yet, when the archetype of Athena is the predominant one in a woman, especially a younger one, she is more a father's daughter than a sister to other women. This stance begins to wear thin as a woman approaches the third stage of her life. If she remembers Metis, she will understand what happened to feminine divinity and to women—and begin to identify herself with them rather than with men. If she acquires Metis, she will be more balanced and whole.

RECOVERING THE MEMORY OF METIS

The return of Metis into the mind of Athena happens when "fathers' daughters" grow psychologically away from their identification with patriarchal misogynistic attitudes toward women and feminine values. Bright, well-educated, ambitious women with a mind for the field they have entered and an affinity with men in power see themselves as exceptional and often look down on other women who do not have either the aspirations or the ability for achievement that they do. If they are ever to remember Metis, they first will need to develop an affiliation with other women, and lose their identification as their fathers' daughters and their allegiance to hierarchy. This often comes about only after a major disillusionment with male mentors and colleagues, or with an institution's principles. The older an Athena woman becomes, the readier she may be for this shift.

An Athena on the fast track to the top may have no inkling of her vulnerability or the tenuousness of her position of power—until she loses her mentor's support and the authority, influence, and status that came with it. Or the disillusionment may result when an Athena's positive relationship to a patriarchal institution is undone when she has gotten ahead on her own merits and finds there is a glass ceiling on how far she can advance because she is a woman. Or when she learns that she is paid less than her male counterparts. Or after she overhears male colleagues describe her in locker-room sexual terms, when she thought that she was an accepted equal.

When she learns that the devotion and loyalty that she has had to her work, her mentor, her team or an institution was not a mutual one, she experiences a deep sense of betrayal and disillusionment; it may shake the premise on which she has built her life. Before then, it might not have been possible for her to have an affiliation with women. It may also be the beginning of feminine wisdom.

In Greek mythology, the goddess Athena never disobeyed or fell out of favor with Zeus. She is an eternal image of the archetype of the father's daughter. The fate of an Athena who disobeys is vividly portrayed by Richard Wagner in *The Valkyrie*, the second of the four operas that comprise *The Ring of the Nibelung*. Brünnhilde is the Valkyrie, who, like Athena, is a divinity and a young woman warrior goddess who wears armor and is her father Wotan's favorite child.* In the *Ring* cycle, Brünnhilde is moved by compassion to go against his orders, and his punishment of her is appalling. He takes her immortality away and plans to leave her unconscious on a rock, to be awakened, sexually claimed, and possessed by the first man who finds her. She pleads with her father to at least let the man who takes her be a hero. At first, he refuses. Then, relenting, he surrounds her unconscious body with a ring of fire that only a hero could cross.

Once Brünnhilde was no longer an obedient extention of Wotan's will and an adoring mirror in which he could see his reflection, he was deeply angered (and narcissistically wounded). Because she disobeyed him, she lost her relationship to him, her armor and weapons, and her immortality; she ceased to be an archetypal warrior goddess and a favored father's daughter, and became a very vulnerable woman. Brünnhilde's mother was Erda, who (like Metis) had been a goddess of wisdom. After she had been seduced and overpowered by Wotan, Erda lost her powers and receded into the earth, where she slept, her wisdom clouded and her foresight lost. Whether wisdom is in the belly of Zeus or buried in the earth, the essential story is the same. The most powerful divinity is a sky god who reigns from the top of a mountain, and a once important goddess of wisdom disappears from sight.

Through her banishment and punishment, Brünnhilde becomes a mortal woman. A metaphorically similar fate occurs to a disillusioned and betrayed father's daughter, who loses her identification with the Athena archetype and finds she is vulnerable and emotional. Only then does she leave the lofty mental and masculine realm of Mount Olympus/Valhalla. Betrayal of a daughter of the patriarchy by the patriarchy is often an initiation into feminism; an Athena gains a first-

---

*Wagner's libretto inspired me to write *Ring of Power*. The main characters are the same archetypes that I had described in *Goddesses in Everywoman* and *Gods in Everyman*, now seen within the context of dysfunctional family psychology.

hand understanding of women's issues that she had previously dismissed, and sees the pattern.

FINDING METIS IN THE BELLY OF ZEUS;
RECOVERING THE HISTORY OF THE GODDESS

When what we have been taught as objective history turns out to be lies and omissions, it is both disillusioning and illuminating. Every woman who has had an academic education has had to develop a linear and logical Athena mind, beginning with the assumption that scholarship is objective. Advanced scholarship brings in an awareness of bias and complexity, but until a feminist consciousness emerges, it is easy to be blind to misogyny and its far-reaching implications. Just as Athena was born out of Zeus's head, an Athena mind is the offspring of male authority and bias, until she remembers Metis. Patriarchal history and theology omit information about the conquest of the goddess and the destruction of the culture that had thrived before. Just as Metis was swallowed and forgotten, the history of such times had been buried and covered over, only to emerge in the last half of the twentieth century.

"The History of Western Civilization" was a required freshman course at my college as it commonly was in most liberal-arts colleges and universities. I was taught that civilization began with the Greeks, and that Athens was the cradle of democracy. Not until I read Merlin Stone's *When God Was a Woman,* did I begin my education in how history is written (or distorted and denied) by the victors. In her introduction to this book, she wrote:

"Why do so many people educated in this century think of classical Greece as the first major culture, when written language was in use and great cities were built at least twenty-five centuries before that time? And perhaps more important, why is it continually inferred that the age of the "pagan" religions, the time of the worship of female deities (if mentioned at all), was dark and chaotic, mysterious and evil, without the light of order and reason that supposedly accompanied the later male religions, when it has been archaeologically confirmed that the earliest law, government, medicine, agriculture, architecture, metallurgy, wheeled vehicles, ceramics, textiles, and written language were initially developed in societies that worshiped the Goddess?"[4]

In *The Civilization of the Goddess*, Marija Gimbutas documents the existence and destruction of the goddess culture in what she describes as "Old Europe," Europe's first civilization, which preceded the establishment of patriarchy. It dates back at least five thousand, perhaps even twenty-five thousand years. From ancient Crete to Celtic Ireland, goddess worship was universal. Archaeological evidence gleaned from ancient sites show that this was an unstratified, egalitarian society that was destroyed by an infiltration of invading semi-nomadic, horse-riding Indo-European peoples from the distant north and east. These invaders were patrifocal, mobile, warlike, ideologically sky-oriented.

The Great Goddess was a trinity: maiden, mother, and crone. Immortal and eternal, she was each and all aspects of the feminine. She was many and she was One. She was the Great Goddess with a myriad of names. She was worshiped as the feminine life force; all life came from her body and returned to her. She was an embodiment of nature, as the creator, sustainer, and destroyer of life. She was like the moon in her cycles, and like the earth in her seasons. All living things were her children which meant that all life shared something of her divine essence.

Women were in the image of the goddess because they, too, brought forth new life from their bodies and could sustain that life with milk from their breasts. The fertile earth and fertility of women were valued. Sexuality was a natural instinct and a pleasure. Society was matrifocal and matrilinear because everyone knew who their mother and siblings were, but not necessarily (and not for sure) the identity of their father.

As Robert Graves pointed out in his introduction to *The Greek Myths*, judging from surviving artifacts and myths, ancient Europe had no gods before the nomadic invaders came from the distant North and East. Until then the concept of fatherhood had not been introduced into religious thought.

When the invaders came, they viewed themselves as superior because of their ability to conquer the more culturally developed people who had long been settled there. Wherever they settled, they subjugated the people of the goddess. The power and attributes of the goddess were either diminished and made insignificant (as unvalued qualities) or taken over and appropriated (swallowed) by male gods. The once Great Goddess was fragmented into many lesser goddesses and incorporated into the religion. They became subservient consorts or daughters of gods.

From the archaeological evidence, Gimbutas described three waves of invasions into Europe: the first invaders came approximately 4300–4200 B.C.E., the second wave around 3400 B.C.E., and the third and most devastating between 3000 and 2800 B.C.E. Gimbutas called them Kurgans after the Kurgan burial mounds found in the arid area near the Caspian Sea. These people were primarily destroyers of the culture that was there. They deified the power to destroy and dominate, idealized weapons, and glorified heroes. Their burial mounds held the remains of powerful chieftains, their possessions, and members of their households, including wives, children, and slaves. The Indo-European languages of the invaders almost completely replaced earlier known pre–Indo-European languages in ancient Europe: the Etruscan language continued to be spoken in parts of Italy until Roman times; only Basque, which is spoken in and around the Pyrenees, between Spain and France, still survives. When the invaders came, sites that had flourished for several millennia were abandoned, the people of the goddess moved to marginal locations, such as islands, caves, or easily fortified hilltop sites, and the major Neolithic technologies of fine ceramic manufacture and copper metallurgy were diminished and lost.

Far from bringing civilization to Europe as we were taught, Gimbutas comments, the Kurgan proto-Greeks brought the end to a civilization and imposed its warrior elite society, its warrior gods, its values and language upon Europe. The social consequences of the Kurgan invaders, as Riane Eisler describes in *The Chalice and the Blade* and *Sacred Pleasure*, was the triumph of the male dominator culture, which reduced women to property.

Greece reached its peak of intellectual, creative, and political power in the fifth century B.C.E. This was the Age of Pericles, when the Parthenon was built, the time of Hippocrates in medicine, of the historians Herodotus and Thucydides, when the plays of Aeschylus,

Sophocles, and Euripedes were first staged. Classical Greece represented the apex and triumph of a male culture that had its roots in the religion and society that glorified war.

Classical Greece was not a "cradle of democracy" for women. All Athenian women were under the legal guardianship of men who had effective control over their persons and property, so much so that women could not, under Athenian law, dispose of any property above the minimal value of one bushel of barley. The legal position of women and slaves in Athenian society during this period was not all that different, as documented by the classical historian Eva Keuls in *The Reign of the Phallus: Sexual Politics in Ancient Athens*. A woman had no protection under the law except in so far as she was the property of a man. She was not even considered a person under the law and could not go to court. Respectable women were segregated, barred from secular education, forbidden to speak or even appear in public except on special occasions. A father could sell his daughter into slavery if she lost her virginity before marriage. Many female children were abandoned and exposed soon after birth, or sold. Slave girls were often used as prostitutes, and could be abused, tortured, randomly executed, or sold at any time. Athens was a harsh slave society in which torture was institutionalized. In legal proceedings, a slave's testimony was admissible in court only if given under torture, and a public torture chamber was maintained for the routine torture of slaves.

The subjugation of women was an inevitable result of the conquest of goddess-worshiping peoples by these waves of Kurgan invaders. However, in their mythology, the Greeks retained the memory of what had gone before. Hesiod's divine genealogy begins with Gaia, the goddess Earth, who was the first parent. She gave birth to the god Uranus, the Sky, and the god Pontus, the Sea. Gaia mated with Uranus and gave birth to the Titans, the first generation of gods and goddesses. Thus even the patriarchal Greeks began their cosmology and creation with the goddess, Gaia, even as Zeus ruled over the Olympians as the chief god in the classical Greek pantheon, and goddesses became lesser images of feminine divinity. While Metis was swallowed, the goddess did not disappear in her entirety into the belly of the patriarchy in Greek and Roman times. It was not until orthodox Judeo-

Christian religions triumphed politically that feminine divinity disappeared altogether.

MEDUSA, A DEMONIZED METIS

The fate of feminine wisdom, goddesses, and women under the Greeks and subsequent dominator cultures was to be disempowered and oppressed; which was Metis's fate. A second fate to befall Metis was to become demonized, a fate which also has been shared, especially by women.

Metis has been equated with Medusa, as both were once revered goddesses of wisdom. Medusa was the serpent-goddess of the Libyan Amazons, representing "female wisdom" (Sanskrit *medha*; Greek *metis*, Egyptian *met* or Maat). Medusa was the destroyer aspect of the triple goddess called Neith in Egypt, Ath-enna or Athene in North Africa. The symbols and attributes of the triple goddess were represented by the three faces or phases or cycles of nature and the moon. Besides maiden, mother, crone, or waxing, full, and waning moon, the divine feminine was seen as creator, sustainer, and destroyer. The Great Goddess was a personification of the Earth. She is the creator from which life comes, the sustainer or nurturer of life, and the grave into which all life returns at the end of its season.

In classical Greek mythology, Medusa was the third and most famous of the Gorgon sisters, who were the once-beautiful daughters of ancient sea deities. Her two sisters were immortal and ageless. Medusa was the only mortal one. They were originally triple moon goddesses, each representing a phase of the moon. In its third phase, the crescent waning moon "dies" as it disappears into the dark, which may be why Medusa as the third aspect of the moon was the mortal one.

Medusa was originally known for her beauty and abundant hair. In mythology, she went from being a goddess to a mortal to a monster with snakes as hair, whose face could turn men to stone. Perseus, a Greek hero armed with Athena's advice and a sword, cut off Medusa's head, put it in a magic bag and took it as a trophy to Athena. The head of the Gorgon Medusa became part of the *aegis,* which was made of goatskin and attached to the breastplate or shield, and worn by Zeus (*aegis* has come to mean "under the sponsorship of a powerful person") or Athena. The power to destroy that is part of the cycle of nature and the third aspect of the goddess was now harnessed and used to turn enemies into stone. Medusa's power, like Metis's was appropriated.

According to Barbara G. Walker, "A female face surrounded by serpent hair was an ancient, widely recognized symbol of divine female wisdom, and equally of the 'wise blood' that supposedly gave women their divine powers."[5]

WHEN ATHENA GAINS METIS

When an Athena woman gains *metis,* she no longer is concerned about achieving power or winning for its own sake; these are the goals of an ego that accepts patriarchal values as her own. Metis the archetype of wise counsel is concerned with using time and energy, talent and resources more judiciously. Metis often comes into the consciousness of women who have acquired power in the world, or whose focus was on furthering their husbands' careers and their social status but whose drive for success has become tempered by having a child or a life-threatening illness, or suffering a loss, or a betrayal, or a humiliation. Such events and introspection, which may come through meditation, psychotherapy, or a spiritual retreat, provide an opening for Metis to enter.

For you to come to know Metis, you must find space in your life for solitude and reflection, which usually are not found until well into midlife. If you are an Athena, something must happen that slows you down and makes you uncomfortably aware that ambition, achievement, and success are not enough. The physiology of perimenopause lends itself to becoming more inner-directed, and the awareness of how short life is, which midlife brings, may invite Metis into your psyche.

It becomes harder to stay identified with the Athena archetype as you grow older. As Athena women turn fifty or become menopausal, or lose their mentors or illusions, or outgrow an identification with Athena as an eternal father's daughter seeking approval from male institutions and individual powerful men, Metis as feminine wisdom is ready to emerge. You have to have evolved beyond being a favored daughter of the patriarchy to find Metis, who is the matrilineal half of your psychological lineage.

I think of Metis as representing a discerning combination of intuition, intellect, and experience, a maturity that comes from becoming seasoned by life, by a loss of hubris, and through learning first-hand about humility and vulnerability. Until then, you may see people as chess pieces, as expendable or protected, to be moved around the board. To have the mind of a successful Athena and be a winning strategist or competitive "player" in the corridors of political, academic, corporate, or even social power, you had to develop the ability to perceive, assess, discriminate, plan, and take action. The mottos of power "to the winner go the spoils" and "might makes right" may have been your own until you felt what it is like to be expendable and realized how much people suffer when they become powerless. As a result, a compassionate and wise Metis may emerge into your consciousness. Then power or status over others, the bottom line, and winning the game will cease to enthrall you and you may become more engaged by issues of social justice, gender equality, ethical standards, and accountability. Perhaps for the first time, you may appreciate and develop friendships with women. You might even become an environmentalist or a late-blooming feminist.

Ellen Malcolm, the founder of EMILY's List (an acronym for Early Money Is Like Yeast—it raises the dough) is an example of a woman with an Athena mind inspired by Metis to make a difference. She saw a need for women to hold political offices (and not just support male candidates) and with a genius for grass-roots organization created a political action committee—that has more monetary clout than the American Medical Association's—to fund Democratic women candidates who can be counted on to support social programs that look out for women and children and the environment.

To form perceptions that run counter to our hierarchal and patriarchal culture is a symbolic representation of Athena breaking with Zeus. To think intuitively upon the evidence and arrive at a different interpretation of the facts, even if it puts you at odds with a mentor, is another. Brünnhilde was punished for disobedience when she did not follow Wotan's orders, but much more was involved than this. She had been affected by what she witnessed, thought about her choices, and acted on her own. At that point, she no longer shared the same perceptions or values as Wotan; she stepped out of the archetypal role of a father's daughter and changed.

It does not always take a personal break with a Zeus/Wotan for this mythic situation to be lived out. It can be a break with patriarchal thought, a break with accepted tradition or traditional values, or a break with accepting the sole authority of (male) logic to arrive at a conclusion.

METIS AS A CRONE-PHASE ARCHETYPE: A REAL-LIFE EXAMPLE

Marija Gimbutas, who unearthed buried images of goddesses and evidence of the Goddess culture at archaeological sites, is an exceptionally fitting example of a woman with a fine Athena mind who became a crone with *metis* in the third phase of her life. She could make connections and draw conclusions from her extensive knowledge of archaeology, comparative religion, mythology, folklore, and linguistics. Gimbutas, who died in 1994 at the age of seventy-three, was a professor of archaeology at UCLA. In 1956, she was the first scholar to link linguistic research (she had a knowledge of twenty languages) and archaeological finds, identifying the homeland of the Indo-European warrior peoples or "Kurgans," as she called them.

Between 1967 and 1980, she directed five major archaeological excavations of Neolithic settlements in Yugoslavia, Italy, and Greece, and began the process of deciphering the engraved and painted symbols that were found at these sites. Gimbutas developed a picture of the prepatriarchal culture that had existed from at least 6500 B.C.E. to 3500 B.C.E., which she described in her last three books, *Goddesses and Gods of Old Europe* (1974, 1982), *The Language of the Goddess* (1989), and *The Civilization of the Goddess* (1991). The initial academic (Zeus) reaction to her work ranged from apathy to violent opposition, but she persisted, published further findings, and is now taken seriously.

I met Marija Gimbutas in the mid-eighties in a house in Malibu,

California. Several of us were being interviewed on film by Tony Joseph, and were houseguests during the filming, which gave the event an aura of a house party in which the main subject of discussion was goddesses and goddess spirituality. Born in Lithuania, Gimbutas was a university student when the Soviets invaded, and became a member of the resistance and later a refugee. She fled to Austria, and got a Ph.D. in archaeology before coming to the United States in 1949. Before she was hired at Harvard, she told us of working as a cleaning lady. She married, divorced, had children, and moved to California in 1963, after securing an academic appointment on the faculty of UCLA, where she became a professor.

She was a short, unpretentious, somewhat grandmotherly European woman who spoke with an accent and had a warm smile. Her work was controversial, and support for her hypotheses about the Kurgan invaders was yet to come. With the diversity and depth of her knowledge across several fields, she had the *metis* to make intuitive connections that made sense of available evidence of a goddess-centered, peaceful culture that had existed for millennia, and the scholarship and authority to offer a radical revision of patriarchal history.

Marija Gimbutas is a particularly elegant example of a woman whose major work and influence occurred in the third phase of her life. Women's creative or work lives characteristically do not follow a linear course, especially if there are children. There are interruptions, moves, periods in which responsibilities for others take precedence over work. In *Silences*, Tillie Olson describes how and why a woman's creative work can lie fallow until she has time for mature creativity in the later part of her life. Mary Catherine Bateson in *Composing a Life* writes of how the making of a quilt might be an apt metaphor for most women's lives. It may only be in the third phase of life that the pieces can come together to create a whole, and when you can finally see that there is meaning and purpose to it all.

Both Olson and Bateson had their work lives interrupted by putting marriage or family first. For many women whose education and work lives make them successful daughters of the patriarchy, having children can cause shift in affiliation from the father world of work to the mother world of relationship, and a new respect for ordinary women and the lot of women. The vicissitudes of ordinary life are not as manageable as work, you can't always maintain a cool head in the midst of ongoing improvisation and adaptation.

Having to make decisions in the emotionally charged moment, trusting instinct or intuition when there isn't adequate information, coping with the situation and learning as you go from mistakes, and developing confidence and an authentic style of your own go into the process of becoming a mother. This is also so when a commitment is made to a craft, a skill, or work that cannot be done "by the book" or under the direction of someone in authority. When you cease to look to experts for authority and trust your own expertise, you find your own *metis*. An Athena mind takes you only so far, after which what is called for is the development of Metis's wisdom.

METIS AS WISE COUNSEL: PRACTICAL AND INTELLIGENT WISDOM

Time passes swiftly and before you know it, you're fifty. Even if you were childless by choice and enjoyed work, chances are that for a time you will feel a loss for the path of motherhood not taken. If you did stop work you loved or diluted what you were doing to have children, even when this was a desired, consciously made choice, prime career years were sacrificed, and as you enter the third phase of your life, chances are that you will regret the loss of opportunities that have passed you by. With *metis* as inner wisdom, feelings of regret and loss, even grief, are likely to be transient. With Metis as the inner wise counselor, you will pause to get your bearings, take stock, put feelings of loss behind you, and then bring a combination of intelligence and wisdom to bear upon what you will do with yourself as a new crone.

This is a stage of life when you may decide to pass on what you know or mentor others. Or, drawing upon the accumulated experience that you have, you may be inspired to teach or to write. Or, having mastered a craft, you may find that it is time to express your own originality and creativity. Maturity and experience foster *metis*.

Metis is practical and intelligent wisdom that you draw upon to make decisions about how to spend the third phase of your life. Metis pays attention to the quality of your life now, to retirement possibilities and to potential disability with age, and plans wisely. Metis is the wise counselor that makes a crone-aged woman a respected elder, someone who others turn to for her perspective and advice. If she is in a position of authority, a CEO, managing partner, or director, and has both Metis and Zeus as her archetypal parents, she uses wisdom and power together in setting goals and the means to achieve them. If she is a craftswoman or a professional and has *metis,* her skills are combined with wisdom in what she does with materials or with clients.

A woman with *metis* is likely to find that the third phase of her life has many satisfactions. She does not harbor illusions about herself or others, and wisely takes reality into account without being either cynical or naive. She has found and values a maternal, feminine wisdom that allows her to express the emotional and nurturing side of herself.

Goddess of Mystical and
Spiritual Wisdom

Sophia Hidden in the Bible

Of all of the goddesses of wisdom, Sophia's name is the most familiar. In contemporary women's psychology and spirituality circles, Sophia has become an archetype of feminine wisdom. New Age spirituality sees her as the Divine Feminine. Hagia Sophia, the magnificent domed church in Constantinople has made her name familiar.* She is a part of the Judeo-Christian heritage of the west, and a forgotten goddess figure within a monotheistic, patriarchal religious tradition that denies feminine divinity. *Sophia* means wisdom in Greek, and her identity as a goddess figure is hidden in the Old Testament by references to her in the abstract and lowercased word "wisdom." She is not mentioned at all in the New Testament, yet Sophia was a major divine figure in the beliefs of first-century gnostic Christians who were denounced as heretics by orthodox Christian bishops and successfully persecuted in the Fourth Century. Information about the Gnostic Christian Sophia resurfaced in the mid-twentieth century, when copies of

---

*The name Hagia Sophia means Holy Wisdom. The Church was built to honor the Divine Mother in the sixth century C.E. by Eastern Christians. It became a Muslim mosque and is now a museum. Roman Christians claim it was dedicated to a minor virgin martyr, Saint Sophia, rather than built in honor of the Divine Feminine. The fate of this magnificent edifice parallels that of goddesses and women. *Hagia* means "holy" in Greek, and was once a title of respect for wise and respected older women; it has been denigrated to "hag."

their gospels (written at the same time or earlier than the New Testament gospels) were found hidden in the Nag Hammadi desert in Egypt. While the psychological focus is on Sophia as an archetype of wisdom, it is very important for women to know how the worship (and then even knowledge) of feminine divinity disappeared because the patriarchy is based upon the negation of women's spiritual authority and denial of feminine divinity. The historical inferior status of women and the suppression of the goddess are related; just as the dominating position of men is related to (male) monotheism.

SOPHIA THE ARCHETYPE OF SPIRITUAL WISDOM: *GNOSIS*

Sophia is the archetype of spiritual wisdom or soul knowledge. Sophia's wisdom is insightful, it is what we know through *gnosis*. The Greek word *gnosis* translates into "knowledge" of a particular kind and source. The Greek language distinguishes between what we can know objectively (*logos*) from what can *only* be known subjectively (*gnosis*). Objective knowledge can be learned through teachers, books, or observation of something outside of ourselves. Gnostic or noetic (an alternative spelling) knowledge is what is revealed to us or intuitively perceived as spiritually true. I think of *gnosis* as what we "*gknow*" at a soul level, it's what we know "in our bones." When I wrote about life-threatening illness as a soul experience, the title I chose for the book was *Close to the Bone*, because when such illnesses strike us or those we love, it can strip away the non-essentials and bring us close to what we *know* at a soul level. At a soul level, we can *know* that we are spiritual beings on a human path, or *know* that life has a purpose, or *know* that we are loved, or *know* God, or *know* that we are part of an inter-connected universe.

As the gnostic Christians used the word, *gnosis* could be translated into "insight," an intuitive process of *knowing* oneself at the deepest level, which, as they believed or mystically experienced, was to simultaneously *know* God. This process has similarities to the individuation work of Jungian analysis that has to do with the Self. A person (or ego) with a connection to the Self has a sense that what she is doing with her life is meaningful. This can only be known subjectively, it is soul knowledge. To have a life oriented to the Self, rather than determined by *persona* (or how we are doing in the eyes of others), is a spiritual orientation. The Self is the "archetype of meaning" in Jungian psychology that can be translated by religious people into their names for divinity or as the invisible oneness (Tao) that underlies and connects everything in the visible universe. What we *know* through a connection with the Self is divine wisdom. This is a wisdom that isn't the exclusive possession of authority above us; it is wisdom that dwells in us and is everywhere.

Gnosis is also that often mysterious way of knowing that men both elevate and demean and call "women's intuition." Far from mysterious, it's a combination of noticing what is going on and processing what we are noticing in an intuitive way. It has to do with *knowing* people, of assessing character, of seeing through the facade—it's insight into the presence or absence of soul. The *click!* insight that sees the underlying sexism or power politics in a situation is *gnosis*. The *Aha!* that happens when something important to you suddenly makes sense is *gnosis*. The moment when you *know* that your spouse is unfaithful, is *gnosis*. That inner twinge of a guilty conscience is *gnosis*.

Growing older *and* wiser is a lifelong process that accelerates in the third phase, especially if you heed *gnosis* in yourself. This is how the archetype of Sophia becomes known to you. She is a way of knowing, a source of inner wisdom as well as an archetypal wisewoman. When Sophia dwells in you, you perceive the soul of the matter or soul qualities in others.

SOPHIA THE MYSTIC

The mystic is an aspect of the Sophia archetype that is evoked by *numinous* experiences. While words are not adequate, those commonly used to describe numinosity are awe, beauty, grace, divinity, ineffability. Numinous experiences are not uncommon—most people may have had them—but a numinous experience is the defining moment for the woman who becomes a mystic. After which, to know God—this particular *gnosis*—becomes the central focus of her spiritual life and her spiritual life becomes her life. She may attempt to convey the experience and the meaning of it and can only do so in metaphorical language. She seeks to enter and stay in a mystical union with divinity. Women mystics flowered in medieval religious communities of women. Hildegard of Bingen was one of a number of them. Others included Teresa of Avila, Julian of Norwich, Clare of Assisi, Catherine of Siena, and Catherine of Genoa. At a time when women in the secular world married young, had many children and a household to run, the place for a mystic was in a religious order. Women mystics flourished in medieval times because it was possible for a nun to seek mystical union with God or Christ, and not have to attend to the daily maintenance of a household. She was celibate and her passion could be directed toward spiritual union, and she did not have the choice or necessity to support herself. Sophia defines experiences as having spiritual or philosophical meaning. The archetype not only has an aptitude for mystical events, but seeks to know their meaning.

Contemporary women mystics may still be drawn to religious communities and find that a Western cloister or Eastern ashram is fertile ground for mystical experience. But since mystics directly experience divinity, and women (especially older ones) no longer automatically defer to hierarchy, question dogma, and are aware of sexism, they also leave if they find the dogma and beliefs of a particular religion constricting and in conflict with what they deeply trust is true for them. Women have more freedom than ever to decide what they will do and one result is that women are inspired by their mystical insights to lead a personally meaningful life. Most may not even define themselves as mystics, but their mystical experiences are at the core of who they are and what they are doing with their lives. With freedom from the need to conform to institutional definitions of the meaning of their mystical experiences, women are redefining spirituality.

The receptivity to mysticism may be a talent or natural ability in a person's psyche, or may come after meditation has become a spiritual practice. This sophianic mystical sense of oneness and revelation may occur in a holy moment or be prolonged in duration, and the insight into its meaning may be instantaneous or a lifetime quest. As more and more people meditate as a spiritual practice or as a means of stress reduction, they are cultivating a space for the Sophia archetype and opening themselves for mystical experience.

In her introduction to *Weavers of Wisdom: Women Mystics of the Twentieth Century* (1989), Ann Bancroft wrote: "Twelve years ago I wrote a book about twentieth-century mystics and they were almost all men. I regretted that at the time but the women's field seemed rather empty. In the very short time between then and now, however, the women's movement has brought in to the public eye a number of profound thinkers."[1] She also wanted to see if it were possible to find authentically feminine insights and ways of being that differed from male thoughts about spirituality; which she did. "Women tend to see all things around them as revelatory, revealing totality and completeness and a numinous quality. To see things in this way a certain attention has to be given, which women are good at. It is not the kind of attention with which one acquires knowledge but rather that which happens when one lets go of all concepts and becomes open to what is there."[2]

In her profiles of women mystics, each renewed and cultivated their mystical relationship with the sacred in their own way; in nature, in creativity, in contemplation, in a deep connection with another person, and had a life other than being a mystic, which is why most did not call themselves "mystics." Their mysticism was a source of wisdom that illuminated the particular path they had taken. For example, Joanna Macy's mysticism matured through Buddhist meditation and deepened her already-formed concern for social justice; this led her to become an anti-nuclear and ecological activist. She practices and teaches others "deep ecology," a meditative and active imaginative way of listening to plants and animals and even stones, to reach a deeply-felt mystical sense of a web of life. Mystical perceptions often seem to inspire activists who, like Joanna Macy, are devoted to their cause because of a visionary and loving connection with what they are trying to save or support.

Mystical experiences are also the inspiration for writing, poetry, and art. Meinrad Craighead is an example of an artist whose mysticism and paintings have become inseparable. She was an accomplished artist who, in prayer, received guidance that she must become a nun, and entered a Benedictine abbey, where she lived for fourteen years and assumed that she would stay in her religious community for life. She painted as an act of worship, and the paintings that grew out of her soul's experience of beauty were of God the Mother. She and her paintings, which are visual expressions of her mystical wisdom, became known through *The Mother's Songs: Images of God the Mother*. Sherry Anderson and Patricia Hopkins interviewed her for *The Feminine Face of God* and wrote of the inextricable connection between her mysticism and art. Drawing was an act of thanksgiving for her, an act that let her express an "overwhelming gratitude just for existence, I don't know if praying made me need to draw, or if drawing made me need to pray. I've never been able to identify one without the other."[3] Meinrad left the abbey and now lives, paints, and teaches in New Mexico, once more following the guidance of prayer and a new element that had entered her paintings—birds soaring over the landscapes. These symbols of freedom preceded her leaving the confines of the monastery. She wrote an article shortly after her departure, in which she said it was impossible for her "to support a liturgy that exalted a masculine God image and encouraged women to lead limited, subordinated, clerically-defined lives."[4]

Contemporary Sophias are often "closet mystics," who may have changed the course of their lives after a mystical experience or whose daily work is sustained through their access to this inner wisdom, and yet this most important element is hidden. Connection or union with divinity is a private and intimate experience that is easily misunderstood by others, and it is always difficult if not impossible to adequately communicate an ineffable experience. Many women who have attempted to describe their mystical insights and found themselves having to defend or justify them arrive at the conclusion that it is enough to live with this connection, especially when what they do in their lives because of their *gnosis* is their individuation path.

When Sophia is not only a source of mystical insight but is also the archetype that fully engages the attention of a woman, then it is accurate to say that she is a mystic and her Self-directed task is to find a means of expression and a way to convey the insight she has acquired. There are women mystics whom we know through their writing. Among twentieth-century examples are Evelyn Underhill, Simone Weil, and Bernadette Roberts.

SOPHIA THE SPIRITUAL LEADER

The religious roles of priest, pastor, or rabbi have until the latter part of the twentieth century not been held by women. Women could not fulfill an inner calling to mediate between divinity and congregation, which is a priestly function, or preach, or be a theologian. Many women recall being ridiculed in childhood when they said that they wanted to be a priest when they grew up. This could not be a vocation for them—even if they felt a deep call to serve God. Just as girls who wanted to be doctors were often told, "You can't be a doctor, but you can be a nurse," they were told, "You can't be a priest, but you can be a nun." This is what girls and women are still being told if they are Roman Catholics.

The women's movement of the seventies had a huge impact on admissions into medicine and law in the decade that immediately followed. Prior to then, medical school classes, if they had any women at all, had a token number. Ten out of a class of one hundred—the number of women in my own medical school class—was an unusually large percentage. A decade later it was not unusual for entering medical classes to be 50 percent women. This change in numbers was true for law schools as well. Theology graduate schools were slower to be affected, lagging behind by at least a decade, but by the end of the twentieth century, seminaries that admitted women also saw a similar rise in admissions of women. There remained overt, religiously sanctioned resistance to the ordination of women by the Roman Catholic Church and in Orthodox Judaism. In most Protestant denominations, and in Reform and Conservative Judaism, however, ordination of women became an issue when individual women sought to be priests, ministers, or rabbis, and met resistance. Most liberal denominations and synagogues now have many clergywomen.

In 2000 the annual convention of Southern Baptist leaders, representing 15.5 million people, revised previous policy, which had resulted in the ordination of fewer than a hundred women pastors and copastors, and declared that the pulpit was for men only. The Reverend Bill Merrell, their official spokesperson, quoted the apostle Paul's assertion: "I permit no woman to teach, nor have authority over men; she is to keep silent." (1 Timothy 2:12).

The mysticism of the Sophia archetype provides insights into the meaning of religious texts, beliefs, and rituals. With Sophia, theology can be the subject of inner dialogue, and writing the means of describing mystical experience. For some women, becoming a priest, pastor, or rabbi is an inner calling that still may not be allowed them. Obedience to male authority and the literal interpretation of selected passages of the Old Testament, Bible, or Koran characterize the religions that reject the spiritual leadership of women.

It is not just the women who are denied access to pulpits, but women in the congregation who suffer from their absence. I remember the time that I was in an Episcopalian church and Barbara St. Andrews officiated. This was in the early eighties, and the first time I ever saw a woman priest in a clerical collar speaking from the pulpit and offering communion. It seemed strangely unfamiliar, and then it liberated something in me. It was similar to when I saw someone who is Asian like me in an honored or respected role for the first time. When I witnessed it myself, my own world grew larger. Wherever there is discrimination, these "someone like me" experiences are heartwarming and affirming, unless there is such internalized self-hatred that affiliation is denied.

A THIRD-PHASE-OF-LIFE TASK

In the first and second phases of a woman's life the tasks that absorb us are: gaining objective knowledge and experience, coping with necessity and reality, and focusing on goals and relationships. This is what we have the "juice" for. At some point after we have crossed into the third phase, priorities shift, and the question becomes: What matters to you now? This is when Sophia, the archetype of mystical and spiritual wisdom, can come into prominence.

Sophia's concern is with spiritual or philosophical or religious meaning, which is a third-phase-of-life task. Soul and spiritual issues come to the forefront if Sophia is an active archetype. Most of us will contemplate our eventual death, not in a morbid way but because it is time to give some thought to this. The third phase is when the subject of death invites us to think about the meaning of life. The death of ail-

ing and aging parents places middle-aged women in the oldest generation, the next to go. You may be caring for a frail and vulnerable mother
and see yourself in years hence. Or you may have a life-threatening
disease or a scare that makes you think about your own death. Prayer
is an almost instinctual act in the midst of a crisis or when death is a
possibility, and prayer activates the Sophia archetype.

Thoughts turn to death and divinity, or mortality and eternity, or our
religious beliefs and personal faith; once Sophia is an active archetype,
what we believe in comes up for review. In earlier phases of life, issues
of faith are much more concrete and have to do with following or challenging one's religion; the beliefs of church and temple have a direct
bearing on a woman's sexuality, reproduction and contraceptive choices,
marriage, raising children, and divorce.

Women, especially in the third phase of life, are usually the most
active and devoted parishioners in churches and synagogues. The
clergy and theologians may for the most part be male, but it's women
who have filled the pews and kept the community going through their
attendance and volunteer work. In their crone years, women may
yearn for a spiritual community or find themselves attending services.
This is so even for women influenced by the women's movement who
have felt at odds with the sexism and yet return to the familiarity of
traditional religion.

As women influenced by the women's movement come of crone
age, many will find Sophia stirring in them and in religious quandaries
that they must personally resolve. They may disagree with beliefs and
yet feel at home in the liturgy, or the church leader, priest, or guru may
be exposed as unworthy, or simply too young for a crone to look to for
spiritual direction, and yet this is her community. Sorting out your own
religious and spiritual feelings, loyalties, and beliefs are sophianic
tasks. With Sophia, having two apparently contradictory feelings can
be resolved by *gnosis* and prayer, or they can remain unresolved but
held as a paradox. For example, a feminist woman may be aware of
how discordant it is with her feminism and yet stay in an orthodox religion because she *knows* that this is the place for her to be. Another
woman, also attuned to her inner Sophia, may take in the same information and *know* that it is time for her to leave a particular community
of believers because she no longer belongs there. The Sophia arche-

type is not concerned with the politically correct response, but with *knowing* and following her particular soul path. Sometimes it leads her back to the church.

Kathleen Norris, author of *Cloister Walk*, is an example of a woman in the third phase of her life who grappled with her faith and the meaning of her religious tradition in an intellectual sophianic way. After twenty years away, she began attending church again and, she writes, "For reasons I did not comprehend, church seemed a place I needed to be. But in order to inhabit it, to claim it as mine, I had to rebuild my religious vocabulary. The words had to become real to me, in an existential sense." Following her *gnosis,* she sought information and drew upon her experience until she *knew* what each word meant to her. The result was her own lexicon of significant Christian words, which she shares in *Amazing Grace*. In the process of seeking meaning, word by word, Norris gradually was converted, although when she began, it was not a foregone conclusion that this book would be her coming out as a Christian.

When Sophia is active as an archetype of wisdom, there is a pressing need to find meaning and reconcile one's beliefs through *gnosis*. Carol Lee Flinders in *At the Root of this Longing* describes her journey from involvement with feminism as a younger woman to being a married woman and a mother residing in a spiritual community. On turning fifty, she was disturbed by a series of events and thoughts and an internal insistence that she reconcile her feminism and her spiritual practice. She wrote, "My feminism and my spirituality have always been closely connected, laying claims on me at the same level. I'd taken up meditation out of a driving and, yes, *aching* need for self-knowledge and meaning. My feminism had arisen out of that same well of feelings, and in many regards the life I'd chosen had satisfied it. Part of me, though—the part that never lost awareness of the attitudes that demean women and girls so universally and systematically—was like a muscle that was sore from continual strain and misuse."[5] Flinders held these apparent opposites in herself until she came to *know* them to be two halves of a spiritual whole; each completed the other. She realized that "feminism catches fire when it draws upon its inherent spirituality"[6] and saw how feminism could even be defined as a resistance movement based in spirituality.

PRAYER

Prayer as the act of communing with the divine is a universal, perhaps even instinctual act and the central focus of the mystic. All spiritual traditions incorporate prayer in their worship services, and most of us have bowed our heads as a priest, minister, or rabbi prayed out loud or said a familiar prayer in unison with others in the congregation. For Sophia, prayer is as much or more about "listening" as speaking, and both halves of the "conversation" may be without words. As Anderson and Hopkins found in their research:

"Communion with the divine is a deeply personal and mysterious experience, and the women we interviewed described again and again how opening oneself to this mystery can be done in any number of ways. Some pray in solitude; others pray communally. Some pray aloud; others pray in silence. Some do both. Some pray inside, and some outside. Some follow the liturgies and formal prayers of their youth, while others make up new liturgies and rituals. Some chant their prayers and some dance their prayers and some paint or perform or swim their prayers."[7]

How Do You Pray?

Think about how and when you have prayed. Widen the definition of prayer to include when you have felt touched by or in touch with divinity—with God, the Great Mystery, Mother God, Goddess, Tao, an unnamed holiness or sense of grace, whenever you had a sense that "this is a sacred moment."

MARRIAGE AND SOPHIA

Women on a spiritual quest go inward when they are finding and developing the Sophia archetype. This private interior communion time and the *gnosis* that emerges shifts a woman's focus away from outer concerns, including her marriage. Achieving balance should be possible, but when Sherry Anderson and Patricia Hopkins interviewed women whose spirituality was an inspiration to others in-depth for *The Femi-*

nine Face of God, their stories raised the question of whether a woman can do this and sustain a marriage or a love relationship with a man.

"We began to notice that no one was inquiring whether women could be true to themselves and raise children, or have deep friendships, or even be in a loving relationship with another woman. The questions were explicitly about long-term relationships between men and women. And the real issues that lay beneath these questions seemed to be: In our male-dominated culture, what happens when women no longer need or want to defer to men? What happens when we no longer automatically modulate our personalities or reorganize our priorities to accommodate our husband or lover? Does the glue that holds male-female relationships together break down?"[8]

In their sampling, seventy-one percent of the marriages ended in divorce.[9] Almost all of the women over fifty were certain that they would not marry again, while younger women believed that it would be possible to maintain a loving marriage and a spiritual path. Since solitude commonly is the developmental ground for contemplation, prayer, meditation, and mystical experience, a conflict will arise between the needs of a relationship and time for Sophia. That this will be a conflict needs to be anticipated, with the awareness that it could become an either/or choice.

SOPHIA AS AN OLD-TESTAMENT GODDESS

Sophia is coming into the western culture as more than an archetype. For many she is feminine divinity or a name for the feminine aspect of God. Women raised in the Judeo-Christian tradition have been ignorant of the fact that the God of the Old Testament, the Christian male trinity, and patriarchal monotheism have not existed from the very beginning, or that there are hidden references to goddesses in the Old Testament. It is enlightening to discover that women's current efforts to bring a sacred feminine into religion, or have women clergy, or language for divinity that is not exclusively male is not a new invention at all, but only the current resistance to the denial of feminine divinity or sacred vocations for women. When women find Sophia in themselves, and then learn about the suppression and subsequent denial of the goddess, the intellectual knowledge enhances the *gnosis* and supports a crone's growing sense of her internal wisdom.

To begin with, there is no word in Hebrew for "goddess," so the word cannot appear in the Old Testament.[10] This nondesignation has the psychological effect of nonrecognition. We learn what something is and attach qualities to it through language. Without a vocabulary, the idea of feminine divinity is even hard to imagine. The theology of patriarchy is that God is male, and that men are created in the image of God, and have dominion over everything else.

But curiously, even if there is no word for goddess and monotheism denies the possibility, there appears to be a goddess in the Old Testament's Book of Proverbs. She was *Chokmah* in Hebrew, became *Sophia* in Greek, and then the abstract and neuter word "wisdom" in English.

Sophia as "wisdom" in the Revised Standard Version of the Bible speaks in the first person. Her description of herself and manner of speaking are that of a divine feminine being. Her attributes are those of a goddess of wisdom. She says: "I have counsel and sound wisdom, I have insight, I have strength," and then gives a biographical account of herself, which I have shortened:

> The Lord created me at the beginning of his works, before all else that he made, long ago. Alone, I was fashioned in times long past, at the beginning, long before earth itself. When there was yet no ocean I was born, no springs brimming with water, before the mountains had been shaped, before the hills, before he made the earth with its fields . . . When he set the heavens in their place I was there, when he girdled the ocean with the horizon, when he fixed the canopy of clouds overhead and set the springs of ocean firm in their place, when he prescribed its limits for the sea and knit together earth's foundations. Then I was at his side each day, like a master workman. I was his darling and delight, rejoicing with him always, rejoicing in his inhabited world and delighting in mankind."[11]

Michelangelo painted this scene on the ceiling of the Sistine Chapel. Sophia is at God's side as God reaches out with his finger to touch Adam's finger, and yet the image that comes to mind is always of the two male figures. Sophia is in plain sight and yet we are seeing only God and Adam. When we do not have the concept or word for goddess, we can't seem to see Sophia even though she is there.

In the *Wisdom of Solomon* (an apocryphal Hebrew text written about 100 B.C.E), Sophia is even more clearly a divine presence. Solomon claims that he learned everything that was hidden or manifest from Sophia, whose skill made all things. In Jewish literature, in a culture which officially maintains that there is but one God, Sophia presented a problem of how monotheism could be reconciled with the existence of a goddess. The solution has been to deny the existence of feminine divinity and consider references to her as poetic expression.

MONOTHEISM ELIMINATES THE GODDESS

The elimination of the goddess was required by the monotheism of Moses and the Israelites. When we read the Bible about warfare over the promised land and struggles against worship of "false gods," we miss the point that the Lord (translation of *Yahweh*) and his prophets were eradicating the persistent worship of the goddess. Goddesses were abominations, and those who made images of them or worshiped them were cursed by the Lord.

The cosmology of Judeo-Christian theology is told in Genesis, the first book of the Old Testament. There is one Great Father God, who is supreme and exists from the beginning. God rules alone. He has no lineage, no family or spouse. On the first day of creation, God decreed, "Let there be light;" and there was light. On each of the next five days, God decreed, and it was done.

In *The Myth of the Goddess*, Anne Baring and Jules Cashford put this into a cultural context: "In Hebrew mythology all the various male deities of earlier cultures—Enlil, Ptah, Marduck, and El—coalesce into the one image of the Great Father God, who enters the stage of the Bible as though he were the first and only deity. The elevation of the god begotten of the mother goddess into the father god was finally achieved in Babylonian mythology; but now it becomes supreme, as though the idea of a mother goddess had never existed in the human psyche."[12]

The Old Testament tells how Moses led his people out of Egypt to

the promised land, which already belonged to goddess-worshiping people whose way of life had made Canaan the coveted land of milk and
honey. After the land and people were conquered, the prophets railed
against the abominations of Asherah, Anath, and Ashtoreth, as false or
foreign gods. Their names did not give me a clue that these false gods
were goddesses, nor could I have guessed that abominations referred to
images of goddesses, shrines to them, and sacred groves on mountains.
I had no idea when I was in Sunday school or even in a college religion
class that the god of the Old Testament and his prophets were obliter-
ating goddess worship, destroying statues or paintings of a divine
woman, or, in the language itself, the word for her.

Asherah was the Semitic name of the Great Goddess. Asherah was
called the "Mother of All Wisdom" and "She Who Gives Birth to the
Gods." Sometimes she was called simply, "Holiness," or in reference to
the moon, she was called the "Lady Who Traverses the Sea." Asherah
and her priestesses were addressed as *Rabbatu,* a female form of *Rabbi,*
which means "Holy One." Her ancient oracles of prophecy were renowned. She alone gave birth to the Seventy Deities of Heaven.
Asherah was the most prominent of the Canaanite goddesses or deities.
Her husband was El, and her daughter was Anath, also called Ashtoreth or Astarte. Anath's husband and brother was Baal, the other cen-
trally important god.

The invasion of Canaan by the Israelites around 1200 B.C.E. was in
many ways a recapitulation of the invasion of Old Europe by the sky
god—worshiping Kurgan nomadic warrior tribes. After wandering for
forty years in the desert, the Israelites who had been slaves of the
Egyptian pharaoh were by then a toughened warrior people. Like Old
Europe, Canaan was a settled and cultivated land inhabited by an art-
making, goddess-worshiping people. Like the Kurgans, once the
Israelites settled in as victors, they were influenced by the people they
had conquered to assimilate their goddess. However, unlike the Kurgans, the Israelites were monotheistic, which made this unacceptable
to Yahweh. Subsequently, there followed, according to the Old Testament, the relentless effort of Yahweh's prophets to eliminate the goddess Asherah and destroy all of her Asherah. ("Asherah" also can be
translated as "sacred grove" and is the name for her sacred tree or image
that was in her temples; at times, even in the Temple at Jerusalem.)

Asherah continued to be worshiped by Hebrew-speaking people for centuries after the invasion of Canaan. In the history of Israel and Judah from 1200 B.C.E. to the Babylonian exile in 586 B.C.E. described in Davies's *The Hebrew Goddess*, there were apparently cycles in which only Yahweh, the god of Israel, was worshiped and cycles when Asherah was also, depending on the power politics of the time. Asherah was in the temple from 928 to 893 B.C.E. (thirty-five years), from 825 to 725 B.C.E. (a hundred years), from 698 to 586 B.C.E. (seventy-eight years) and from 609 to 586 B.C.E. (twenty-three years).[13]

Efforts to eliminate the goddess eventually did succeed. Virtually all that was known about Asherah was from the Old Testament, until, in the 1930s, a few tablets were found inscribed with various myths that were written about 1350 B.C.E. In the Old Testament, "Asherah" is translated "grove," without explanation that the sacred grove represented the goddess's genital center, birthplace of all things.[14]

The first and second commandments are directly related to eradicating the goddess. According to Leonard Shlain's analysis in *The Alphabet Versus the Goddess*, the First Commandment, "I am the Lord thy God. Thou shalt have no other gods before me" (Exodus 20:2–3), announces the disappearance of the goddess and declares that Yahweh will not tolerate mention of a goddess.[15] The Second Commandment, "Thou shalt not make unto thee any graven images, or any likeness of *any thing* that *is* in heaven above, or that *is* in the earth beneath, or that *is* in the water under the earth" (Shlain's emphasis), forbids making a likeness of *anything*. If the commandments are listed in their order of importance, the commandment against making images is more important than killing, adultery, stealing, and the rest of them. The prohibition against making representational art meant that it was a sin to make paintings or sculptures inspired by the beauty and power of nature or by the feminine face or body. It was a commandment of a jealous god, whose rival was a goddess.

GNOSTIC-CHRISTIAN SOPHIA

In the New Testament, divinity is also exclusively male. Father, son, and holy spirit (male) comprise the Christian trinity. However, kept literally hidden until the mid–twentieth century was the existence of early Christian gospels that were written at the same time or even before those in the New Testament. These have come to be called the Gnostic Gospels. In some of these texts, Sophia is described as a Judeo-Christian goddess, Yahweh as the son of a great mother goddess, and the Trinity as comprised of father, mother, and son.

The discovery and translation of the Gnostic Gospels coincided remarkably with the emergence of feminism in the psyches of American women. The timing has struck me as synchronistic, the information came at such an auspicious time. Originally written in Greek, these Coptic translations had been concealed and preserved for 1,500 years to be found in an era when scientific methods could preserve them, when scholarship existed that was able to translate them— scholarship that was not beholden to the church and to the maintenance of the orthodox faith—and there was interest by women scholars and theologians in Sophia and in knowing about women's participation in early Christian communities.

In December 1945, an Arab peasant made an extraordinary archaeological discovery in a mountain honeycombed with caves in Upper Egypt near the town of Nag Hammadi. He uncovered thirteen papyrus books sealed in a huge earthenware jar, which contained gospels of the heretical gnostic Christians. Described in the text is a divine feminine creator and teacher called Sophia. Long concealed, Sophia—who was revered as a divine figure in these texts—was now being revealed as a Judeo-Christian goddess.

These papyri came to the attention of the Egyptian government when they were sold on the black market through antiquities dealers in Cairo. Officials bought one of the books—called codices—and then confiscated ten and a half of the thirteen, depositing them in the Coptic Museum in Cairo. A large part of the thirteenth codex, containing five extraordinary texts, remained at large, and was discreetly offered for sale. They had been smuggled out of Egypt and were hidden in Belgium. Word of the availability of this codex reached Professor Giles Quispel at the University of Utrecht in the Netherlands, who urged the Jung Foundation in Zurich to provide funds for their purchase. Professor Quispel acquired the papyri and smuggled what is now called "The Jung Codex" across the border; a dramatic story of the scholar as an unlikely secret agent.

An excellent account of the Nag Hammadi texts and their significance can be found in Elaine Pagels's *The Gnostic Gospels,* published in 1979. When the Nag Hammadi manuscripts were translated, there were fifty-two texts from the early centuries of the Christian era, including a collection of early Christian gospels. They were Coptic translations, made about 1,500 years before, of still more ancient manuscripts, originally written in Greek, the language of the New Testament. The research efforts to date them concluded that some originated possibly as early as the second half of the first century (50–100 C.E., which means that they were written as early or earlier than the New Testament gospels). These texts and others like them were in circulation among the early Christians. In the middle of the second century C.E. they were denounced as heresy by orthodox Christians, those who accepted the power of bishops to determine faith and practice and who came to be called the Catholic Church. Until these early texts came to light, all we knew of them came from what bishops wrote attacking them.

Christianity became an officially recognized religious cult in 313 C.E., and in 323 C.E., a mere decade later, it became the state religion of the Roman Empire (following the conversion of the emperor Constantine). Once in power, Christian bishops took possession of all texts they had determined were heretical, made possession of them a criminal offense, and burned and destroyed all of them. The campaign against them was an admission of their persuasive power, and until the Nag Hammadi books were found, all we knew about the heretics and their beliefs were through the condemnatory writings of orthodoxy. As Elaine Pagels pointed out, those who wrote and circulated these texts did not regard themselves as heretics.

Gnostic congregations or groups were autonomous. There were many variations in beliefs, and many different scriptures or gospels. Many were ascribed to contemporaries of Jesus, including his brothers. Like the gospels in the New Testament, there were sayings and words attributed to Jesus. One text claimed that the true revelation of Christianity came through a woman, Mary Magdalene, who was also Jesus' beloved. Some gnostic Christians prayed to a divine mother and a divine father. Many texts were mystical works similar in the visionary quality to the book of Revelations. Their cosmological writings were either very different than what was recounted in Genesis, or they focused on the second version of the creation of man told in Genesis 1:26–27: "Then let us make man in *our* image, after *our* likeness . . ." Some considered the God of Israel ignorant of his own mother, in others, Yahweh is castigated for his arrogance and jealousy.

Pagels noted that the gnostics tended to regard all doctrines, speculations, and myths—their own as well as others'—only as approaches to truth. Their ways of perceiving and understanding was in marked contrast to the authoritarian style of the bishops, for whom there was only one truth, one church, one system of organization, and, therefore, only one legitimate Christianity.

The gnostic Christians were egalitarian, which especially rankled the church fathers. Tertullian charged them with lacking distinctions: "They all have access equally, they listen equally, they pray equally—even pagans, if any happen to come." He found it offensive that "they share the kiss of peace with all who come," and considered them all arrogant, because "all offer you *gnosis*." The place of women in gnostic congregations was especially offensive. They had authority. He charged, "These heretical women—how audacious they are! They have no modesty; they are bold enough to teach, to engage in argument, to enact exorcisms, to undertake cures, and, it may be, even to baptize!"[16]

The orthodox Christian churches were patriarchal. The "Precepts of Ecclesiastical Discipline," which Tertullian saw as proper behavior for women, specified: "It is not permitted for a woman to speak in the church, nor is it permitted for her to teach, nor to baptize, nor to offer the eucharist, nor to claim for herself a share in any masculine function—not to mention any priestly office."[17]

Also in marked contrast to orthodox Christianity, which vested power and authority at the top, with a major class distinction between the laity and the clergy, the gnostic Christians rotated positions and changed roles in their services. Bishop Irenaeus said that when they met, all members drew lots. Whoever received a certain lot had the role of priest; the one who drew the lot to offer the sacrament, functioned as bishop; another would read the scripture; and others, as prophets, would address the group, offering extemporaneous spiritual instruction. The next time the group met, they would draw lots again, so that the people taking each role changed continually. All initiates, men and women alike, participated equally in the drawing; anyone might be selected to serve as priest, bishop, or prophet, which also appalled Irenaeus.

To draw lots and rotate positions of authority and service is another example of egalitarianism, but more than this, I suspect that this was an expression of having an implicit trust in the unfolding of events. They let fate or meaningful coincidence (rather than meaningless random chance) determine who would be the vessel through which divinity would speak or act. Since Jung coined the word "synchronicity" for meaningful coincidences, we would say that they let synchronicity decide. Synchronicity has been defined, tongue-in-cheek, as "God acting anonymously," which nonetheless alludes to an awe that can accompany an especially uncanny and significant synchronicity. Maybe we should think of it as "Sophia acting anonymously," when we *know* through the synchronicity that there is no adequate explanation for how this could happen other than that we are part of an interconnected spiritual universe that has just shown us that we matter.

TO SPEAK OF SOPHIA

The fear of ridicule, of appearing superstitious, or being irritational inhibits us from sharing the mystical *gnosis* that may have been or still could be a turning point or a defining event once it is acknowledged by us and supported by others. When you were younger, anything mystical may have been labeled "foolishness" by pragmatic parents, or even "of the devil" by fundamental clergy or families. Friends of your youth may have reacted similarly, or listened and left you feeling that they were just humoring you. If you took part in consciousness-raising groups, you may remember that there was no place for spirituality then. And, while most subjects can be discussed with a therapist, I think it reasonable to be concerned that bringing up mystical experiences risks having them labeled as magical thinking or delusions. Obviously, insights gained from *gnosis* are rarely welcomed as topics of conversation at social gatherings. To break the silence and speak about what you know to be your spiritual reality, or tell another about a numinous experience or your philosophical insights or take up a religious vocation becomes possible for many women only when they are over fifty and have found friends with spiritual depth.

While some women have been in touch with Sophia's wisdom as children and remained so all their lives, the Sophia aspect of most may remain dormant or neglected until they are over fifty because the second phase of most women's lives is characterized by a shortage of time, with everyday life requiring a deft juggling of roles and tasks. There often is no time to cultivate Sophia until you are a crone. If you have a circle of women with whom you can share your spiritual journey, the circle can become a vessel for Sophia to develop in each woman. The receptivity to spirit, the ability to listen and value mystical experience, learning that *gnosis* was behind major life choices that others have made creates a safe space for Sophia's wisdom.

Goddess of Intuitive and
Psychic Wisdom

Hecate at the Fork in the Road

In Greek mythology, Hecate was the goddess of the crossroads who could see three ways at once. When you arrive at a fork in the road, she is there. She can see where you are coming from, and where each of the two paths at the crossroad might take you. If you are someone who pays attention to dreams and synchronicities, draws upon a store of past experiences and uses intuition to decide which direction to take, you know this archetype.

Hecate is a goddess of intuition. Her three-way perspective allows her to see the connection between past, present, and future. This ability to see patterns that link past situations or relationships and present circumstances is an intuitive way of perception. Seeing how a situation evolved—or where someone is coming from—is not uncanny or mysterious to an intuitive person. At significant junctures, Hecate is silently present as an inner witness. Hers is wisdom learned from experience; she is what makes us grow wiser as we grow older. At significant forks in the road, she recalls the shape of the past, honestly sees the present, and has a sense of what lies ahead at a soul level. She does not make your choices, nor judge you. To know her wisdom, you must come to a stop and consult her. You must listen to what she says in the voice of your own intuition.

Sometimes in life something happens and you know that nothing in your life will be the same again. You know it is no longer an option to go on as before, but you are not sure what to do. A younger you might have responded impulsively by letting your emotions carry you away without much thought or consideration. Those same emotions may arise, but a maturity (often having to do with being responsible for others) stops you from acting on them. You know that whatever you decide to do here matters. It is time to call on Hecate to help you see the larger picture, to stay at the crossroad until it is clear to you which path to take.

You may find yourself at a significant fork in the road not because of some external event, but because your psyche is urging you to make changes. It's not uncommon for the focus—or archetypal direction—that a woman has had for decades to shift as a woman enters the third phase of her life. If you feel that you have reached a point where whatever you are doing no longer holds much interest, you are at a crossroad with Hecate.

Hecate is the goddess at the threshold of major transitions. She is embodied by the midwife who assists at births, and by women who help ease the passage of the soul as it leaves the body at death. Metaphorically, Hecate is an inner midwife, whose perspective aids us when we birth new aspects of ourselves. She helps us let go of what is ready to die: outmoded attitudes, outgrown roles, whatever elements in our lives are no longer life-affirming.

Hecate can be found at the threshold between old and new millennia. We anticipate the possibility of a new age for humanity, but until we arrive there, we are betwixt and between—in a *liminal* time (from the Latin word for "threshold") where a shimmering potential has not yet become solid. At the beginning of the twenty-first century, humanity is at a critical juncture where change is needed to avert turning where we live—from neighborhoods to the planet—into a wasteland. Many women enter the crone phase with some sense of wanting to make a difference, or have an urge to "give back" in appreciation of opportunities that feminism provided them and first-hand experience that it is possible to bring about change. Women born just before, during, and in the first decade after World War II were in a movement that was peaceful and yet revolutionary in its influence.

Hecate is at the crux of the situation when a woman enters the third phase of her life and heeds a pull inward. She appears indecisive or as if her energy is lying fallow, when she is in this liminal phase. If she stays at the crossroad until she intuitively knows what direction to take, she emerges renewed and replenished.

HECATE THE GODDESS

Even if you took a course in Greek mythology or have a current interest in the gods and goddesses as archetypes, at best Hecate is a vague figure. She is mentioned as accompanying Demeter in the story of the abduction of Persephone, depicted as the third and least important goddess. Hecate is invariably the crone goddess when classical mythology describes goddesses in threesomes; a pattern derived from the unacknowledged triple goddess of pre-Olympian times. Besides Persephone the maiden, Demeter the mother, and Hecate the crone, there were three goddesses who personified the phases of the moon: Artemis, goddess of the waxing moon; Selene, goddess of the full moon; and Hecate, goddess of the waning and dark moon. A third triad was Hebe the maiden, a cupbearer of the gods; Hera, the goddess of marriage; and Hecate, the goddess of the crossroads. Women who saw themselves in the archetypes of Persephone, Demeter, Artemis, or Hera in *Goddesses in Everywoman*, may realize that by the third phase of their lives, the paths converge in the wisewoman archetype of Hecate.

Metaphorically and mythologically, she is dimly seen. She is associated with the underworld but did not reside there. Her time was twilight. Offerings—"Hecate suppers"—were left for her at crossroads, usually when the moon was dark, sometimes when it was full. In later times, when women were feared as witches, Hecate was called a queen of the witches or queen of the ghostworld, and seen as a diabolical figure. The poet Sappho called her queen of the night.

Her mythological origins are unclear, with discrepancies in the few accounts of her genealogical tree. Usually she is described as a Titan, who remained a goddess after these earlier divinities were defeated by Zeus and the Olympians. Hesiod, in *Theogony* (about 700 B.C.E.), said that her name means "she who has power far off" and that she was honored more highly than other divinities and given power over land, sea, and sky by Zeus. These were realms clearly divided among and ruled over by male divinities, thus for Hecate to be accorded "power over" them must not have been the same as ruling over a domain. This may have had to do with a psychic ability or clairvoyance. It also may have acknowledged another once valued aspect attributed to her, that of goddess of magic and divination.

Hecate is described as a moon goddess who wears a gleaming headdress or a headband of stars, and holds flaming torches in each hand. She was thought to walk the roads of ancient Greece accompanied by her black hounds. She was an invisible presence at the three-way crossroad, or materialized in the form of a pillar or Hecterion, a statue with three faces that looked in the three directions. Over time, as she was denigrated, Hecate became transformed into the goddess of trivia (from the Latin word *trivia*—three ways—which meant "crossroads").

Demetra George in *Mysteries of the Dark Moon* describes an ancient image of Hecate, depicting her with three heads and three pairs of arms. She carries three torches and a key, a rope, and a dagger. Her torches allow her to see in the dark, the key unlocks the secrets of the occult or hidden mysteries and knowledge of the afterlife; the rope is a symbol of the umbilical cord of rebirth, the knife, which became a symbol of ritual power, the power to cut through delusions.

Greek divinities were linked with animals who were sacred to them or had their characteristics and became symbols of them. The dog was Hecate's primary symbolic animal. She was sometimes addressed as a black bitch. When people saw black dogs howling at night, she was thought to be invisibly present. Instead of having three faces or three heads, statues representing Hecate sometimes were composites of three animals: the dog, the snake, and the lion; or the dog, the horse, and the bear. Besides the dog, the other animal strongly associated with Hecate was the frog, a symbol of the fetus and of gestation, a totem image of the midwife.

The yew, alder, and poplar were funeral trees associated with Hecate as the goddess of the gateway between the upperworld of the living and the underworld of the shades. The yew has an association with immortality, which sees death as merely a transition.

DESCENTS INTO THE UNDERWORLD
AND THE ACQUISITION OF WISDOM

The story of the rape or abduction of Persephone is told in the Homeric *Hymn to Demeter*. The maiden Persephone was gathering flowers in the meadow. Attracted to a particularly beautiful, large bloom, she left her companions in order to pick it. As she reached for it, the earth opened up before her. Out of a deep, dark vent in the earth, Hades the Lord of the Underworld emerged in his black chariot drawn by his black horses, abducted her as she screamed in terror, and took her with him back into the underworld. When Persephone disappeared from the meadow, her mother, Demeter, searched the entire world for her, to no avail.

Finally, after nine days and nights, Demeter returned, defeated and in grief, to the meadow. There Hecate came to her, saying that though she could not see what had happened, she had heard Persephone's screams. Hecate suggested that they seek information from the god of the sun, who was overhead when Persephone disappeared. He could tell them what had happened. Accompanied by Hecate, Demeter now hears the truth: Persephone was abducted by Hades, with Zeus's permission.

Hecate is not mentioned again in the myth, until Persephone returns from the underworld and is reunited with Demeter. Hecate greets Persephone with much affection, followed by a cryptic line that reads, "And from that day on that lady precedes and follows Persephone."[1]

For Hecate to precede and follow Persephone would be impossible physically. It suggests that Persephone would now be accompanied by a spirit or consciousness that she acquired upon her return from the underworld. The story of the rape of Persephone and her abduction into the underworld applies to everyone. We've all had periods when we were Persephone gathering flowers in the meadow, when all was well. Then the unexpected happened, and we were terrified as our secure world was violated by a sudden loss. It could be a betrayal and the end of a relationship, a death, the onset of an illness, financial loss, or an end of innocence. If we are plunged into the dark world of hopelessness, depression, or despair, or into cynicism, bitterness, or revenge, we are for a time held captive in the underworld, wondering if we will ever return.

If you return from your own descents into the underworld, you have learned that love and suffering are parts of life. By making it through the hard times, you grow in depth and wisdom. A wise Hecate then becomes an inner companion. Women friends or women in support groups gain this perspective by listening, and witnessing, and caring about each other as well.

Hecate consoled Demeter in her grief and loss but she was more than a comforter and a witness. She suggested that they seek information from the god of the sun who saw what happened to Persephone. Hecate's counsel was to *seek the truth*. She accompanied Demeter and was with her when Demeter learned that Persephone was abducted by Hades. The god of the sun urged her to accommodate and accept Hades as, after all, he was an Olympian like herself, and thus would not make a bad son-in-law. When Demeter heard this, and that it was done with Zeus's permission, her grief turned to anger. She decided to leave Olympus and, in disguise, wander among people, and her determination eventually led to Persephone's return.

People may think that they cannot face what is true, and so they adapt, often by keeping the truth at a distance through rationalization, denial, or addictions that serve to numb us to the truth. Only when a woman has learned from experience that reality can be faced, is she a wisewoman like Hecate.

A Hecate Meditation/Active Imagination

Ask yourself: "What have I learned about life from my own experience?" and "What truth do I need to face?" Answers are likely to come when you really want to know and are receptive. They may come into your mind if you are quiet and wait.

Or you might visualize Hecate and ask her these questions.

HECATE THE WITNESS

Hecate is a witness within us at every juncture, even if the ego denies, represses, distorts, and cannot acknowledge what is happening. This observer makes connections and speaks to us in the symbolic language of dreams. Dreams come to you in the half-light, they are liminal messages that come from the dreaming unconscious and require conscious effort to grasp and remember, just as the insights that could illuminate a painful emotional situation also come and will recede and be forgotten unless you pay attention and learn.

As an archetypal figure, Hecate, too, can be ignored. She can also become an observing part of your psyche that you draw upon daily. Psychotherapists come to depend upon Hecate, and to some extent serve as embodiments of Hecate for their clients. People are at a crossroad when they seek psychotherapy. A therapist observes, hears, and bears witness to what is revealed. Like Hecate was for Demeter, the therapist encourages the client to seek the truth of the situation, which includes her genuine feelings and perceptions that denial covers. Hecate the witness is there when you pay attention to your dreams, heed your intuitive perceptions, or listen to an inner voice. It's as if she accompanies us, holding up her torches so we can see in the dark.

People with multiple personalities reach Hecate's juncture each time a new personality emerges. This disorder arises out of terrible abuse in childhood when the child learns to dissociate from pain and memories too awful to bear. Multiples are usually unaware of the existence of other personalities in them, experience unaccountable lapses of time, and puzzling and distressing occurrences. In the absence of a consistent "I" there is a hidden observer who functions like Hecate and bears witness to the "birth" of each personality. Ralph Allison, M.D., a psychiatrist who worked with integrating multiples, called this part of the psyche the "inner self-helper." Allison characterized the inner self-helper as androgynous, as feeling only love and goodwill, and knowing all of the personalities and the circumstances in the patient's life.[2] Allison and other clinicians have found that with the help of this inner witness, the many fragmentary personalities can become aware of each other, and eventually integrate into one personality. The inner self-helper is another name for Hecate.

Unlike people with multiple personalities, we may not have amnesia and have chunks of time we cannot account for, and yet we, too, are "multiple selves." Observing this in others is easy and begins in childhood, when we see how adults put on a "different face." Seeing the "multiples" in ourselves is harder. The compassionate gaze of Hecate the witness does not blame or shame anyone, and so does not foster defensiveness or denial. Instead, she enables us to see ourselves, especially those parts that might otherwise be kept hidden. While Hecate may develop early in a person's life or come into the foreground of the psyche when traumatic circumstances call her forth, Hecate usually grows in significance as we grow older and can see patterns and reflect upon events that have taken us unaware into dark places of depression, jealousy, vengefulness, or hopelessness. The older we become, the more likely it is for us to know Hecate as a wise counselor who reminds us of lessons learned from experience. In these ways, Hecate facilitates the integration of our multiple selves into becoming a consistent and authentic person.

HECATE AS MIDWIFE

A midwife stays with the pregnant woman throughout the stages of labor. She is a reassuring, experienced presence, who reduces fear and pain as the woman labors to give birth. She knows when labor is progressing normally and recognizes the signs of trouble. The midwives were the first to be condemned as witches during the Inquisition because they eased the pain of childbirth. Quoting the Old Testament account of the banishment of Adam and Eve from the Garden of Eden, to ease difficulties and pain in labor and delivery went against God: women were supposed to give birth to children in travail and pain.* For midwives to ease labor was a sin and against the will of a punitive God. Women also sought the help of a midwife for various women's ailments and ways to avoid or abort pregnancy.

Midwifery is an earthy calling, one that assists nature and calls upon an instinctual awareness as well as an observing eye about the signs of physical transitions—the stages of labor and the stages of dying. Like mothers are with their children, a midwife has to be

*"To the woman, he said, 'I will greatly multiply your pain in childbearing; in pain you shall bring forth children, yet your desire shall be for your husband, and he shall rule over you.'" Genesis 3:16.

unbothered by the body fluids of birth, sickness, and death, knowing all are part of nature.

The midwife is a priestess to the Great Mother who, like the earth itself, is womb and tomb for all life. To see divinity in nature and her creatures, and to be able to assist at such times, is a sacred calling. Physicians who are most trusted by their patients are archetypally midwives, as well. When what you are doing draws upon the archetype of the midwife, you know that you are engaged in sacred work. Your skills or knowledge can help bring forth new life or assist healing.

The midwife may be a hospice volunteer, who is concerned that a dying person not suffer in pain or fear. She is a midwife at the time of death, this time helping a soul to leave the body. Her presence at this natural passage is comforting and may ease the passage. Just as there are stages of pregnancy preceding the onset of labor, there are stages in which the body and soul prepare for this delivery. Many women instinctively seem to know the first time they are with a dying person when the end is near and what to do or say, even when the dying person has been in a coma for some time. When the soul leaves the body of a person who is ready to die, the moment of passing is a holy moment shared by those present.

Dr. Elisabeth Kübler-Ross's *On Death and Dying* grew out of listening to patients who had terminal illnesses and were dying. She noticed that there were four stages that people go through when they are told the diagnosis, and also recognized that they sensed that death was close, even when it was not obvious to a physician. Kübler-Ross and others who work with the dying to ease the transition are enacting Hecate as midwife.

For the soul to leave the body, there is sometimes a period of labor—when the groans of a dying person (who may be in a coma) even sound similar to those made by a woman in labor, particularly in the transition phase immediately before the delivery. This is when the mother often must gather up whatever energy she still has for one last intense push, before the baby will leave her body, and it will be over. Sometimes labor is easy and the delivery is also, just as dying can follow a quiet and peaceful last soft breath. In either case, it helps to have Hecate there, in the comforting presence of an experienced, wise woman.

Hecate as the archetype of the midwife is present in those who assist others who are going through a difficult birthing process: in vocations such as editing, coaching, directing, teaching, or psychotherapy, where it is possible to be a midwife for the expression of another person's creative life. Caroline Pincus, for example, understands this perfectly well. She is an editor who calls herself a "Book Midwife" on her business card. The older and wiser you become, the less invested you are on an ego level, thus making it more likely that you will be able to assist the creative process of another.

HECATE AS MEDIUM AND PSYCHIC

Hecate the psychic is at home in the "twilight zone" of the medium, who mediates between the visible and the spirit worlds. She may be a clairvoyant who sees with the third eye, or the mind's eye, or through visions. She may have intuitive or extrasensory ways of gathering information. She may understand the precognitive meaning of dreams. Hecate's time was twilight, that threshold zone through which we pass from day to night. She was in her cave when Persephone was abducted; in myths, caves are the entrances to the underworld, a passageway between the world of the living and the "shades of the dead." In Greek mythology, afterlife existed in the underworld, where the shades of the dead were transparent and recognizable figures; metaphorically, the underworld is the personal and collective unconscious. A channeler or trance medium who receives information either from her own unconscious or the psyche of the inquirer or from the spirit world, the medical intuitive who is able to diagnose accurately without information or examination, the psychometrist who can hold an object in her hand and tell you its past are uncanny Hecates.

Reading omens, using oracular means of knowing such as the Tarot, or the *I Ching*, Medicine Cards, or Runes, interpreting dreams, or going on soul retrieval journeys are all nonrational ways of perceiving, knowing, or healing that are in Hecate's realm. Since psychic abilities are discounted, ridiculed, or feared, people with Hecate's mediumistic gifts usually don't develop them when they are young. As women grow older, they have had opportunities to learn from experience to pay attention to psychic or intuitive perceptions.

As women enter menopause, circumstances enhance the likelihood that they will become aware of Hecate. When parents and friends are dying, you may become aware that they are sensing the presence of loved ones, often long-ago deceased. Or, after their death, you may feel their presence yourself, or have what I think of as a "visitation" in a vivid dream that usually does not take place in a recognizable location. In the dream itself, you know that the person has died and that you are seeing them after their death. They look very well and often have something to say to you. Such dreams commonly let survivors know that their deceased loved ones are all right, and that the dreamer is loved. It is a dream that is so real that you may have a sense of not just seeing and hearing the person, but of touching, even smelling his or her scent. You awake with the memory of an experience that was so much more than just a dream—it was as if you entered Hecate's between-the-worlds realm.

In menopause, with its sleep disturbances and introspective times of solitude, "the veils between the worlds" may seem thinner. An awareness that you are entering the last third of your life, which ends in death, is, after all, a major shift in direction, when questions about an afterlife become relevant. Or it may be that after menopause, you no longer care if people think you a little weird,[3] and are willing to come out of the psychic closet. When you emerge, Hecate will be accompanying you.

When a woman develops her psychic abilities, what she does with them can be issue for her. Manipulation of people, misuse of information, being exploited, becoming obsessed with occult power, are shadow possibilities. The more integrity and maturity a woman with occult abilities has, the more likely it is that she will use her psychic powers well. I have seen younger women heed an inner wisdom of Hecate, and hold off on pursuing the development of their psychic abilities until they are crones. Hecate's counsel has also cautioned psychic women to keep their psychic abilities hidden and to use them discreetly in their work. This is especially true of physicians whose diagnostic and healing abilities are enhanced by these talents, and yet their reputations would suffer if others knew about this. Some are aware of having healing ability in their hands. Others are able to perceive energy fields around organs, or can sense what treatments will work, or have telepathic connections with their patients, and when something they do as a consequence is uncannily accurate, fall back on "professional intuition" as an explanation.

HECATE AS FEARED WITCH

Hecate was said to have power over earth, sea, and sky, not in terms of ruling over these realms, but in being able to affect them from a distance. Occult powers were attributed to older women who were supposed to be able to cast spells and enchantments, hex people, or practice black magic. Hecate has become the archetype of the witch because of her uncanny powers and association with twilight. We can speculate that old women were irrationally feared because of mankind's suppression of the triple goddess, whose crone phase was the most mysterious and awesome.

Women fear being called a witch, for good historical reasons. The Inquisition was established in 1252 by Pope Innocent IV, and continued with officially sanctioned torture for five and a half centuries until it was abolished by Pope Pius VII in 1816. Between 1560 and 1760, the persecution of women for witchcraft was at its height. Feminists have called this "the women's holocaust" with the number of women condemned to the stake estimated from over a hundred thousand to as many as eight million.

The women who were most feared or respected became the most persecuted. The first women to go to the stake were the midwives and healers; older women who eased the pain of childbirth and delivered babies, who knew herbal medicine, whose powers came from observation and experience. Women with authority, independence, or knowledge, eccentric women, or women with property (usually widows) were also denounced, tortured to confess, and condemned. Any woman of crone age was at risk for having supernatural powers including poor, outcast, powerless, demented old women, who were routinely persecuted as witches. It was, in fact, heretical to say that such old women were harmless. Any woman of crone age was at risk. To survive, an older woman needed to be unnoticed and undistinguished; only "invisible" older women stayed alive.

Barbara G. Walker's encyclopedic compilation of information on witches and witchcraft[4] is an appalling litany of pathological fear and persecution of women, especially crones. Witches had descriptive titles such as "one who gathers herbs," "one with the evil eye," "screech owl," "keeper of an ointment box," "wisewoman," "worker of charms," "poisoner," "seeress," or "evil doer." In Italy a witch was a *strega* or *Janara*, an old title of a priestess of Jana (Juno). In England a witch was called a hag or a fairy.

One epithet for a witch was "stick rider." Broomsticks were associated with witches because of their use in pagan rituals of marriage and birth. In Rome, the broomstick was a symbol of Hecate's priestess-midwife, who swept the threshold of a house after each birth to clean it of evil spirits that might harm the child. Old wedding customs included jumping over a broomstick, which was retained in gypsy weddings and unsanctioned ritual weddings between slaves in nineteenth-century America. Broomsticks were phallic symbols, especially when ridden. The woman astride or "on top" was considered a perversion of power as well as a sexual perversion.

Today the inquisitors' fear of old women and their power would be diagnosed as pathological. There was a preoccupation with sexual intercourse between the devil and women designated as witches who were blamed for anything that went wrong, from miscarriages to impotence. Inquisitors' handbooks directed them to wear a bag of salt consecrated on Palm Sunday, to avoid looking in a witch's eyes, and to cross themselves constantly when in their presence. When these tortured women appeared before them, the inquisitors required them to be naked, walk toward them backward, and never look at them.

A motivation for making accusations of witchcraft was greed, to acquire the witches' property or be rid of competition. The accusers of the midwives, for example, were physicians. Widows who owned anything that someone else coveted were denounced. There was avarice on the part of the Inquisition itself. The estate of a woman of any means who had been denounced as witch and burned at the stake was charged for the cost of her jailing, her torture, and even for the cost of burning her.

It was decidedly dangerous to be noticed, envied, or feared. Any unusual ability in a woman instantly raised a charge of witchcraft. "The so-called Witch of Newbury" was murdered by a group of soldiers because she knew how to go "surfing" on the river.

Country women burned as witches were nominally Christian, but if they observed the summer and winter solstices, spring and fall equinoxes, planted according to the phases of the moon, could predict from animal behavior how cold a winter could be expected, and had knowledge beyond the learned churchmen, they became personifications of evil. All of this because their herbal remedies worked like magic for some people and their knowledge of the cycles of the seasons, which came from the old religion of the goddess.

The Catholic Church called any woman who criticized church policies a witch. For example, women allied with the fourteenth-century Reforming Franciscans and burned for heresy were described as witches, and as instigated by the devil. Jewish Talmudic scholars also viewed women in a similiar light. Walker quotes them as writing, "Women are naturally inclined to witchcraft," and "The more women there are, the more witchcraft there will be."

While being called a witch no longer leads to the torturer and then to the stake, it still feels dangerous. This was the cause of the tension in the air at a large conference on Women's Spirituality held in Seattle in the 1980s. Negative newspaper attention had been focused on the conference, especially on Starhawk, an author and teacher of Wicca. Outside of the auditorium, we encountered men handing out flyers that proclaimed across the top: "Thou shalt not suffer a witch to live" (Exodus 22:18), a Biblical quote that had given scriptural support to the Inquisition. The flyer had a small blurred photograph of "Starhawk the Witch" on it. Rather than avoiding the man in her path who was handing out these flyers, Starhawk engaged him in a friendly conversation about what was on his flyer, and then introduced herself and spoke to him for several minutes about Wicca beliefs and how she felt reading the flyer he was handing out. Her quiet courage and manner were impressive; maybe the encounter left him a little more enlightened than he had been.

A more recent incident had the emotional impact of a burning cross, which served as the Klu Klux Klan warning. The words "Burn the Witches" were spray-painted on the garage door of an ordained woman minister in Northern California who had attended "The Re-Imagining God" conference held in the midwest in the early nineties, which brought feminine imagery into Christian worship. She was one of over several hundred women who attended, mostly clergywomen from major Protestant denominations. Many were censured from pulpits, had letters written attacking them, and found their positions in jeopardy. The accusation of being a witch is (unofficially) still used against women who challenge church authority.

HECATE PRESIDES OVER MOMENTS OF TRUTH

"Let us go to the god of the sun, who was overhead. He saw what happened to Persephone and can tell us," were Hecate's words to Demeter. To seek the truth rather than stay in ignorance or denial, or speak the truth rather than remain silent are critical, at-the-crossroad decisions.

Whenever you tell the truth to someone else, especially if that truth shakes a premise, this moment becomes a fork in the road. Likewise, whenever you ask for the truth, Hecate is the inner wisdom that prepares you to hear it. Sometimes, you may unexpectedly find yourself at Hecate's junction when something is being done or said that puts you on the spot. It may be a public moment that will put you on record. Or, knowing that "silence is consent," you alone may realize that this is a moment of truth that calls on you to do what you know will be hard but true to yourself. Apart from the effect that you may or may not have on the situation itself, such moments of truth decisions are soul-shaping.

Sometimes when you know that what you are about to do will appear "heretical," an irrational fear arises, an emotional reaction that seems to anticipate hearing the cry, "Burn the witches!" This is a transpersonal fear that seems to lie just below the surface in women's psyches, where the fear of being labeled and persecuted as a witch lurks. To feel this fear and do it anyway takes courage. With a morphic field effect, the more women confront this collective fear, the easier it will become for others.

When Persephone returned from the underworld, Hecate accompanied her from then on. This is so for us as well. Hecate's wisdom is acquired through our own life experiences—from having lived this long. With Hecate, older is, indeed, usually wiser.

Goddess of
Meditative Wisdom

Hestia as the Fire at the
Center of the Hearth

One of the most important Greek goddesses had no persona, no physically identifiable characteristics that can be seen in statues or paintings. She is Hestia, the goddess of the hearth and temple, one of the original twelve great Olympians, and the eldest. Hestia was the older sister of Zeus, Demeter, Hera, Poseidon, and Hades, and the aunt of Artemis, Apollo, Hermes, Ares, Aphrodite, and Athena. Although she was not visible, she was the center of every house and honored with the best offerings in the temples of all the divinities.

As a goddess, Hestia was the sacred fire at the center of the round hearth, present in the flames and in the glowing coals, a source of light and warmth. As an archetype, Hestia is the still point, the center of the psyche, what many think of as the Self.

It is Hestia you wish to be with when you yearn for time alone, when solitude is a sanctuary, and your soul is at the center of your being. If you know Hestia's symbolic fire as a spiritual center or inner presence that warms and illuminates your psyche and your body, you will have a feeling of being at home in yourself and in a universe that is both ordinary and sacred.

Of all the stages of adult life, it is in the phase of the waning moon that there is the most time for Hestia. This "archetype of meaning" comes into her own when ego strivings and how we look to others, or the need for a particular relationship, or the needs of others no longer are at the center of our lives. The goddess Hestia was one-in-herself, as many older women who have a sense of themselves as whole can be. These wisewomen are beyond the need or the delusion that something or someone outside of themselves will complete them. They are at peace with themselves just as they are.

Hestia is the only goddess archetype that has a chapter of her own in both *Goddesses in Everywoman* and *Goddesses in Older Women*. In the world of achievement or the traditional roles of wife and mother, the other Olympian goddesses are clearly visible as images and as forces within the psyche of women, while Hestia is not. When Hestia is the predominant archetype throughout a woman's life, she may feel out of step and inadequate, unless she develops other aspects of herself as well, or until she sees and honors who she inwardly truly is and finds a place where she can be herself in the world, or finally comes into her own in her older years.

HESTIA'S HEARTH FIRE

Living as I do, on the side of Mount Tamalpais, north of San Francisco, where storms commonly cause electrical outage, I've often had to do without electricity. Sometimes it takes quite a while before the electricity returns. At night it is dark and often cold inside. During these times I've realized how much of a difference a fire makes, and am reminded how Hestia's sacred fire transformed a house into a home, and a building into a temple.

Staying near the fire in the dark also reminds me of summer camp and the campfire that was the source of heat and light around which we gathered after dark. It was laid out with great care and ritually lit, as we sang, "Rise up O Flame." The tinder, and then the small branches, and finally the logs caught fire, creating an inviting island of light in the dark night.

For many millennia, fire was the only source of light in the dark, the only way to cook food, the only source of heat in winter; it kept wild animals away and people together. Think of what it meant to people to have fire, and how cold, dismal, bleak, and even dangerous it could be without it. Home and hearth fire went together. The hearth fire was the center around which everyone gathered for warmth and safety. Tending the fire, feeding the fire, banking the coals, keeping the fire alive would have been a serious responsibility, even a sacred one, upon which the survival of the group could have depended.

In classical Greece, Hestia was a presence in all the marble temples to the gods and goddesses. The fire burning on the temple's round hearth invited the divinity, whose temple is was, to be present. Similarly, for the body to be a temple, there must be a source of warmth and illumination within.

A Hestia Visualization

Imagine that your body is a temple. The center of the temple is inside your chest, and in the center of this space, there is a glowing fire upon a round hearth.

Sense the light and warmth that emanates from this glow, radiating out to fill your whole body with warm inner light.

Place your hands over this place.

Then, with each intake of breath, breathe in peace.

Hold your breath for a moment and be still.

And then slowly exhale.

Breathe in peace, and hold, breathe out peace.

And in the Stillness, Hestia is present.

HESTIA'S MYTHOLOGY

In Greek mythology, Hestia was the first child born to Rhea and Cronus, the Titan parents of the first-generation Olympians. By birthright, she was one of the twelve major Olympians, yet she could not be found on Mount Olympus and made no protest when Dionysus, god of wine, grew in prominence and replaced her as one of the twelve. Thereafter instead of six gods and six goddesses, the Olympian pantheon was comprised of seven gods and five goddesses. She was the only divinity of classical Greek mythology without a persona—she had no characteristic image or pose, was not represented in art, and did not take part in any of the conflicts or erotic pairings that make up much of Greek mythology. Yet she was greatly honored, receiving the best offerings made by mortals to the gods. She was known as Vesta by the Romans.

Poseidon, the god of the sea, and Apollo, the god of the sun, desired Hestia, who refused them both and instead took a great oath to remain forever a virgin, averting a conflict between the rival suitors. A grateful Zeus gave her the privilege of being at the center of every house, honored in the temples of all the gods, and the recipient of the first offerings.

HESTIA'S RITUALS

Unlike other Greek gods and goddesses, Hestia was not celebrated by storytellers or artists. Instead, she was honored in rituals, in which she was the sacred fire. In ancient Greece, when a couple married, the bride's mother lit a torch from her own household fire and, followed by the newly married couple, carried it to their new house where she lit the first fire in their hearth. This act consecrated the new home. The symbolic meaning of this ritual was to make the goddess Hestia present in the center of the house. Since the fire was brought by the mother to the new household of the bride through the generations, each woman—by being hearthkeeper and torch carrier—would symbolically perpetuate a matrilinear continuity of the goddess.

A second significant ritual took place after a child was born. When the newborn was five days old, guests were invited to the house to witness the ritual in which the child was carried around the hearth fire and, in the light and warmth of Hestia, acknowledged as a member of the family.

Just as each household had a hearth in which Hestia dwelled, so did every city or city-state. The common hearth was the sacred fire in the main hall or temple. Just as in the formation of a new household, whenever people set out from the home city to establish a new colony, they took the sacred fire from the common hearth to their new community; from the mother fire to the daughter fires throughout the settled world. Hestia linked the old home with the new, the capital city with all of its colonies.

In Rome, Hestia would become worshiped as the goddess Vesta. Vesta's sacred fire united all the citizens of Rome into one family. The sacred fire was tended by the Vestal Virgins, who embodied the anonymity and virginity of the goddess.

VIRGIN GODDESS

In Greek mythology, Hestia was one of three Olympian virgin goddesses (along with Artemis and Athena). They were the only divinities impervious to the arrows of Eros or the love spells of Aphrodite. Hestia did not take part in the conflicts, struggles for power, or contests that are the subject of so many myths. It was enough to be present in homes and temples. As a virgin goddess archetype, Hestia is "one-in-herself," meaning that she did not need anyone else to be complete, not a spouse, not a child, not a lover.

The virgin goddess archetype, as described by Esther Harding in *Women's Mysteries*, is motivated by a need to follow her own inner values rather than a need to please, be liked, or gain approval. When a woman is one-in-herself, she does what has meaning for herself, and is not deterred by what other people think. This usually becomes easier to do the older one becomes. Sometimes, Hestia comes into the psyche only after loss and grief lead a woman to discover the richness of an inner spiritual life or the sweetness of peace and quiet.

MEDITATION

Many people have come to know Hestia through the spiritual practice of meditation. The Latin word for "hearth" is *focus,* and this inward focus comes to many people only through a commitment to meditation. Her meditation is a focus on being in the moment, of emptying the mind and stilling the emotions. Persona and ego, comparisons, criticisms, the gamut of thoughts having to do with past and future, the attachments we have to seeing ourselves or others in certain ways that lead nowhere, all drop away when we still the mind. Meditation as a practice to achieve this works for many.

However, to women in whom the archetype of Hestia is present, the state of mind that others achieve in meditation comes naturally. Tending to household details is a centering activity, a means through which a woman puts her house and herself in order. As a "hearth-keeper," she finds inner harmony through outer order. With Hestia, there is no rush, no eye on the clock, nor an internal critic. What she does pleases her and absorbs her in the same way that concentrating on the breath absorbs a meditator. As she sorts and folds laundry, irons or cleans up clutter, picks and arranges flowers, prepares dinner, or puts her closet in order, she is totally in the present moment.

During this time, a thought or feeling may surface in her mind, and be seen with some clarity and detachment. Hestia provides us with access to meditative wisdom, perceptions that come to us when we are in harmony with the Self.

In religious communities, work, service, and ritual come together as one cleans the sanctuary or prepares a table or an altar. Wherever and however a woman brings order, beauty, and harmony to an environment, she is creating a sacred place. There is something nurturing about doing this sort of work and in entering a space that has been cared for in this way. From the time of prehistoric cave dwellers, the fire at the center of a hearth not only provided light and warmth, but a sense of family. The fire was where meals were cooked, and around it meals were eaten. Hospitality meant sharing the fire and food. Hestia's presence now warms the heart, nourishes the soul, and makes others welcome.

HESTIA'S SPACE

As an archetype, Hestia represents an invisible feminine presence or energy that permeates a situation, a place, or a psyche, and transforms it into a sacred space. Hestia's hearth fire has to do with soul and home, with being rather than doing. Her wisdom is the wisdom of being centered, with an emotional warmth that is generous and not possessive. She is the archetype that we associate with soulfulness or the still point in the center of the psyche.

Without doing anything or saying anything directly to bring about a shift in the relationship or a situation, a woman who is embodying this archetype has a subtle, transformative influence on others in her environment. She does not polarize anyone because she is at home in the quiet in herself. In her presence and her invariably serene environment, other people also can just be. When one enters a Hestia space, comparisons and competitiveness are left outside the door.

HESTIA AND SHEKINAH

There is a similarity between Hestia as goddess of the hearth and the Shekinah, the feminine aspect of divinity in Judaism, who is also unseen and unpersonified. The Hebrew word "Sh'kina" meant "dwelling place," perhaps meaning "where God lives." The Shekinah comes into a Jewish home on Friday, when women light the candles for the Sabbath meal, and the Sabbath begins. She is in the household while the Sabbath is observed, a time when work comes to a standstill, and the house can be considered a temple.

The Japanese tea ceremony is another Hestian sanctuary. While the task is merely to make and serve tea to a guest, it is elevated into an art form that brings the participants into an inner state of serenity and a timeless space.

A THIRD-PHASE-OF-LIFE ATTRIBUTE

When being needed, or being productive, or being attractive, and staying so are a woman's major concerns, there is no place for Hestia in her psyche. Even when these are not compelling, juggling work and relationships, and taking care of responsibilities require more hours than we often seem to have. It is no wonder then that a woman may not find much time to have an inner life, much less periods of solitude, until she is in the third phase of her life. But it isn't only a matter of the availability of time. To find solitude soul-satisfying, the archetype has to be present.

When Hestia emerges as an important archetype, a woman is able to both value what has gone before and see herself and others in a more objective light. Like the hearth fire that illuminates, there is more clarity in all aspects of a woman's life, and an inner center around which the diverse aspects of a personality can come together. Hestia is an archetype of integration and inner wisdom.

I think of Hestia as a yearning for a place of one's own and the time to be there. A Hestia space, real or imagined, is not disturbed by anyone else's presence, emotions, or belongings. It is a place to return to and find as we left it. As our need for solitude makes itself known, women begin to fantasize about such sanctuaries or even dream of them.

Women drawn to meditation as a spiritual practice are heeding the Hestia within themselves. For them, solitude and silence are nourishing and centering. It may be the first time in their adult lives that they have the time to spend with their own thoughts, or to observe their feelings. They are more detached from family, marriage, or career, which may still matter enormously, but if Hestia becomes active, there is a marked inner shift.

If in the midst of your active life you begin to have fantasies of retreating into a cloister, or joining a convent, or crossing through the mists to an imaginary Avalon, it is an inner call to shift your focus inward, to find some solitude, or to be with other women who are spiritually centered. Or if you are drawn to something new in your life, as if to a bright warm fire, it may be because it is illuminated by Hestia, and is a potential source of meaning.

A PRIVATE CHRYSALIS

The sleep disturbances, middle-of-the-night thoughts, and hot flashes that mark the perimenopausal phase of a woman's life demand that you pay attention to this transition. Many women report mood swings, the urge to write poetry, feelings that well up, and memories that suddenly intrude on their thoughts. The onset of menopause can throw women into an identity crisis and a hormonal readjustment that is as disturbing as in adolescence.

At this time, it is common for women to want to retreat into a Hestia space, to seek time alone, to tend the inner fire, to muse and meditate upon change and making changes. It's almost as if there is an urge to make a private chrysalis to cocoon the Self through this time of physiological transition and potential transformation. When a woman emerges as a wisewoman-crone from this chrysalis stage, her sanctuary exists inside herself.

FROM INNER COMMITTEE TO INNER CIRCLE

In *Goddesses in Everywoman*, I used the committee metaphor to describe our complex personalities. The inner archetypes that express the many aspects of ourselves are sometimes in competition with each other. They are male and female, young and old. In most women, the goddess archetypes are the basis of the major patterns within us. If we function well, it's because we have a competent ego "chairing the committee," deciding who will be heard and heeded, keeping order, allowing discussion before decisive actions are taken. Different situations call for different aspects of ourselves, sometimes an archetype or part of us has to "wait her turn."

The most compelling archetypes act upon us. When thwarted, they can lead to painful obsessions, and when fulfilled, they can be sources of meaning. Whether it is to have a faithful spouse, a healthy child, or a lover, or to be a competitor or a winner, these are the powerful drives in young and middle adulthood. As menopause approaches with its downshift in hormones, there is an easing of intensity. By then, the dominant archetypes have had their day, as has the ego. A woman who passes through menopause is not only older in years, she has, more than likely, to have been seasoned by her joys and sorrows, accomplishments and losses.

I think of a wisewoman-crone as a woman who has experienced a shift in her inner world. The Self, rather than the ego, has become the center of her personality. Instead of a committee meeting with the ego as the chair, a circle meets around the hearth with Hestia's fire at the center. Once Hestia is the centering archetype in a personality, it's as if the members of the inner council sit around the fire, speaking or listening, until there is clarity about the situation. With inner consensus, there is an integrity to what you do and how you live: outer actions become a manifestation of the inner person. An *inner-directed* person, I might add, can be very active and effective in the world. This is something that sometimes takes becoming a crone to learn. As Gloria Steinem said about herself:

"Who would have imagined that I, once among the most externalized of people, would now think of meditation as a tool of revolution (without self-authority, how can we keep standing up to external authority)? or consider inner space more important to explore than outer space? or dismay even some feminists by saying that power is also internal?"[1]

Her Name Is Wisdom

In Hestia's presence,
with Hecate as witness,
trust Sophia's *gnosis*,
listen to Metis's wise counsel.

Use of Imagination
For Hestia

Enter a serene room, a temple, a sacred space
or even a clearing in a forest.
See a glowing fire in the center of a round hearth
and be drawn closer.
Watch the fire.
Feel warm and safe.
Hestia is here.
You can sense her presence,
maybe even see her in the fire.
Find her in your heart center
and feel at home.

Use of Imagination
For Hecate

It is twilight,
neither day nor night,
the mysterious time in-between.
You are on a country road or a path.
You are approaching a place where three roads meet.
Where the one you are on
comes to a fork in the road.
There are two paths to choose from.
Which direction will you take?
Hecate is here.
You may see her or sense her presence.
Hear or feel what she has to say.
She is a wisewoman who knows you
very well.

She is the deep intuitive wisdom
you can draw from if you are receptive.
Ask the right questions
and wait for her answers to come.
What is this intersection?
What are your choices?
Where does each path lead?

Use of Imagination
For Sophia

Imagine:
a gateway or doorway is opening.
A threshold to cross.
For you to meet Sophia.

Sophia is inside of you
as *gnosis*.
She *knows* that
you are a spiritual being on a human path.
She *knows* that
you have a soul and a purpose.
She *knows* that
you are a part of a vast, beautiful, and meaningful,
visible and invisible universe.
She *knows* that
divinity dwells in you
and is feminine.

Might you cross over this threshold,
know her
and *know* what she *knows*?

Use of Imagination
For Metis

Talk to Metis.
Visualize her.
Ask for her guidance
and give her time
to counsel you.

The inner wise counselor
is a strategist of the highest order;
has learned from experience
of risk and retribution.
Knows to be vigilant and patient,
to adapt to inevitable change.
Has developed particular skills
and a deep familiarity with the material that she works,
which may be people.
She has developed a craft or mastered an instrument
or ran a household or managed an office,
raised children,
commanded troops,
or is a scientist or scholar.
Whatever she has done in the world,
however successful she may have been,
it was only a learning ground for a higher wisdom
beyond ego.
Metis is skill plus experience plus wisdom.
Seek her counsel
when you want to know:
What is the wisest course to follow?
(Not merely how to accomplish a goal).

You Can Know Wisdom

Be present and centered.
Be an intuitive observer with memory.
Trust what you know in your bones.
Let wisdom be your guide.

PART 2

SHE IS MORE . . .
THAN WISDOM

And, above all other prohibitions, what has been forbidden to women is anger,
together with the open admission of the desire for power and
control over one's life (which inevitably means accepting
some degree of power and control over other lives).

In the end, the changed life for women will be marked, I feel certain,
by laughter. It is the unfailing key to the new kind of life. . .
It is the laughter of women together that is the revealing sign,
the spontaneous recognition of insight and love and freedom.

—Carolyn G. Heilbrun

The capacity to feel another's pain as your own,
the nucleus of reform politics, is a spiritual quality.

—Carol Lee Flinders

In part 2, I introduce goddesses that often come into full expression in the third phase of women's lives. They represent archetypal qualities that need to be balanced and accompanied by wisdom—often for the woman's sake, sometimes for the sake of others. I've grouped them by their traits into three categories: the goddesses of transformative wrath, the goddesses of mirth and bawdy humor, and the goddesses of compassion. When you can tap into the energies of all three, and also have wisdom, you are an internally free woman and a juicy crone.

When I look around at my contemporaries growing older, I see some wonderful women among them. What seems to make them special is that they are uniquely themselves. And yet, there are some characteristics they have in common. Each has reached a "This is who I am" self-acceptance. They have strong feelings and are passionate about what matters to them: each is capable of acting on her own behalf or in the best interest of someone else. They have spontaneity: each woman has a genuine laugh or giggle that can become infectious hilarity. Each is also compassionate. These qualities are not the same as wisdom, yet it is because each woman is *also* wise, that these qualities enhance her.

HER NAME IS OUTRAGE

Outrage is good healthy anger that finally is directed at changing an unacceptable situation. The depression and anxiety that women suffer from in the first and second phases of their lives are usually the result of feeling angry and powerless, afraid to express it because of the consequences, either real or imagined, and bottling it up so well that it is no longer recognizable as anger. By the time a woman is in the third phase of her life, she may no longer be intimidated by parents or others who taught her that anger was unacceptable either to them personally or for a "good girl" to express, or held emotionally captive by an abusive or domineering person.

Or she may not have been depressed or felt oppressed personally at all, and now, in the third phase of her life, becomes angry at what she is seeing beyond her personal situation. Her anger may be directed at injustice, stupidity, narcissism, addictions, carelessness, and cruelty that affect others who are disempowered, or at social evils that institutions and politicians are ignoring.

This is when she can tap into what I call the "Enough is enough!" archetype. These are the energies of the goddesses of transformative wrath, powerful agents of change. Chief among them are Sekhmet, the ancient Egyptian lionheaded goddess, and fierce Kali, the Hindu goddess. These goddesses were called forth when needed. They are inhuman in appearance and became appalling in their respective mythologies when they were carried away by their wrath against evildoers and became bloodthirsty. By the time a woman is in the third phase of her life, if she has gained wisdom—and has the resources of compassion and humor—she will not be impulsive, one-sided, and carried away by fury. The outrage of Sekhmet and Kali will provoke her to action, but not until there is a consensus of her "inner council" of crone goddesses.

You can call upon the fierceness and power of Sekhmet or Kali through the use of intention and imagination. This is what the character played by Kathy Bates did in the movie *Fried Green Tomatoes* when she called upon Towanda, the Amazon queen, and transformed herself from a compliant and stepped-upon woman into a formidable and authentic person. With a cry of "Towanda!" the Bates character did what she had dared not do before. It was an amusing touch that drew upon a deeper reality—the transformative power of myth to evoke archetypal energy.

Third-phase women are most able to become authentic people—juicy crones—who know what they feel and live accordingly, when this is their intention and they have the tools that imagination and consciousness can provide and the support of others and other archetypes. The wisdom of Hecate and Metis restrains impulsive action and holds rage in check. The ability to stay centered, found in Hestia, and the spiritual meaning from Sophia contribute to restraint until a woman can act effectively rather than be taken over by the fury of this archetype, which needed to come into her consciousness, before transformation is possible. Women who reach the point of enough is enough and have wisdom, compassion, and humor, are formidable forces for change.

Her Name Is Mirth

A sense of humor can support us in a difficult situation. The antics of the Japanese goddess Uzume brought sunlight back to earth. In Greek mythology, the maidservant Baubo humored Demeter out of her silent grief. Mirth and dance, bawdy and body, are related in this archetype. When our bodies change and become inelegant, humor brings together an earthy spontaneity and reality. When troubles happen, gallows humor can help. There is a wisdom to black or rueful humor; it connects and comforts, heals the isolation of suffering alone. In an instant, a bleak mood is transformed by laughter. A belly laugh is radically authentic and is most often heard among women outside the earshot or judgment of men.

The goddesses of mirth have an earthy perspective that is a commentary on reality; a wise humor that is not mean or demeaning to others. Humor without wisdom and compassion is often sadistic and cruel, a means of feeling superior at someone else's expense. The intellectual and verbal talent that gives rise to a rapier wit in the company of equals is also not the same as mirth.

Women who can embody Uzume or Baubo are women who accept their own bodies growing older and can laugh with each other about the changes. It's necessary to be beyond the need to perform or look good for others even to laugh freely, which is also why these are crone goddesses. Ladies are supposed to cross their legs and not laugh uproariously, after all.

HER NAME IS COMPASSION

Older and wiser women are also compassionate. I don't think it is possible to be emotionally mature without learning compassion. When we were younger women, most of us judged others and ourselves harsher than we do as crones. We may have felt entitled, or had expectations of people derived only from surface appearance, and needed lessons in reality and humility to know better.

Kindness and generosity are childhood qualities that often go underground in the first and second phases of women's lives. We may have been warned against being gullible or had our generosity abused. Or a cynical adult may have made us feel foolish when we were motivated by kindness. The deluge of requests for donations from charities may have had a deadening effect on our compassion as well. Maybe we adopted the prevalent patriarchal attitude of contempt for weakness.

Although there is no divinity of compassion in Greek mythology, in Eastern religion and mythology she is a prominent goddess. She is Kuan Yin in China, Kannon in Japan, Tara in Tibet. Catholics have the Virgin Mary, and I think that Americans have an unrecognized goddess of compassion in the Statue of Liberty. These are feminine archetypes with maternal compassion for the poor and powerless, for suffering humanity.

Missing an Archetype?

A wisewoman-crone has the wisdom to hold within herself "opposing" qualities. She is able to be outraged and compassionate, fierce and tender, spiritual and bawdy; she can love solitude and be an activist in the world. She can be one-in-herself and be deeply committed to another person. She is unique and authentic because she has many facets and an integrity that holds them together. She works at integrating the diversity within her, which is why she is a whole person but not a perfect or "finished" woman.

The crone phase is a time of self-knowledge, when shifts occur in outer and inner life and you may find new archetypes as sources of change and vitality. It is a time that does call for reflection and contemplation of your life so far and the "work in process" that you are. The goddesses in part 2 may have unfamiliar names, and yet they may already be an active part of you. If so, you'll recognize them and come to know this part of yourself better. It may be of even more value, and definitely something to think about—if you find that one of them is "missing." If Sekhmet, or Uzume, or Kuan Yin were a conscious part of your psyche, how would your life have been different? If you find them now, how will your life be different?

Goddesses of Transformative Wrath:
Her Name Is Outrage

Sekhmet, the Ancient Egyptian
Lionheaded Goddess
Kali-Ma, Hindu Destroyer Goddess

The goddesses of transformative wrath are markedly different from the goddesses of wisdom that we met in the preceding chapters. They come to the fore when it is time to take action to change an unacceptable situation, when *enough is enough*. These are goddesses who were called forth when male gods or men were not able to defeat evil and only a powerful goddess was equal to the task. The most prominent goddesses of transformative wrath are depicted as nonhuman in appearance. The Egyptian goddess Sekhmet has the head of a lion and the body of a woman. Kali-Ma, the Hindu goddess, has a frightful inhuman face and a many-armed woman's body.

I include them as crone archetypes because they come into this phase of women's lives. Gloria Steinem has frequently observed that women become more radical as they get older. Men are likely to be radicals in their youth, and upholders of conservatism later in life. In their personal lives and political thinking, crones appear radical when they act upon what they know and feel. They may end long-standing dysfunctional marriages. They may fire authoritarian experts and take medical and financial reins into their own hands. In the political sphere, they may look around at how men are running things and become outraged at the tolerance of evil or the indifference to suffering. Sekhmet/Kali arises in them and fuels their determination to bring about change.

These archetypes of transformative wrath are most effective when balanced by wisdom. Without wisdom, they can be destructive to the woman and others. Rage without wisdom feeds on itself and makes a woman fear she is going crazy or out of control, and some do. The abused wife who doused the marital bed with gasoline and set her sleeping husband afire and killed him, and the mother of a sexually abused son who took a gun into the courtroom and shot the perpetrator are extreme examples. It is uncomfortable to grapple with intense feelings of wrath and hostility, especially after a lifetime of accommodation and making the best of it. However, when such is the case in crone-aged women, there are other strong archetypes that can balance and contain these raw feelings.

With wisdom, the goddesses of transformative wrath are not unleashed in outbursts of rage, nor acted upon impulsively. With wisdom, anger is channeled into a commitment to bring about change, and a determination to find the best way. With wisdom, blame and shame do not immobilize or divert a woman from facing the truth or being angry. And when wise strategy and outrage come together, an older woman is transformed into a formidable crone.

SEKHMET, THE LIONHEADED GODDESS

No Greek goddess had the attributes and power of Sekhmet, the ancient Egyptian goddess of divine order. She was a protectress with the strength and ability to spring upon evildoers and transgressors. Egyptian gods and goddesses often were either visualized in an animal form or with the head of an animal, unlike the divinities of the ancient Greeks who were portrayed as idealized human beings. Sekhmet had the head of a lion and the body of a woman. She was a goddess of wrath and a goddess of peace. Her name means simply "the powerful."

Sekhmet was one of the triad of powerful Memphite divinities with her husband Ptah and her father, the sun god Ra. Memphis had become the administrative capital of Egypt after the unification of north and south kingdoms, around 3000 B.C.E. Sekhmet was adopted by the pharaohs as a symbol of their own unvanquishable heroism in battle. As such, she was portrayed as the goddess who breathed fire against pharaoh's enemies, expressing his wrath toward those who rebelled against him.

No other deity of ancient Egypt was represented by so many large and impressive statues. Close to six hundred were placed at Karnak, and a great many others were erected nearer the Nile at Thebes during the reign of Amenhotep III (18th Dynasty, 1411–1375 B.C.E.). Sekhmet's statues were made of dark basalt or black granite, both igneous rocks—solidified volcanic magma—that were appropriate for a fierce or fiery goddess. In her mythology, she did not initiate or provoke conflict, but when the divine order was threatened and the gods called upon Sekhmet for help, she responded with the direct savagery of a protective lioness.

Most of the existing statues of Sekhmet are in museums. There was one, however, that I saw at the ancient temple site of Karnak in an insignificant-looking building not usually visited by the hordes of tourists who come daily. When I entered the small room in which she stands, I gazed at this statue of a standing Sekhmet and felt as if I were in the presence of a powerful and protective figure. I was traveling with a small group of women and each of us felt as though we had entered a sanctuary.

This Sekhmet was a tall figure made of dark smooth basalt stone. She stood on a base that hugged the ground; the tallest among us reached barely to her shoulder. Her lioness face was not only peaceful but kind. She wore emblems of power on her head, a large representation of a solar disk with the standing cobra (uraeus) before it. Her human body was slender with small breasts. She grasped an ankh, a symbol of eternal life in her right hand, which was at her side. In her left hand, extended immediately in front of her body, she held the stem of a tall papyrus, a heraldic plant of north Egypt. The small room she inhabited was bare of any ornamentation. The only source of light was the sun, which streamed through a small aperture in the ceiling into the dim room.

When we entered the chamber, the sun's position overhead was such that an intense beam of sunlight fell across the front of Sekhmet.

First it illuminated her face, and then, as the sun moved across the sky, the beam of light traveled down her body. One woman in our group, who learned as a child to look after herself because no one would protect her from violence in her alcoholic family, instinctively sat down at the feet of Sekhmet and leaned up against her body, and as she sat there, the beam of sunlight moved across her hair. She looked like a little girl and, in her stillness, she and Sekhmet formed a tableau. She stayed there for some time, and told us later that she had felt young and safe, and had not wanted to leave.

This was my introduction to Sekhmet. I saw her as a serene and strong feminine figure, a maternal protector, in whose presence a youngster was safe. But with the head of a lion, I could also imagine her ferocity, the attribute for which she is known best. As a goddess of divine order, Sekhmet was called upon to bring balance back into the world, to overcome the destructive and evil forces that threatened that order when no other divinity, including the most powerful male divinities, could. In Sekhmet's most famous myth, "The Destruction of Mankind," once this ferocity was called forth, and her wrath unleashed against evildoers, she became intoxicated by the aggression. On a rampage and overcome by madness, she could not be controlled or contained. Finally, she was tricked into drinking a mind-altering potion, which restored her sanity. The story that I retell here is found in most accounts of Sekhmet, among which Robert Masters's version[1] was the most helpful.

The Myth of Sekhmet and the Destruction of Mankind

The gods had given men powers so that they could flourish on earth and become great, but instead of gratitude for these gifts and reverence for the gods, mankind plotted to overthrow them. They blasphemed against Ra, the sun, who with other ancient divinities was present in the primeval waters before there was life. Evil priests and magicians conspired to use the very powers the gods had given them to destroy the gods. Ra heard their plans and called the gods together to decide what to do.

They decided that Sekhmet, "the force against which no force pre-

vails," should manifest on earth to bring an end to the rebellion. They called her forth to punish those with evil thoughts and wicked plots. So she walked among the evildoers and destroyed them. With the ferocity of a rampaging lioness, she slaughtered humans, tore their bodies apart, and drank their blood. The carnage went on. Her rage fed on itself and she became intoxicated on human blood. Then the gods realized that she had to be stopped before she destroyed all human life, but none had the power to restrain her.

So Ra had certain plants brought to him, from which powerful mind-altering drugs could be brewed, and sent them to the god Setki, who added these to a mixture of beer and red ochre. Setki filled seven thousand enormous jars with this mixture and took them to a place where Sekhmet would pass. There he poured out the contents, inundating the earth and filling the fields with what appeared to be blood. When Sekhmet came with her bloodthirst, she thought that it was blood and drank her fill, which calmed her mind. After this, she no longer was bent on destroying mankind.

Sekhmet then rejoined the company of the gods and was welcomed back by Ra, who addressed her as "One Who Comes in Peace."

Besides her wrathful nature, Sekhmet was associated with healing and perceived as having the power to counteract illness. Her priesthood had a role in medicine. They recited prayers to Sekhmet as an integral part of medical treatment, while the physicians carried out whatever was done physically. She was an intimate of death, her presence was invoked in situations where a patient could live or die, and on the battlefield, where life and death were also in the balance as a warrior goddess.

She had a beneficent and an aggressive aspect. She was a goddess of healing and also of pestilence. She preserved order and was goddess of war. Yet it was her terrible aspect with which she is most identified. In this role, she enacts the destroyer aspect of the Great Goddess in her triple functions as creator-sustainer-destroyer. Even if no image or memory of a Great Goddess or a powerful goddess as destroyer remained in western mythology after the Greeks, the configuration was dimly kept alive in the three Fates of classical Greek mythology, who were usually portrayed as old women that held each person's life in their hands; one spun and created the thread that represented a life, the second held the thread in her hands, until the third—as destroyer—cut the thread. The Scandinavian Norns and the three Wyrrd or Weird Sisters (from the Teutonic word *wyrd*, meaning fate) were very similar mysterious and mythic female figures whose power over life and death was feared. In their respective patriarchal mythologies they were minor figures, and yet they had a grip on men's imagination.

The Great Goddess was an embodiment of the earth in its cycles rather than the moon in its phases: she was the creator who brings forth new life, the sustainer of life, and the destroyer. Women often come to know the dark destroyer aspect of the goddess, especially as they age. In their traditional roles as caretakers, women become intimately aware of the ravages of age and sickness, and of the deterioration of personality, spirit, and mind as well as the body. The older we get, the more of this reality we are likely to see. Life also exposes us to the shadow aspects of human nature, to the dark and destructive elements in others and in ourselves. We live long enough to see the damage from neglect and abuse on next generations, and realize that a lot of suffering could have been prevented. It is this longer view that can evoke Sekhmet as the outraged and fierce protector of values and of people, determined to bring about a change for the better.

If a woman is taken over by a raging Sekhmet, however, and is not balanced by wisdom or compassion, she becomes a woman possessed. It may take a potion (many psychiatric drugs can do exactly what Ra's concoction did for Sekhmet), for her to recover. These powerful drugs can be used like a chemical straitjacket, silencing this archetype and making a woman docile; they can also help her to be in control and become a person who can feel angry and decide what to do. Some women fear that they are going crazy when they (finally) become angry instead of depressed, which is their old pattern. Friends who listen and share their own "enough is enough" stories are usually all that they need to realize that they are sane.

The more patriarchal and fundamentally religious the family, the more likely that girls and women were punished or shamed if they expressed anger or became assertive. In these circumstances, adaption supports being numb and dumb, suppressing what you perceive and how you feel, saying nothing that puts you in conflict with authority. But increasingly, there are cracks in all authoritarian institutions and keeping the lid on women is no longer easy. Sekhmet can emerge into the psyche of a crone-aged woman as a force for change.

THE HINDU GODDESS KALI

A Sekhmet-like myth is told about the Hindu goddess Kali, whose worshipers throng her temples in India to this day and revere her as Kali-Ma or Ma-Kali, the Divine Mother. She is also a fierce protectress. Her appearance is far stranger than Sekhmet's and, to the western mind, bizarre and terrifying. Kali has black skin and white teeth or tusks, her tongue hangs out, her mouth drips blood. She has three eyes, with the third in the middle of her brow, and four arms. She commonly holds a knife in one left hand, and the severed head of a giant dripping blood in the other. Her right hands are both open. She dispells fear with one, and blesses worshipers with the other. Her body is naked except for her hideous ornaments, and she is dancing on the white body of the god Shiva. While Sekhmet is portrayed in her peaceful aspect, statues of Kali emphasize her fierce nature and remind worshipers of how Kali was created to defeat the demons and became intoxicated with blood.

The Hindu pantheon of divinities and their mythologies are complex, and like most rich mythologies with an oral tradition, there are variations and a wealth of detail in the story of Kali and the demons. My retelling draws the basic story and some details from Elizabeth U. Harding's *Kali*.[2]

The Myth of Kali and the Demons

The gods were exhausted from warring with the buffalo demon Mahishasura, the evil king of the demons, and his legions, who were defeating them. If Mahishasura won, the gods would be destroyed and chaos would result. The demons were winning because Mahishasura had an advan-

tage: he was invincible, except to a woman. So the gods created Durga for the express purpose of defeating Mahishasura. This goddess was a beautiful golden woman adorned with a crescent moon. She had ten arms and rode on a lion. She was created out of the flames that came out of the mouths of the gods Brahma, Vishnu, and Shiva. She held weapons and emblems in each of her ten hands, each one a symbol of the power given to her by a specific god.

Durga defeated Mahishasura, but even Durga was not powerful enough to defeat three other demons, Sumbha, Nisumbha, and Raktavira. Durga's lion and a mere sound—a Hum from the lips of the goddess—destroyed armies of the demons, but when this was not enough, Durga became terrible in her anger, and from her frowning forehead came the awesome goddess Kali. Kali mounted her great lion and, armed with her sword and the sound Hum, defeated Sumbha and Nisumbha and their armies. The third demon, Raktavira, appeared to be invincible. Every drop of blood that fell from his body and reached the earth produced innumerable demons like him. Kali defeated this demon the only way possible. She held him above the earth, mortally wounded him with her sword, and drank all of his blood as it gushed out, so that none would reach the ground.

Then Kali went through the battlefield with her sword, beheading and slashing at demons, killing elephants and horses, intoxicated by the blood of her enemies. Only the god Shiva could stop her, which he did in a very unusual way. He smeared his beautiful naked body with ashes and lay down, motionless, among the corpses. Kali in her intoxicated state staggered across the dead bodies until she found herself standing on top of a whitened, perfect male body. Awed, she looked down and gazed into the eyes of her husband, Shiva. When she realized that she was touching her divine husband with her feet, she regained her mind.

In Harding's interpretation, Kali's bewildering and hideous appearance and her destruction of the demons are seen allegorically. The legend then represents the war that goes on within all of us, between our divine and demonic natures. Kali's appearance and her repulsive ornaments can be intellectually understood as symbolic, but they still make identifying with her difficult.

However, a woman who has felt the raw ferocity of this archetype in her may find Kali's inhuman and hideous appearance quite fitting. That Kali came back to her senses when she came back into relationship with her husband Shiva also rings true. When a woman is "possessed," or taken over by Kali, she is, in Jungian terms, caught up in a Kali complex. She may need someone she cares about deeply to bring her back to herself, to help her remember that she is more and that there is more than wrathful fury, however much her outrage is justified.

In another version, which China Galland tells in *The Bond Between Women*,[3] Kali, as an emanation of the Great Goddess Durga in her battles with the demons, saves the world from destruction and then, when Kali is no longer needed, Durga absorbs her back into herself, and withdrew from the world with a promise: "Do not worry. If the world is ever in danger of being destroyed again, I will return." When a woman has a fierce feminine warrior within her that she can count on to do battle, especially when enough is enough, and recall from active duty afterward, she is like Durga in this respect.

While we are likely to see Kali as hideous, she is not fearsome to the worshipers who appeal to her kindness and benevolence. To them, she is Kali-Ma, a fierce and maternal figure. They cover her basalt statues with garlands of flowers and tie prayer ribbons to the trees around her temples. To them, she is a powerful feminine devi or goddess, who knows the horrors that are in the world and is able to be ferocious on their behalf and responsive to their prayers.

THE ARCHETYPE OF KALI/SEKHMET

If the goddess Kali were a person, we might say of her, "She's been there." By this we mean that because of what she has been through, there is nothing too terrible or horrible that we can tell her that would be beyond her comprehension. Kali is an archetype that, once evoked and felt, even if not unleashed and expressed as rage, takes a woman into her dark side and into this aspect of others. An inner encounter with Kali is a shock, especially to a woman who has kept a lid on her negative feelings and thought of herself as a nice person, as someone better or more evolved than this. It's deeply informative to find yourself capable of rage and fantasies worthy of Kali; not only do you dis-cover a side of yourself you may not have known, but it gives you a bet-ter understanding of those who act on their rage. An evocation of Kali can happen at any time in a woman's life, though one of the most com-mon and devastating provocations often happens about the time a woman enters her third stage of life, and her husband leaves her for a younger woman.

When you are reckoning with the archetype of Sekhmet/Kali, the psychological and spiritual task is to hold the opposites of wrath and wisdom. When you are rejected or humiliated, have been badly treated, attacked physically or verbally, the immediate impulse may be to retaliate. Wisdom tempers wrath and reins in the savage lioness or bloodthirsty Kali. Wisdom realizes that tit-for-tat invites escalation. Even worse at a soul level, when you "do unto them" as was done unto you, you risk becoming just like them. You can turn into an angry, hostile, obsessed person, so taken over by rage that you become "pos-sessed" as were Sekhmet and Kali. The task of holding it in and distill-ing it into purposeful action is the immediate challenge.

This is very different from either bottling up anger or directing it against yourself, which causes depression. Or from suppressing anger and even forgetting the reasons for it, which is denial and leads to codependency. Obviously, depression, codependency, and victimiza-tion are not attributes of Sekhmet or Kali, but they are the flip side of this archetype. The ferocity of Sekhmet/Kali needs to be harnessed rather than suppressed or unleashed in a blind rage. Then Kali ener-gizes the insistence that a problem be faced and solved, and Sekhmet persists and is not diverted, and you become a force to be reckoned with. The mother who won't take no for an answer when her child's needs are ignored by a school system and perseveres until the situation is changed, is one example. MADD (Mothers Against Drunk Driving) is another. In the crone, third-phase of life, a woman's concerns often go beyond her immediate family to the larger community, where there is much to be outraged about. When she encounters the evils of incompetency, malpractice, or abuse of power, she can become a Kali with a knife in one hand and, if successful, she'll have the head of the malefactor or perpetrator in the other.

The lioness could be the totem animal for the "exceptional patient" that Dr. Bernie Siegel described. She is the cancer patient who is an advocate on her own behalf. This woman is usually described by her physician as "difficult," because she does not just do as she is told. She is informed, asks hard questions, wants to know why certain tests or treatments are proposed and not others. She gets second opinions and changes physicians when she perceives this to be in her best interest. She explores alternatives and makes important decisions herself. She is committed to doing all that can be done to be healed. And, Siegel notes, these are the qualities that enhance the possibility of beating the odds, of going into remission, or healing the illness.

Sehkmet was onstage and in the audience on Mother's Day 2000, when the Million Moms March brought 750,000 people to Washington, D.C. to protest against the easy availability of guns, the appalling toll of death and suffering, and the power of the National Rifle Association to influence Congress and block legislation. Antonia Novello, M.D., a past U.S. Surgeon General, ended with the words "We are tired of taking it!" "No more!" was the rallying cry of Carol Price, whose thirteen-year-old son was killed by a nine-year-old neighbor. But the outrage of Sekhmet was most expressed by the actress Susan Sarandon when she finished her remarks with "We are pissed off!" and the audience spontaneously erupted and repeated her words, "We are pissed off!" "We are pissed off!" "We are pissed off!" in a rising crescendo of wrath and power.

ERESHKIGAL, THE SUMERIAN GODDESS

In *Close to the Bone*, a book about serious illnesses, I described the Sumerian goddess Inanna's gate-by-gate descent into the underworld, as analogous to a patient's experience of being stripped of persona and psychological defenses. I think of a life-threatening illness as a descent of the soul into the underworld, a journey into the realm of Hades and Pluto (the Roman god of the underworld, whose name means "riches underground"), which is the personal and collective unconscious. We encounter our worst fears as we make such a descent, and we also may find abandoned parts of ourselves and powerful archetypes that we have been cut off from. In the myth,[4] a humbled Inanna who was queen of heaven and earth, came face-to-face with a wrathful Ereshki-gal, who is archetypally similar to Sekhmet and Kali.

Naked and bowed low, Inanna went through the seventh and last gate to encounter Ereshkigal, goddess of the Great Below, a dark goddess of death. Ereshkigal struck Inanna dead with a baleful look and hung her body on a hook to rot. After three days, when Inanna had not returned, her loyal friend Ninshibur sought help and, as a result, Inanna was restored to life. She was, however, not the same as before. She had acquired attributes of Ereshkigal—demons now clung to her skirts, ready to claim anyone she designated. On her return to the upper world, Inanna could discern who had mourned her and who had not, she could decide who would stay in the upper world with her, and whom she would turn over to the demons and consign to the underworld. She saw Nin-shibur, without whose help she would never have returned, and when the demons inquired, "Shall we take her?" Inanna said, "Never!" She saw her sons in mourning clothes in grief for her, and would not allow the demons to claim them. Then she went into the throne room of her city and saw her husband Dumazi dressed in finery and lolling on the throne, obvi-ously not mourning her. She pointed a wrathful finger at him and told the demons, "You can take him!"

When Inanna returned from the underworld, her encounter with Ereshkigal had changed her in ways that women are changed when they face the possibility or likelihood of death. Many such women have said to me, "Cancer was a cure for my codependency." Cancer was a crisis that made them take a long look at uncaring friends, narcissistic rela-tives, and a lack of joy in their lives, and act with anger and clarity. Like Inanna, they realized whom to keep and cherish, and whom to cull.

The publication date for *Close to the Bone* was set for October 2, 1996. When I announced this in a lecture, I was delighted to learn from a woman who was born on October 2, that this date is Guardian Angel day on the Roman Catholic calendar. It seemed like a syn-chronicity for this book that I had written to help people to also be born on this day. Besides, I had written a chapter on prayer, in which I said that I like to think that when we pray, we are sending guardian angels to sit on the shoulders of those we pray for. Because of these coincidences, readers knew that October 2, 1996, was the publication date, and it was because of this that I received a letter from Caryl Campbell, a reader for whom this date, her menopause, cancer, and Kali were linked. She wrote:

"First, my birthday is Ocober 2. Second, I celebrated my 1996 birth date as the beginning of a transformed self following a successful journey 'to and from Kali's temple.' I had just completed radiation treatment for breast cancer.

"I thought you might be interested in the metaphor that I developed to handle my experience. You well describe the shocked feeling that vigorous, fit, healthy people experience when they discover that they are very vulnerable. I describe this as an encounter with Kali. October was also my menopause, so I was already feeling a sense of transformation, when the jolt of possibly dying sooner than planned required a more urgent metaphor. I picked Kali because I had used her in previous art work, and I liked the image of a dramatic, bloody Goddess. I felt the need for a powerful expression of the dangerous line that I was walking. This was a real life-and-death situation and it called for a real life-and-death metaphor . . .

"I learned that initiates of the Kali temple had to enter her dreadful underworld, stay and see the face of death, and then leave as a new person. The radiation center at the hospital was underground at the end of a maze of hallways . . . The patients in the center seemed horrific to me, hairless, maimed, some near death—all people I was afraid of, and that I did not want to admit that I was one of. This was Kali's temple. I decided that I needed to enter the temple, face the people there as one of them, accept the healing photons of Apollo, and walk out as an initiate into the Cancer Clan, as a healed initiate . . ."

As this writer describes, a descent into the dark realm of diagnosis and treatment can be transformative psychologically and spiritually. You face the dark goddess of death and wrath, transformation and healing, and if you return to the Upper World of ordinary life, you are different. Once you encounter the archetype that can be nameless or Sekhmet, Kali, or Ereshkigal, you are no longer the same person.

CROW MOTHER/MORRIGAN

Crow Mother was one among many kachina dolls on a shelf at a trading post on the Hopi reservation. When I saw her, I recognized that she was another expression of this archetype of transformative wrath. Kachina dolls are representations of the *katsina,* plural *katsinam,* the spirit beings who live among the Hopi for about six months each year. This doll wore a turquoise helmet with large, black crow wings attached on either side. The face of the helmet was a black inverted triangle outlined in white and framed by red and black stripes.

The inverted triangle is a universally recognized symbol of a woman's pubic triangle, a shape associated with the fertility of the goddess. It was the crow wings that made me realize that she could be a crone figure. In ancient Ireland, the triple goddess was Ana the maiden, Babd the mother, and Macha or Morrigan the crone, who appeared on battlefields as the raven. Once again, as I recalled how the crow or raven symbolized the awesome destroyer aspect of the triple goddess, I was reminded how the once feared or revered names or symbols for the crone or crone goddess are all derogatory put-downs. To call a woman "an old crow" is as bad as calling her a "hag," which once meant "holy woman."

I asked Alph Secakuku, an elder of the Snake Clan on the Second Hopi Mesa and a kachina-doll expert, to tell me more about Crow Mother.[5] Secakuku pointed out that she was carrying a bundle of green yucca whips, and that another name for her in this particular ritual role was "Mother of Whippers." In February, when the katsinam-spirit beings are invited to appear among the Hopi, the Whippers (fearsome male kachinas) appear in the village to evaluate whether the villagers have maintained standards of morality and virtues, and to punish and bless accordingly. At this time, the Mother of Whippers and the Whippers also play a prominent role in initiating children into Hopi beliefs and culture. The initiation ceremony takes place in the *kiva,* a round underground chamber that is the center of the religious life of the Hopi villages.

With her supply of green yucca whips and Whippers, Crow Mother drives out the impurities or the demons. She is aggressive and full of fury. I think of her as whipping people into spiritual and moral shape.

"Mother of Whippers" knows that "nice" doesn't do it. She is the archetype in women who organize their neighbors to drive the drug dealers off the streets. She is the archetype in women who organize workers and blow the whistle on poor working conditions. She works to end genital mutilation, child prostitution, the burning of brides whose dowries were small. Crow Mother is the formidable crone in all walks of life, who says "Enough is enough!" and leads a troop of "whippers" onto the streets or into voting booths, the courtroom, or boardroom. Whether as Mother of Whippers, Sekhmet/Kali, or after lessons from Ereshkigal, when a woman decides that "enough is enough," she discovers the inner strength and the responsibility that comes with that decision. When they were younger, these same women often assumed that men would take care of the problems. At fifty and older, women individually and collectively are realizing that if changes are to be made, it is up to them.

LIONHEARTED WOMEN

The archetypal energies of Kali/Sekhmet are expressed as "the fierce compassion of the feminine" that China Galland[6] found in women who are addressing major evils in our contemporary world. They have qualities that I think of as being "lionhearted." The fury of a lioness is that of a protective mother or a bereaved mother whose response is retaliatory. Kali rides out on a lion to defeat the demons, while Sekhmet is both a lioness and a woman. Theirs is a heart-motivated fury at evil that threatens to overwhelm and destroy what they hold sacred. To be a woman who is outraged and protests against powerful authority takes courage—a word derived from *coeur* or "heart." In Argentina, for example, the Mothers of the Plaza de Mayo, who have demonstrated every week since 1977 in spite of harassment and the very real possibility of danger, are lionhearted women. Individually and together, they are fierce in their determination to know the fate of their loved ones who disappeared when Argentina was controlled by a military dictatorship. Every one of them lost at least one child or member of her immediate family. Once a year, the Mothers are joined by the Grandmothers of the Disappeared and by members of other human-rights organizations. They have become the conscience of Argentina. Galland found that same fierceness in women whose efforts are directed at stopping the international trafficking in child prostitution.

LIONHEARTED AND WISE WOMEN

From-the-heart emotional responses and the ability to be empathic are qualities of women who are nurturers and caretakers of families and friendships; they also motivate women into action on behalf of girls being genitally mutilated or children sold into prostitution or subjected to incest, neglect, or abuse. While girls are not exclusively vulnerable to these evils, they are the primary direct victims (the families and cultures that allow this are indirectly greatly damaged for generations). Unless a woman has become callous or has armored herself against having feelings and can live in her head, it is uncomfortably easy to mentally and viscerally imagine how it feels at a body-and-soul level to be so treated, and be helpless and totally vulnerable. Bad or scary experiences enhance this: if you became lost as a child yourself, or were scared and confused when a man exposed his genitals, or were in physical pain or raped yourself, it is all too easy to imagine. Without the archetype of Sekhmet/Kali, however, brutality and vulnerability result in becoming numb, passive, and docile. To be moved to overcome such evils, women need to be lionhearted in having both empathy and courage, fury and restraint. While a dark goddess might do this alone, women need the support of each other; like the Mothers and the Grandmothers of the Disappeared, there is some protection in numbers, but whenever women protest or take action and meet opposition and resistance, it is the doing this together that makes it possible for them to not lose heart and sustain the effort.

In the history of western civilization since the Greeks, patriarchal laws and institutions have systematically enforced vulnerability in women by making women the property of men, which was so in the United States until the end of the nineteenth century. In the psyche, that which is suppressed is not allowed into consciousness and becomes feared, which helps explain why every effort toward equality for women has been achieved against strong emotional, fear-based resistance. The presence of Sekhmet/Kali in the archetypal layer of the collective unconscious may help explain why men fear women's retaliatory anger. Women also fear becoming angry: this is learned both as a culturally enforced fear (an angry woman provoked punishment and shunning), and a deeper, vague fear of the archetype. This fear has lessened considerably.

The "enough is enough" goddesses may bear unfamiliar names and inhuman faces, but their energy and outrage are no longer foreign to us. With wisdom and maturity that are best supported by being in the company of others with these qualities, the wrath of Sekhmet/Kali becomes channeled into effective action. When women can do this, they become lionhearted wisewomen, whose wrath holds the promise of transforming our institutions and culture.

Goddesses of Healing Laughter:
Her Name Is Mirth

Bawdy Baubo
Uzume, the Japanese Goddess of
Mirth and Dance

Baubo, a minor crone figure in a major Greek myth, has a counterpart in Uzume (Ama-No Uzume) a Japanese goddess with a prominent role in the most important myth of ancient Japan. Each brought healing laughter to a dire situation. While humorous remarks were made in one myth, and there was dance and drumming in the other, the specific act that was responsible for the laughter in both was the same: Baubo and Uzume lifted their skirts and exposed their vulvas. This gesture and the laughter it provoked restored a mother goddess's ability to nurture and brought sunlight back to the world; it could not have been the hostile laughter of ridicule nor the snickering laughter at an obscenity. Something deeper and more significant was revealed.

Women who are comfortable being themselves laugh a lot together, especially crone-aged women. In *The Metamorphosis of Baubo,* Winfred Milius Lubel observed that "references to Baubo usually carry a special quality of laughter. It is a chuckling, wry sort of humor, compounded of irony, compassion, and shared experience between women . . . it is Baubo's sacred belly laugh." Baubo (also called Iambe) was only a maidservant with a bit role in the myth of Demeter and Persephone and yet she captured a crone spirit in women that is earthy, funny, compassionate and, ultimately, wise. She was described by Marija Gimbutas, the noted archaeologist, as an embodiment of an "important but little-known deity, who has touched the human psyche for millennia."[1]

Bawdy Baubo

Once the goddess Demeter learned that her daughter Persephone had been abducted by Hades with Zeus's permission, the pain of her loss was even sharper. She left Olympus and withdrew from the company of the gods, and wandered on earth, hiding her divine beauty disguised as a woman beyond childbearing. One day she appeared in Eleusis and sat by the well where the daughters of Celeus, the ruler of Eleusis, came to draw water. Curious about the stranger in their midst, they talked with her and found that she sought employment as a nursemaid. They led her home to meet their mother Metanira who had given birth to a baby boy. When the goddess put her foot on the threshold and touched her head on the ceiling, momentarily the doorway filled with divine light. Awed, Metanira, who had been seated with her infant son in her lap, immediately offered Demeter her own splendid couch and finest wine, which the goddess declined. The sight of a mother and child must have stirred memories and longing for her missing daughter because Demeter became mute and stood with her eyes downcast, until the servant Baubo brought her a simple chair. She then sat in grief-stricken silence from which no one could draw her out, until Baubo cheered the goddess with her bawdy humor. Her jests brought a smile, and then, when she lifted her skirt and exposed herself, Demeter laughed and was restored. Then she accepted a simple drink of barley water and mint, and agreed to become the baby's nursemaid (a temporary solace in the midportion of the myth).[2]

Baubo's jokes have not been retained through the ages, but what she represents even now is something women intuitively understand: the notion that in the midst of loss and betrayal, a woman might cry, sob, swear, even throw up, or feel benumbed in her grief and outrage, but if "Baubo" is present, someone can say something that can bring tears of laughter to the situation. It is often in laughter that we share our courage and know that we are survivors. In being able to laugh together, we affirm each other's strength. Baubo's jokes and gestures are a bawdy and belly-laughter humor that can arise among women in the midst of a disaster. A good friend can say something that evokes laughter at a very bad time, and healing begins.

When Baubo lifted her skirt in jest, as recounted in the classical Greek myth, it was an exposure of her vulva, an act called *ana-suro-mai* (literally meaning to lift one's skirt) in Greek religious writing. The gesture was bawdy and evoked laughter but it was much more. Lubell traces this gesture from its prepatriarchal roots as a faint reminder of an earlier matriarchal time when the pubic area of the goddess was the holy gate through which all life came, and the inverted triangle was a sacred symbol. Baubo's skirt-raising, vulva-exposing gesture can be found in artifacts and art from the paleolithic through the middle ages, and from old Europe and Egypt through Siberia to the Americas.

Some of the small clay "Baubo" figurines that have been found by archaeologists invite us to smile. They are women who have their clothes raised above a full belly and are mostly legs and abdomen. Sometimes a smiling face was actually represented on the belly. The cleft in the vee-shaped smooth chin is the vertical vulvar slit between her legs. While Baubo and these statuettes are minor images amidst the Olympian divinities and marble statues of ancient Greece, when her origins are traced back to prepatriarchal times, we understand that she is a faint and depreciated reminder that images of women's sexuality and fertility were sacred, not prurient. Once the vulva was the entrance to the body of the goddess, and cleftlike cave entrances were painted earth-red in reverence.

Rufus C. Camphausen in *The Yoni: Sacred Symbol of Female Creative Power* also focused on artifactual evidence, widening the geographic range from which these images originated and widening the time span from paleolithic to contemporary time. *Yoni* is a Sanskrit word for female genitals that translates as "vulva," "womb," "origin," and "source." Camphausen chose to use this term because it had neither a clinical nor a pornographic connotation and derived from a culture and religious tradition in which female genitals are seen as the sacred symbol of the Great Goddess.

Representations of female genitals, breasts, and pregnant women from carvings, cave paintings, and other artifacts, provide circumstantial archaeological evidence that paleolithic and neolithic peoples worshiped goddesses. With the rise of patriarchy, the vulva went from being a place of reverence to a puritanical, unmentionable and "dirty" part of a woman. It went from a symbol of the goddess to one of the most demeaning and hostile words ("cunt") a woman can be called.

In seeking the meaning of Baubo, Lubell made connections between women's laughter, sexuality, and restoration of balance. "The spontaneity of Baubo's laughter flashes out like graffiti across the ruins of the past. Her jests have vanished, but her wry and startling gesture and the record of her comic wit remain. Many have suggested that laughter among women is the hidden side of women's sexuality. That kind of laughter—often associated with the trickster figure and with fertility—was often used in sacred and joyful rituals to ease a stressful situation, to set painful matters in perspective, to restore balance . . . She is irreverent and she is sacred."[3]

Baubo apparently played a part in the Mysteries that were celebrated in Eleusis, northwest of Athens, for two thousand years until the shrine was destroyed in 395 C.E. The *Homeric Hymn to Demeter* says that after Persephone's return from the underworld, Demeter gave the Mysteries to humankind. There were public portions, which we know about, and the Mysteries known only to initiates who were forbidden to reveal the secrets. Men and women participated in the Eleusinian Mysteries. The little we know about them is through the writings of Christian bishops who were hostile to these rites. According to Clement of Alexandria (150–215 C.E.), sometime during the Eleusinian Mysteries, Baubo "hoisted up her robes and displayed all of her body in a most unseemly manner."[4]

Instead of being present in these solemn rites in Eleusis, it is more likely that Baubo was a presence at the Mysteries of Thesmorphia, a women-only, three-day festival held at Eleusis in October at the time of the autumn sowing of the grain. Women gathered together to mourn with the goddess and to console her for the loss of her daughter (reenacting the original abduction, which would be cathartic for them in the shared grief). After the solemn rites and communal mourning, there was hilarity, with jokes, gestures, foul language, and song.[5]

Uzume, the Japanese Goddess
of Dance and Mirth

The irreverent and the sacred, healing laughter and lifting one's skirts are found together in another myth across the world from Greece. This is a major myth of Japan, in which the grieving goddess is Amaterasu, the goddess of the sun and the ancestress of the emperors. When she withdrew into a cave, endless night resulted, and none could draw her out until Ama-no-Uzume, the goddess of dance and mirth, told jokes and lifted her skirt. This myth was recorded in the *Kojiki* ("Records of Ancient Matters") and again in the *Nihongi* ("The Chronicles of Japan") which were written in the eighth century C.E. from much earlier oral versions. Lubell[6] and Merlin Stone in *Ancient Mirrors of Womanhood*[7] have longer versions of the myth, which I retell as follows:

The Myth of Amaterasu

Amaterasu Omikami, called the Heavenly Shining She, the Great Woman Who Possesses Noon, and She Who Reigns Over the Plain of High Heaven, watched over the earth and its fields of growing rice (a similarity to Demeter, the Greek goddess of grain). Amaterasu also presided over her weaving women in the great Weaving Hall of Heaven. Her brother Susanowo (referred to as the Outrageous Male), the god of the sea and storms, was resentful that she had the greater power. One day, he announced that he intended to visit their mother and gained the right to approach Amaterasu's heavenly realm to tell her of his plans. Instead, he came and trampled his sister's newly planted heavenly rice fields. Then he defecated inside Amaterasu's sacred temple. Next he took and killed a colt of heaven, broke into her weaving hall, and flung the bloody carcass among the sacred silk looms, which caused a great uproar among the weaving priestesses.

(In the differing versions of this myth, either a priestess was killed by a shuttle, or Amaterasu herself was wounded in the vagina by a shuttle or was raped by her brother.)

Filled with anger and fear, Amaterasu then fled into the cave of heaven, fastened the great door tight behind her, and withdrew her light and warmth from the world. There was now only endless night. Without Amaterasu, nothing would grow on earth. Eight hundred divinities gathered before the cave and many tried to lure her out, with no success.

Finally, Ama-no Uzume, the goddess of mirth and dance, came forward with a plan. Uzume climbed upon a large upturned tub that resonated like a drum, and began her dance. Her feet drumming, her dancing ecstatic, she removed her undergarments and then, once she had the undivided attention of the eight hundred divinities, she lifted her kimono and exposed her vulva. They laughed, clapped their hands, and shouted; roosters crowed, and the sounds of hilarity reached Amaterasu in her cave. Curious, she looked out of the cave to see what was happening and faced the bronze mirror that had been placed outside the cave entrance. Her reflected light was so great that she could not see and so Amaterasu ventured out of the cave. When she did, those that watched closed the door behind her. Once Amaterasu came out of the cave, sunlight once again shone upon the earth, the pattern of day and night returned, and the earth was fertile once more.

This myth of the return of the light and life to the world was annually celebrated in Japan in a Shinto ritual, in which Uzume's *Kagura*, a laughter-provoking, obscene (a Western characterization) dance was performed in temples. The Ise Shrine of Amaterasu, the holiest Shinto shrine in Japan, houses the Most Sacred Mirror. In nonwestern and unpuritanical Japan, Uzume is an esteemed goddess. Her drumming dance steps, jokes, and the exposure of her vulva are essential elements in this major myth of Japan.

In *When the Drummers Were Women*, Layne Redmond traced the drum as a sacred ritual instrument used by women as far back as the sixth millennium B.C.E., where it appears painted on a shrine room in ancient Anatolia (Turkey). The drum was a tool for many spiritual experiences. Different rhythms altered consciousness, facilitated childbirth, induced ecstatic and prophetic states. From sacred caves of old Europe through the mystery cults of Rome, women danced and drummed until they were forbidden to do so by the early church fathers.[8] She speculates that drumming probably began as an echo of the human pulse, the rhythm we heard in the womb, and that the brain-wave state that it induces is the basic rhythm of nature. In teaching other women to drum and by being in a women's drumming circle, Redmond became convinced that women have been dispossessed of a heritage, tradition, and sense of identity that was uniquely their own.

HEALING LAUGHTER

Healing laughter is a relief from tension and an expression of joy and hilarity. Bawdy humor is juicy humor that is also an earthy and sexual commentary about human nature, appetites, and foibles. At its most nurturing—which humor can be—there is an afterglow of good feeling. In the shared laughter, there is a sense of commonality about vulnerabilities and strengths. In making ribald comments or responding to them with laughter, women are acknowledging their sexuality and sexual experience and also revealing the sexual vanities or habits or proclivities of men, which is what men fear most.

To be Baubo/Uzume, a postmenopausal woman has to live in her aging body comfortably and unself-consciously. Her sexual energy is a component of her zest and vitality. With Baubo as an inspiration, she refuses to stop being herself just because she is older: she is a sensual, sexy woman who laughs and dances. Good humor and experience become enhancements to earthy sex. It would be in the tradition of Baubo to take up belly dancing after fifty. In fact, many celebrated belly dancers are postmenopausal women.

It may seem a stretch to appreciate Baubo as an archetype of wisdom, but she is. Hers may be a wisdom that only women can appreciate because she grows out of the numerous inelegant though profoundly important body experiences we have had from the onset of menstruation through pregnancy and menopause. In laughing or joking about what women go through biologically, we can be bawdy Baubos. This sharing often leads to more sensitive and serious talk about sexual experiences, miscarriages, abortions, infertility, and loss. In the telling, we are metaphorically lifting our skirts and revealing our vulnerable underside and our source of strength. Each woman's story becomes a mirror for another woman to see herself and her resiliency. In sharing the pain and laughter, we go through these transitions and experience the healing power of humor, wisely coming to the conclusion that "such is life."

Baubo is all that remained in Greek mythology of this bawdy aspect of the Great Goddess. When Baubo lifted her skirts and revealed her naked body to Demeter, she revealed a body that once had been a nubile maiden, and then was a full-breasted woman, and now, with her thinning pubic hair and sagging breasts, was the body of a crone. Each phase is part of a cycle, an expression of the dance of life. When we remember our divinity and not just our mortality, we know that everything that happens is part of life, and we are part of a divine dance. The danger of being a mortal is forgetting this. Demeter, in her identity as a human woman, was alone with her sorrow until Baubo raised her skirt and made her laugh. Maybe it helped Demeter put her loss in perspective, or perhaps she was reminded of the creative and sexual power that she had as a woman and a goddess of fertility. Baubo had lost her youth, her looks, and was past her childbearing years, but she was a juicy, bawdy woman, whose mirthful compassion for Demeter's grief drew laughter out of the goddess. Only when sexuality is natural and pleasurable, can sex and mirth mix.

When I thought about contemporary embodiments of this archetype, Bette Midler—"The Divine Miss M," a "goddess of mirth"—came to mind. This juicy and bawdy comedienne first became a star in the gay bathhouse culture of pre-AIDS New York, and continues to be earthy, sexual, and funny. Then there is the *ana-suromai* gesture of lifting one's skirt, which seems so instinctual that little girls have to be trained out of doing it. Put a little girl of two or three in a skirt, and she will impulsively lift it up and down, "flashing" her underpants; from her delighted expression, she may know she's being naughty and definitely is not ashamed (this has to be taught). It is also not unheard of for a group of grown women to "get away" for a weekend and become bawdy together.

The healing humor that women bring out in each other is spontaneous and natural. It suffers in the retelling because "you had to be there" to appreciate the in-the-moment, unself-conscious provocation for whoops of infectious laughter. In its full-blown splendor, it's uproarious and raucous, emotionally juicy and wet, as in "I laughed so hard, I cried," and "I laughed so hard, I wet my pants." Especially when the humor is bawdy, but even when it is not, this kind of laughter resembles an orgasm; the laughter is uncontrolled and pleasurable, there is a physiological release, followed by well-being, and a sense of being spent. It's good for the immune system and releases endorphins, which are healing elements physically, but what I see most healing is the instantaneous sharing that dissolves isolation and celebrates life. Green and juicy crones know this archetype well. It is a humor that is wise about the nature of life and has compassion for the foolishness and pain of it.

Men accuse women of not having a sense of humor or not getting the point of certain jokes that women do not think are funny. But women do get the point. Freud's contention was that humor is disguised hostility, which is very evident in mother-in-law, dumb blonde, and male-bashing jokes. Laughing at the butt of the joke releases hostility, temporarily allies those that laugh together and feel superior, and has a sadistic edge. There is a world of difference between this kind of wounding humor and the healing humor of Baubo and Uzume. Like Amaterasu's sunshine and Demeter's laughter, this humor brings hope and renewal.

Goddesses of Compassion:
Her Name Is Kindness

Kuan Yin, She-Who-Harkens-to-
the-Cries-of-the-World
The Virgin Mary and Lady Liberty

The development of compassion is like wisdom: it grows through life experience. But just as growing older does not necessarily mean growing wiser, so it is with compassion. The dictionary definition and the spiritual one are the same: it is an empathic sympathy for the distress of others, coupled with the desire to alleviate suffering. Through our maternal and caregiver roles, through sharing confidences with women friends, and hearing men reveal themselves to us—something they are much more likely to do with us than with another man—we learn about vulnerabilities and the suffering of others as we grow older. In midlife and our crone years, our parents are likely to become old and dependent; and even if we have been angry or resentful at them, this, too, often changes because they are not the same people they used to be. Given circumstances such as these, the older the woman, the more opportunities she may have to know the truth about people's lives and circumstances and if she feels for them and is thoughtful and responsive, her compassion will grow with age. However, forgiving and caretaking are not always an expression of compassion or altruism. They may express codependency.

Many women mistake codependency for compassion because both are often about feeling another person's pain. The concept of codependency comes from the psychology of addictions; it developed from seeing a characteristic marriage pattern. One person, the alcoholic, dominates the other with selfish needs and irresponsible behavior, and can be abusively angry. The codependent partner repeatedly makes excuses and forgives, and if abuse continues, she becomes emotionally numb and unable to look out for herself or her best interests. Codependency is about putting yourself second to someone else who is self-centered. The other person may not be addicted to alcohol, but could be a driven workaholic, or obsessed by something else. The resulting match—between a narcissist and a codependent—is not made in heaven. It is a dysfunctional relationship in which the codependent learns that what she perceives or feels doesn't really matter.

Even when a goddess of compassion is an active archetype in the codependent, the wise crone sees a clear and distinct difference between codependency and compassion. It is not as simple as saying that compassion without wisdom is codependency; a woman with wisdom and compassion might see the situation clearly, know what course should be taken, and (without Sehkmet) still be immobilized by her inability to act. As positive as these goddesses of compassion are, to identify with them is fraught with the potential to become a martyr or an enabler of another person's worst or weak qualities.

Development of compassion is a spiritual task as well as a psychological one, and like all human capabilities that have to do with nature and nurture, easier for some than others. Girls are encouraged to be so; boys often learn that it is a liability. With an emphasis on hierarchy, on the acquisition of power or profit, on warfare and other ruthless means of domination, compassion is seen as weakness in patriarchal cultures. It is no wonder that the Greeks lacked a divinity of compassion. The Olympian gods raped mortal women and goddesses in a mythology in which obsessive or possessive sexual passion rather than compassion was emphasized. In order to find archetypes of compassion, it was necessary for me to look elsewhere, where they were to be found in female or androgynous figures.

KUAN YIN, CHINESE GODDESS OF COMPASSION

Kuan Yin means "She-Who-Hearkens-to-the-Cries-of-the-World." For over a thousand years, in China, Korea, and Japan, Kuan Yin has been popularly revered as a goddess of compassion. Her importance and comfort to common folk who assumed that she listened to their sorrows, gives her the same meaning as the Virgin Mary in Roman Catholicism. Neither Kuan Yin nor the Virgin Mary are goddesses in their respective theological traditions, but in practice, both are prayed to as divine and holy. From a psychological perspective, they are similar archetypes.

Kuan Yin and the Virgin Mary wear robes that conceal the body; a viewer is drawn to the serenity of the face. In contrast, statues of Aphrodite as the goddess of sexual love are usually of a mostly undressed or totally nude woman. Aphrodite had the compelling power to cause gods and mortals to fall in love (or obsession); she could be without mercy or consideration of the consequences.

Kuan Yin was often depicted in paintings as standing upon a floating lotus or seated on a rock gazing out across the water. Statues of her are of a graceful and ageless robed woman, often holding in one hand a vase of "sweet dew" symbolizing the nectar of compassion, and in the other hand, a willow spray to sprinkle this nectar on the heads of those who call upon her mercy. There are also splendidly robed and bejeweled depictions of Kuan Yin that could almost be mistaken for that of Mary arrayed as Queen of Heaven. In whatever form, her chief attribute is "pure, unwavering compassion, utterly free from pride or vengefulness and reluctant to punish even those to whom a severe lesson would be salutary."[1]

Just as an archetype might manifest with a different name in Greek, Roman, and Norse mythology and have slightly different characteristics, so it is in eastern religious traditions that Kuan Yin (sometimes spelled Guanyin) was known as Kwannon-Sama (Kannon) in Japan, Quan Am in Vietnam, and as Tara in Tibet. Tara is a beautiful female divinity able to manifest herself in twenty-one different forms in order to come to the aid of sentient beings.

John Blofeld, a renowned scholar of eastern religion, described in *Bodhisattva of Compassion* the many ways in which Kuan Yin has been perceived and understood. She was worshiped as a folk goddess whose shrines were found in pre-Communist China, throughout the length and breadth of the country, usually placed near running water or overlooking a lake or the sea. Provided only that one's wish was not evil in itself, all that was required to pray for aid to Kuan Yin was a belief in her power to help. No degree of piety or strict conduct was required.

As Blofeld discovered as he sought Kuan Yin, she is regarded as a mental concept by some and as a goddess by others; how one sees her depends upon one's expectation and attitude of mind. The more sophisticated perception of Kuan Yin is as a bodhisattva, which Blofeld described as similar to the Jungian concept of an archetype.

Taigen Daniel Leighton, an American Zen priest, explicitly described Kuan Yin and other bodhisattvas as archetypes. In *Bodhisattva Archetypes*, he describes the images that we have of them as representations of awakened qualities within our own selves, and within all beings. Bodhisattvas are dedicated to the universal awakening or enlightenment of everyone. They exist as guides and providers of support to suffering beings, and offer everyone an approach to meaningful spiritual life. The Sanskrit name for the bodhisattva of compassion is *Avalokiteshvara*, of which Kuan Yin is the most famous. The qualities associated with bodhisattvas of compassion are kindness, gentleness, responsiveness, empathy, and helpfulness. Simply giving people what they want and need is one of her attributes. Leighton notes that this provides the experience of generosity, which can be contagious, encouraging caring for others and loss of self-centered concerns.

To take compassionate action, one must be capable of feeling compassion for oneself and others, and the most natural way is to grow up in an environment where there is justice and love, where a child matters, and where empathy and compassion are taught by example and by story in families and in the culture. As Robert Coles, M.D., author of *The Call of Service: A Witness to Idealism*, observed, "A child who has been treated with kindness and has been able to summon others successfully is more likely to respond to the dire straits of others."[2]

The golden rule "to do unto others as you would have done unto you" is a universal message that is at the heart of compassionate action, just as the sayings that counsel us to "walk for a day in another's shoes" are lessons about empathy. Abusive families and institutions that are indifferent to suffering and social justice teach fear instead of love, and perpetuate abuse and indifference through action and attitude.

Bodhisattvas are an ideal in Mahayama ("Great Vehicle") Buddhism, which is the dominant branch of Buddhism in Tibet, China, Taiwan, Mongolia, Korea, Japan, and Vietnam. A bodhisattva has vowed not to personally withdraw from the world as a fully awakened buddha until he or she can assist all sentient beings to become enlightened and free from suffering. Leighton makes the point that bodhisattva qualities appear in people of all religious and cultural backgrounds, citing exemplars as diverse as Martin Luther King Jr., Mother Teresa, Gloria Steinem, Bob Dylan, and many other contemporary figures.

The historical Buddha was Siddhartha Gautama in sixth-century B.C.E. India. The bodhisattva of compassion, of which Kuan Yin is the most popular and well known, appears in more different forms than any other bodhisattva. There are male and female bodhisattvas of compassion, and many images are androgynous in appearance. There are systems that have described from seven to one hundred and eight manifestations of this bodhisattva. In Tibet, he is named Chenrezig. The current and fourteenth Dalai Lama is considered an incarnation of Chenrezig.

Just before he received the Nobel Prize in 1989, the Dalai Lama engaged in a series of dialogues in compassionate action at a conference. It was a lively three-day discussion between his holiness and seven psychologists and psychiatrists—of whom I was one—before a rapt audience. He changed my understanding of compassion; before this, I had thought that compassion was the same as empathy. The point he made was that genuine compassion generates a spontaneous sense of responsibility to do something to alleviate the suffering. The Norwegian Nobel Prize committee quoted a verse that His Holiness recites daily, which contains the central themes of the Bodhisattva vows:

As long as space remains
As long as sentient beings remain
Until then, may I too remain
And dispel the miseries of the world.

Compassion is presented in the bodhisattva tradition by figures that are male, female, or could be either. Psychologically, as we grow older, women and men become more androgynous, and since compassion is an evolved human quality, it is appropriate that there be a gender ambiguity in many representations of the bodhisattva of compassion, who also appear ageless. Compassion is ageless as well as the nonexclusive attribute of either sex. Many children come into the world with an inherent compassion that many adults either have lost along the way, or develop only after they have had experienced suffering themselves.

Though compassion is a universal quality and an attribute found in men, women, and children, I am calling Kuan Yin a crone archetype because the conscious awareness of its development is such a common experience in older women. Some comment that when they were younger, they were judgmental and unforgiving toward parents, and now they have compassion for them and a relationship with them. Others describe how bitter and even vengeful they had been and now they aren't the same person. Many can remember how ignorant or afraid they were of people who were of a different social class, religion, or race, or were homosexual. Many also recall that they had no compassion for themselves, and say, "I'm not so hard on myself." Kuan Yin makes us kinder, easier on ourselves and others. Growing older and wiser seems invariably linked with also growing kinder.

When I was in Kansas City a number of years ago, I went to the Nelson-Atkins Museum to see a stunningly beautiful statue of Kuan Yin, a painted wooden statue from about the eleventh–early twelfth century C.E. There was a serenity, strength, beauty, and grace about this Kuan Yin. Something about it, a "suchness" or presence, gave this stationary figure both a fluidity and a stillness, qualities enhanced by the similar colors and flow of lines in the ancient mural on the wall immediately behind it. This Kuan Yin was seated in what is described as a royal ease position, from which she could rise easily in response to those in need. *She* could be a graceful *he*, as the androgyny of the figure made the gender ambiguous, yet it was neither an effeminate male nor a masculinized female figure. Strength and grace, serenity and intensity came together in this Kuan Yin that drew me into a timeless contemplation.

Seeing this particular statue of Kuan Yin helped me to understand the archetype of She-Who-Hearkens-to-the-Cries-of-the-World. It's the ability to listen empathically, accepting the person and his or her feelings, without becoming judgmental or defensive. It's an ability to hear and bear another's pain, anger, and suffering, which can help to relieve it. It is a responsive act that involves *feeling and doing,* even if no physical action can be observed. It is this kind of response that heals. This is how people who feel that what was done to them or by them makes them outcasts can be healed when they risk speaking of the reasons for these feelings. Telling this kind of secret with courage and listening with the compassion of Kuan Yin are two halves of a healing process.

The archetype of compassion is present in recovery group meetings, in psychotherapy sessions, and in any other relationships which can become vessels for healing psychological and spiritual wounds. To listen as well as to tell involves risk. It is difficult to bear witness, to listen with compassion without becoming personally affected by the story. When we listen empathically, we take what we hear into our imagination, heart, body, and soul. When what we hear from another is beyond our own experience and even our comprehension, the task and opportunity is to become "bigger" and be able to hold what we are hearing and feeling. The listener is at risk of becoming vicariously traumatized by her empathy or becoming emotionally distant when it becomes hard to listen. Kuan Yin is the archetype that we call on to be able to hear and bear our own pain and the pain of others and have mercy.

THE VIRGIN MARY

In the Roman Catholic Church, Mary, the mother of Jesus, is the "Blessed Mother." For nearly two millennia, she has been the predominant female figure in Western culture, in religion and art, and as the inspiration for the construction of some of the most magnificent edifices in the world. The cathedrals built throughout Europe in the eleventh and twelfth centuries, such as Chartres and Notre Dame, were consecrated to Mary. Patriarchal and monotheistic religions supplanted and suppressed the Triple Goddess, and yet in the figure of Mary, the goddess continued to be in the world.

Mary has absorbed and transformed the Triple Goddess as maiden, mother, and crone. Mary was the immaculately conceived Virgin to whom the Archangel Gabriel appeared. She was the Mother, who parthenogenically gave birth to Jesus and is depicted in her most characteristic pose as the Madonna and child, holding the infant Jesus on her lap. And, as the grieving mother of the crucified Christ, Mary was also an embodiment of the Crone.

Prayers for mercy and comfort are directed to Mary because people relate to her as a mother and as a woman who has known grief and suffering herself. In the Eleusinian Mysteries of ancient Greece, her equivalent was Demeter the mother goddess and goddess of the grain, who grieved for her abducted divine daughter, as Mary grieved for her crucified divine son. In the solitary figure of Mary, the three phases of women's lives that correspond to the Eleusinian trinity of Persephone-Demeter-Hecate or maiden-mother-crone, can still be found.

It is the older Mary, the crone, who knew suffering herself, and not the pure young virgin, nor even the young mother of an infant that people appeal to with their prayers and offerings when they ask her to intercede in their lives. This is the Mary in Michelangelo's *Pietà*, the mother who holds her dead grown son in her arms. Common folk pray to her, consciously or unconsciously making the connection between her suffering and her compassion for their suffering.

MARY AS THE GODDESS OF THE CHRISTIAN ERA

In *The Mists of Avalon*, Marion Zimmer Bradley retold Arthurian legends from the viewpoint of the women in the story, as if this were the time in which the goddess and Avalon as the realm of the goddess disappeared from the world and was replaced by patriarchy and the Christian religion. This book stirred the collective unconscious of her readers. Women read it like amnesiacs, sensing there was something familiar and yet not quite remembered about a time when there was a goddess. (It contributed to the experience that led me to write an autobiographical book, *Crossing to Avalon: A Woman's Midlife Pilgrimage*).

At the end of the book, Morgaine—the main character who is Arthur's half-sister and the last priestess of the Goddess—despaired at the passing of Avalon until she visited the new Christian nuns at Glaston-bury and realized that while Avalon has passed into the mists, the god-dess is still in the world:

> "Morgaine followed the young girl into the small side chapel. There were flowers here, armfuls of apple blossoms, before a statue of a veiled woman crowned with a halo of light; and in her arms she bore a child. Morgaine drew a shaking breath and bowed her head before the Goddess."
>
> "Morgaine looked on the statue of Brigid, and she could feel the power coming from it in great waves that permeated the chapel. She bowed her head . . . *But Brigid is not a Christian saint,* she thought, *even if Patricius thinks so. That is the Goddess as she is worshiped in Ireland* . . . Exile her as they may, she will prevail. The Goddess will never withdraw herself from mankind."[3]

Mary replaced the goddess not just as an archetype or as a divine fig-ure, but literally so when cathedrals or churches dedicated to Mary were built on sites that were once sacred to the goddess. As Barbara G. Walker noted, "Rome's cathedral of Santa Maria Maggiore was built over the sacred cave of the Magna Mater. Santa Maria in Ara-coeli on the Capitoline Hill was formerly a temple of the goddess Tanit. Mary's churches throughout Italy were founded on shrines of Juno, Isis, Minerva, Diana, Hecate. One church was even naively named Santa Maria sopra Minerva, Holy Mary over (the shrine of) Minerva. In the sixth century, the great temple of Isis at Philae (Egypt) was rededicated to Mary. Aphrodite's sanctuaries on Cyprus became churches of Mary, whom the Cypriots continued to address by Aphrodite's name."[4]

For psychological and archetypal reasons, common people turned to Mary for compassion easier than to her son, and asked her to inter-cede for them to him or to God the Father: human beings have expec-tations that mothers will listen, forgive, comfort, and be understanding and accepting much more than fathers. Even when one's personal mother has not been so, the archetype of the good mother predisposes us to project these attributes onto maternal figures.

MARY AS A RETURN OF THE GODDESS

Catholics are often surprised that Mary is so little mentioned in the New Testament. Sally Cunneen, author of *In Search of Mary*, commented about this from her own experience: "What is striking in the Gospel stories is how seldom Mary is mentioned. Many of the scenes and characters I assumed were there are not; they were added by legend, art, and devotion in later centuries. No St. Anne, for example . . . *The New Testament* tells us nothing of Mary's parentage. Nor does it have Jesus appear to his mother after the Resurrection, something later believers found hard to accept."[5]

References to Mary in the Gospels are mainly related to the birth or childhood of Jesus, reported only by Matthew and Luke. Mark begins his narrative with the baptism of Jesus at the beginning of his ministry. There is precious little, fewer than two dozen mentions of Mary in the New Testament. Her only biblical role was as the human mother of Jesus, which is also the only importance she has for Protestants. There are no remnants of the goddess in Protestant Christianity except the structure of divinity as three in one: only now, the trinity is Father, Son, and a (male) Holy Spirit. In the last half of the twentieth century, a feminine dimension has entered most mainstream Protestant churches, however. Women priests and women ministers have been ordained by Protestant denominations, and gender-inclusive language has increasingly been adopted in rewritten liturgy. God is sometimes referred to as She as well as He. There have also been theological revisioning by some who see the Holy Spirit as feminine. The Holy Spirit appeared in the form of a dove in the New Testament, which is an ancient goddess symbol, associated with Aphrodite in classical Greek mythology and a feminine archetype.

In contrast, in Roman Catholicism, the Virgin Mary has been elevated in significance to where one could say that there is a Christian quaternity of Mary and the Trinity. It could be even said (especially by others outside the Roman Catholic Church) that the goddess is return-

ing into the culture through Mary. Common people have long worshiped her as common people did the goddess before Christianity,
even if her divinity was not claimed by the church. However, within
the theology and dogma of the Roman Catholic Church, a deification
of Mary seems to be proceeding.

Mary was declared Mother of God in 431 C.E. at the third Council
of Ephesus. In 1854, Pope Pius IX declared the Immaculate Conception, in which Mary was preserved from original sin because she had
been chosen by God to be the mother of Christ. In 1950, Pope Pius
XII invoked papal infallibility and proclaimed the Assumption of Mary,
which declared that Mary was taken up into heaven, body and soul.

There is now a major movement within Catholicism directed
toward a receptive pope, asking him to exercise the power of papal
infallibility once more, to declare that Mary is "Co-Redemptrix, Medi-
ator of All Graces and Advocate for the People of God." If this drive
succeeds, the result would be what theologians call "High Mariology."
It would proclaim that Mary participates in the redemption achieved
by her son, that all graces that flow from the suffering and death of
Jesus Christ are granted only through Mary's intercession with her
son, and that all prayers and petitions from the faithful on earth must
likewise flow through Mary. If proclaimed, so say the theologians, it
would not make Mary God. In practice and in the psyche of those who
pray to her, however, she becomes (if she is not already) the Divine
Mother, the Mother Goddess.

In many parts of the world, the most beloved and revered image of
Mary is as a dark or black madonna, whose immediate precursor in the
Roman empire was black Isis, the Egyptian goddess who also suffered
loss with the death and dismemberment of her husband Osiris.
Shrines and temples to Isis were established in Rome and on Delos,
the sacred island of the Greeks. The goddesses of the dark moon were
black, the color of the crone aspect of the goddess was black, and now,
in this century, there has been a great resurgence of worship and reverence for black madonnas such as Our Lady of Guadalupe in Mexico,
and the black madonnas of Montserrat in Spain, Einsiedeln in
Switzerland, and Pope John Paul II's beloved Black Madonna of
Czestochowa in Poland. In the black madonnas especially people see
the compassionate face of a maternal God.

Mary's increasing significance is also expressed in the increasing number of appearances or apparitions of Mary all over the world. In the twentieth century, four hundred apparitions of Mary were reported (*Newsweek*, August 25, 1997). Her appearances, the interest in black madonnas, and the growing Mariology movement are catholic expressions of the return of the Goddess into the culture and a yearning for compassion.

LADY LIBERTY

We in the United States have our own version of the goddess of compassion. I realized this one morning shortly before dawn on the deck of a cruise ship as we passed by the Statue of Liberty. How breathtaking *she* is. This "graven image" is Our Lady of Liberty or Goddess of Liberty, or goddess of compassion. Lady Liberty (my best name for her) holds her torch aloft as a homecoming beacon and, in the words of Emma Lazarus, inscribed on the base, is saying: "Give me your tired, your poor/ Your teeming masses yearning to breathe free . . ." As we passed by, I remembered the Chinese students in Tiananmen Square who erected their "Goddess of Liberty" and were shot and imprisoned after their demonstration for freedom. Even if current immigration policies close the door to the world's tired and poor, "Lady Liberty" remains as an American Kuan Yin, an archetype of "she-who-hearkens-to-the cries-of-the world."

Time and time again, Americans have responded to natural disasters and postwar devastation around the world with an outpouring of compassionate action through volunteer efforts, donations from individuals, and aid from the government. It's part of our national character to hearken-to-the-cries-of-the-world and rush in with help. Immediate aid efforts crop up on the heels of devastating earthquakes and hurricanes. These and long-established nonprofit organizations that help people are expressions of the Kuan Yin archetype.

Community-based organizations count most upon women in the third phase of their lives, whose children are grown and whose energies now go into volunteer work. Even with the two-career family now more the rule than the exception, this still seems to be the case. Compassionate action is a challenge to "walk your talk," and as baby boomers come of crone age, they'll find that Kuan Yin opportunities come their way.

COMPASSIONATE CRONES

Crone archetypes are those potentials for development in individual women who come into their crone years and continue to grow spiritually and psychologically. Compassion is the essential one, without which the others cannot be all they can be. Wisdom in its several forms becomes compassionate wisdom. Outrage demands justice, but outrage and compassion together becomes justice tempered by mercy. When compassion is present, the laughter and humor of mirth is never unkind. Compassion acts to relieve suffering, one's own as well as others.

Compassion is unpossessive love that does not need to be reciprocated and is unrationed: the more you give away, the more you have. It is a wise crone who has learned the difference between codependency and compassion, usually through her own experience of each.

Use of Imagination
For Sekhmet
(Calls on dramatic skills)

Feel yourself morphing into a lioness
with muscles and a golden coat,
with the grace of a cat
and power to spring upon wrongdoers
or protect what you love.
No one messes with you.
"I am a Lioness . . . I can Roar."
So ROAR, and ROAR, and ROAR some more.
And then,
be silent.
Become aware of your inner Sekhmet,
of the lioness energy that is in you.
If "enough is enough" in some facet of your life,
call upon Wisdom and Compassion
for counsel.
And Sekhmet for Lionhearted Courage.
When it is time to do what you know you must do.

Use of Imagination
For Uzume and Baubo
(Dance)

Put on music with a beat,
Loud Music.
Music that moves through the cells of your body
and makes you want to move.
grinding, sensual, tingly music
for the bawd in you.
This dance is not directed outward,
is not about seduction or attraction,
not about seeing yourself as if in a mirror
but about being alive in yourself.
In your belly, in your hips, in your breasts,
in your down-below.
In your vulva.
"I am a Woman." "I am a Goddess."
Such good exercise.
What if (fill the blank) could see you now!
Makes you smile, makes your belly smile
at the thought.
And if you try this with your friends,
there will be Belly Laughter.

Use of Imagination
For Compassion
(Meditation)

There are Buddhist meditations for the well-being
of all sentient beings,
and Catholic recitations of the rosary that touch the same chord.
There are many traditions
and prayers for compassion for oneself and others.
What might you do?
What do you do?

The prayer of St. Francis begins,
"Let me be an Instrument of Thy Peace . . ."
Thich Nich Han, the Vietnamese monk,
teaches a walking meditation.

Breathe in—
breathe out—
is at the heart of meditation.
What is it you want to breathe in,
transform through compassion,
and breathe out?

PART 3

SHE IS A GODDESS GROWING OLDER:
GODDESSES IN EVERYWOMAN, REVISITED

There are in the beach-world certain rare creatures, the "Argonauta"
(Paper Nautilus), who are not fastened to their shell at all.
It is actually a cradle for the young, held in the arms of the
mother argonaut who floats with it to the surface,
where the eggs hatch and the young swim away.
Then the mother argonaut leaves her shell and starts another life.

—Anne Morrow Lindbergh

Though I've worked many years to made marriage more equal,
I never expected to take advantage of it myself.

—Gloria Steinem commenting on her first marriage—at age sixty-six.

The goddesses I have so far described come into our lives as we become older, wiser, more compassionate, and able to take decisive action in ways that we may not have been able to as younger women. These crone goddesses develop if we learn soul lessons through what has brought us joy and suffering. They deepen us but don't change the basic archetypal underpinnings that have shaped our personality and priorities from the beginning. Observant old and good friends know this: whatever our age—from fifty to ninety-plus—we still retain qualities that we had as children and as much younger women. We come into the world with tendencies that vary depending upon which archetypes are active in us; these patterns shape our personalities and determine what most matters to us. These are the archetypes that I described in *Goddesses in Everywoman* and they are based upon the familiar Greek goddesses that we recognize and know of through their myths.

Most women of any complexity have several important and active goddess-archetypes in them. Depending upon "the climate" of family and culture, some fit in and others spell trouble, even at a time when women are not burned at the stake or stoned for expressing suppressed goddesses. There is also more inner conflict—between goddesses—when real choice is possible. I think of the Greek goddesses of Mount Olympus—each of whom was unique, some of whom were antagonistic toward each other—as a metaphor for diversity and con-

flict within women who are complex and many-sided. All of these goddesses are potentially present in every woman and yet we do seem to
be born with innate characteristics of one or some of them more than
others. When several compete for dominance in a woman's psyche,
she needs to decide which aspect of herself to express and when.

There is personal and spiritual meaning in the experience when
there is a depth connection between a woman's role and an archetype.
When there is not, a woman who fulfills the very same role is adapting
to a life that is "not her own."

In the first two phases of our adult lives, we may not have been able
to embody a particular archetype and yet longed to do so. In the third
phase, we may feel grief or depression over this missed possibility.
Some women deny that they are older, and in maintaining the illusion
of being younger become increasingly inauthentic. Psychological and
soul growth comes through the crone archetypes *and* through the *evolution* of the "goddesses in everywoman." For these reasons, it is
important for women who are familiar with the rich imagery and
mythology that helped us understand ourselves through these goddesses to revisit them, and for others who are learning about archetypes to be introduced.

The goddesses that have been active in us through our first two
stages of adulthood often continue to be so in the third phase. At each
stage of life, there are characteristic patterns for each archetype, which
I described in *Goddesses in Everywoman*. Although I included a short
section of the "Later Years" in every one of the goddess chapters—
Artemis, Athena, Hestia, Hera, Demeter, Persephone, Aphrodite—now
that I have reached this stage myself, I have considerably more to add.

A particular goddess-archetype may have been compelling, a problem, or an asset when we were younger or in a particular phase: it was
Aphrodite when we were in love, Demeter if we yearned to become
pregnant or embraced motherhood, Persephone when we wanted to
be swept off our feet. It was Hera who impelled us toward marriage or
consumed us with jealousy, Artemis who drew us into the women's
movement and made it easy for us to focus on a chosen career, Athena
who was an asset when we entered the male world, and Hestia who
preferred solitude.

Women who are now coming of crone age and those who were

young women in the 1960s and 1970s have had complex lives, juggling work and relationships, keeping an eye on the biological clock while on a career track, breaking with old traditions and exploring new ground, facing more complex situations and personal choices than women have ever had. Circumstance and choice—and these goddesses—shaped the course that each of us has followed. Revisiting these goddesses may provide retrospective insights or be an opportunity to take stock, both of great value, particularly if we stand at the threshold of the next stage.

For some crone-aged women, a single archetype may be the wellspring that she has drawn from all her life. Then this one goddess is the essence of her character, while others may have been important for a phase of her life and then receded. A goddess that has been dormant may also come alive for the first time and, as a late-blooming archetype, be an unexpected source of delight and new growth.

CATEGORIES AND QUALITIES

In *Goddesses in Everywoman*, I placed these archetypes into three categories: the Virgin Goddesses, the Vulnerable Goddesses, and the Alchemical Goddess; based on their psychological qualities and mythologies. I created these three archetypal categories after realizing how well the major patterns in women's psyche fit into them, and how cultural expectations affect each category. Two powerful forces, archetypes and stereotypes, act upon us, whether we are conscious of them or not. The Greek goddesses existed in a patriarchal society. Male gods ruled over the earth, heavens, ocean, and underworld. Each goddess and category adapted or was affected or dominated by this reality, and women have been ever since.

When the ancient Greeks described Artemis, Athena, and Hestia as virgin goddesses, it was because they were virginal—they were goddesses who retained their chastity. Of all of the gods, goddesses, and mortals, they were unmoved by the otherwise irresistible power of Aphrodite. As I describe women in whom these archetypes predominate, you will see that psychological virginity is not the same as physical virginity. The vulnerable goddesses—Demeter, Persephone, and

Hera—can be deeply fulfilled or wounded by their relationships. Aphrodite I placed in a category of her own as the alchemical goddess. She is the archetype of the lover, which is definitely not a virgin goddess, but with the power to pick and choose her lovers, she had an autonomy denied the vulnerable goddesses, as well as an alchemy all her own.

Each of these three categories have a different quality of consciousness. Focused consciousness typifies the virgin goddesses, diffuse awareness is characteristic of the vulnerable goddesses, and Aphrodite consciousness is what we shift into when we are engaged in creative work or are in love.

The Virgin Goddesses

The three virgin goddesses of the Greeks and their Roman counterparts were Artemis (Diana), goddess of the hunt and moon, Athena (Minerva), goddess of wisdom and crafts, and Hestia (Vesta), goddess of the hearth and temple. These three personify the independent, nonrelationship aspects of a woman's psyche. Each has a self-contained quality. Artemis and Athena have attributes that allow a woman to focus outward and lead to achievements in the world, while Hestia is inwardly focused. All three represent inner drives in women.

The virgin goddess aspect is that part of a woman that is unowned by or "unpenetrated" by a man—that is untouched by her need for a man or a need to be validated by one. This is a psychological virginity. When a virgin goddess is the dominant archetype, a woman is "one-in-herself," and does not need another person to feel whole or complete.

Women who are like these three goddesses have the ability to concentrate their attention on what matters to them. They can easily become absorbed in what they are doing. In their focus, they can easily exclude or "tune out" everything that is extraneous to the task at hand or to the long-range goal. I think of focused consciousness being like a willfully directed, intense beam of light that illuminates only what it is focused on, leaving everything outside of its radius in the dark or in the shadows. When a woman can focus on solving a problem or achieving a goal or sit for extended periods in meditation, she can ignore her own needs for food or sleep, as well as not attend to the emotional needs of those around her. There are advantages and drawbacks to this ability.

The Vulnerable Goddesses

The three Vulnerable Goddesses are Hera (Juno), the goddess of marriage, Demeter (Ceres), the goddess of grain, whose primary mythological role was as mother to Persephone, and Persephone (Proserpina), the maiden goddess and queen of the underworld. These three goddesses personify archetypes that represent the traditional roles of women—wife, mother, and daughter. They are the relationship-oriented archetypes in women. Hera and Demeter, especially, express the need for a significant relationship in order to be fulfilled. In their mythologies, these three goddesses were overpowered and dominated by male gods. They were raped, abducted, or humiliated. Each suffered when an attachment was broken or dishonored. Each experienced powerlessness and became psychologically symptomatic. Women in whom these archetypes predominate are likewise vulnerable and can become depressed like Demeter and Persephone, or obsessed and jealous like Hera. When these archetypes are fulfilled by positive relationships, a woman finds spiritual depth and meaning in traditional roles.

Diffuse awareness is their characteristic quality of consciousness, which is like the light of a living-room lamp that illuminates and casts a warm glow on everything within its radius. It is an attentiveness that a woman has to others in her circle of concern that enables her to notice subtle emotional shifts in them or hear the whimper of her child over the din of adult conversation. It is a receptive attentiveness that is attuned to others and felt by them subliminally.

The Alchemical Goddess

Aphrodite (Venus), the goddess of love and beauty, I placed in a category all her own as the alchemical goddess, a fitting description for the power that she alone had, a power that was compelling and transformative. Aphrodite was initially an awesome and revered presence (until she became denigrated). She had the power to cause mortals and deities to fall in love and conceive new life.

The alchemical power of Aphrodite remains awesome: whomever or whatever Aphrodite imbues with beauty can feel irresistible. To come into contact with Aphrodite results in a magnetic attraction, a powerful urge to get closer, to consummate—or "know"—the other. While this drive may be purely sexual, the impulse is often deeper, representing an urge that is both psychological and spiritual.

The quality of consciousness that I call "Aphrodite consciousness" is like theater lighting which contributes to the magic that can happen between the audience and actor, speaker, or musician. It is more focused and intense than the diffuse awareness of the vulnerable goddesses, but it is more receptive and attentive to what it focuses on than the focused consciousness of the virgin archetypes. Whatever is in the limelight onstage, enhances, dramatizes, or magnifies the impact of the experience on us, and our response, in turn, affects those on stage. An alchemy takes place between audience and performers when this is so. We take in and react to what we behold. The special lighting helps us become emotionally transported. It contributes to an onstage illusion.

When this quality of consciousness is focused by an attractive woman on susceptible men, the alchemy that results is Aphrodite's. If she is unconscious of what she generates, she herself falls in love often, which plays havoc with her life and those who fall under the temporary spell with her.

Aphrodite consciousness is present in all creative work whether it is being done with people or in solitude. The creative person becomes both lost in the work and, at the same time, is sensitively observant, like a lover. There is an absorption, an intensity, and a fascination in the creative work. Both elements—the work and the person—are affected by the process.

In this section, my brief descriptions of each of these goddesses will introduce or refresh your memory. If you are learning of these archetypes for the first time, and have an *Aha!* of recognition, you may want to read more about them in *Goddesses in Everywoman*. In the following, I present "each goddess, growing older." My focus is on positive ways a goddess may be expressed in the lives of older women and the characteristic problems and difficulties that arise with aging. I also note the affinity that each of these goddesses has with certain of the crone archetypes.

Artemis, the Goddess of the Hunt and Moon

Sister, Feminist, Goal Achiever

Artemis, known to the Romans as Diana, was goddess of the hunt and moon. The tall, lovely daughter of Zeus and Leto roamed the wilderness of forest, mountain, meadow, and glade with her band of nymphs and hunting dogs. Dressed in a short tunic, armed with a silver bow and a quiver of arrows on her back, she was the archer with unerring aim. As goddess of the moon, she is also portrayed in statues as a lightbearer carrying a torch in her hand, or with the moon and stars surrounding her head. Symbolized by the crescent, waxing moon, Artemis represented the maiden aspect of the once-worshiped triple goddess, with Selene being the mature or full moon, and Hecate the crescent, waning moon. As a trinity, Artemis's realm was earth, Selene's the heavens, and Hecate's the underworld. Of the three, only Artemis was a major Greek divinity.

As the goddess of wildlife, she was associated with undomesticated animals that shared her qualities. The stag and doe symbolized her elusiveness, the bear her role as a fierce protector of the young, and the boar (which she once unleashed in anger to ravage a countryside) her destructive aspect.

Artemis was the daughter of Zeus and Leto (a pre-Olympian nature deity), the firstborn twin sister of Apollo, god of the sun. As soon as Artemis was born, this divine child witnessed the most difficult labor in Greek mythology. For nine days and nights, Leto suffered atrocious pain, finally delivering Apollo with Artemis as her midwife. This is why Artemis was a goddess of childbirth, prayed to by women in labor for delivery from pain.

When Artemis was three years old, Leto brought her to Mount Olympus to meet her father. Zeus was delighted with his little daughter and promised to give her whatever she wanted. At three, Artemis knew exactly what she wanted: a bow and arrows, a pack of hounds to hunt with, nymphs to accompany her, a tunic short enough to run in, mountains and wilderness as her special places, and eternal chastity. Zeus granted her all of her wishes, plus the privilege of making the selections herself. Artemis was granted autonomy and would never be violated or overpowered by male power.

As an archetype, Artemis personifies an independent feminine spirit that enables a woman to seek her own goals on a terrain of her own choosing. She had qualities that were idealized by the women's movement such as sisterhood and independence. She acted swiftly and decisively to protect and rescue those who appealed to her for help and was quick to punish those who offended her. In her mythology, she alone of all the goddesses came to the aid of her mother; once a giant attempted to rape Leto and was swiftly punished (rape is a usual occurrence in Greek mythology, punishment a rarity). She was the protector of young wildlife and young girls. She was the archetypal big sister to her nymph companions, and an equal and competitor of her twin brother, Apollo.

With an affinity for the wilderness and animals, the Artemis archetype is active in women who backpack, ride horses, and have a spiritual connection to nature. An athletic Artemis is a fierce competitor and a team player. She is concerned about equality, fairness, and justice for people and animals, and most likely articulated these values as a child. When she was treated differently from a brother because she was a girl, she protested, "It's not fair!" Motivated by these same values as an adult, she may become an activist. In her advocacy, she can be merciless. In the early years of the women's movement, for example, such feminists trashed others for not being pure enough, as well as directed their wrath (righteous destructiveness is a shadow aspect of this archetype) toward sexist people and institutions. The metaphoric wilderness of uncharted terrain attracted many Artemis women to fields never before open to women. Armed with the attributes of the huntress with unerring aim, this was the active archetype in goal-oriented young women who single-mindedly set their sights on personal targets.

Artemis at Ephesus is probably the most famous statue of the goddess. More stately than the usual representations of her as a huntress, it often is called "the many-breasted Artemis" because of the numerous rows of rounded protuberances covering her chest. In the middle adult years, women usually juggle several roles and many responsibilities; the part of her that is Artemis can feel more constrained than fulfilled in the traditional roles of wife and mother or nurturer—"like an Artemis of Ephesus, with someone hanging on each breast" is how one Artemis woman put it. Yet it is through these same commitments to people that an Artemis woman grows in maturity and compassion. Until she has made such commitments, or had her own experiences of physical pain, dependency, jealousy, or emotional loss, she may be unable to have empathy for the suffering of others or awareness of her own vulnerability.

Humility is another of her teachers. With strong feelings and high principles, the Artemis woman can be righteous and intolerant. She can also be quick to act in anger and can do harm. However, because she is capable of reflection and has the ability to feel remorse as intense as her outrage, it is through these lessons that she can learn humility and grow wiser as she grows older.

CRONE-AGED ARTEMIS

It's not unusual for a woman to have her Artemis qualities not only persist into her crone years but enjoy a renaissance at this time. If she is an active person in good health, the later years can be the best years of her life. The events that are major losses when other archetypes predominate—retirement, the end of a marriage through divorce or widowhood, children growing up and leaving the nest—can free a woman to be her Artemis self. A crone-aged Artemis retains an affinity for the young and an ability to think young, which keeps her from feeling middle-aged long after others might consider her old. She is an explorer who likes to travel to new and foreign places, and retains passionate interests in whatever fascinates her. She may be more free to follow her own inclinations and can more readily than most leave house and home behind and strike out for new terrain. In an age of recreational vehicles, she may take to the open road in her mobile home (there are networks and organizations of crones in RVs who report on conditions up ahead on their mobile radiophones or cellular phones and rely on each other's awareness of where they are for a measure of safety). She may go to foreign countries or onto reservations as a volunteer, not shirking from the deprivation or hardships of living among tribal people, or she may travel on her own, making up an itinerary as she goes along, glad for the many elder hostels that now exist. Or she may be drawn to Esalen, Findhorn, and other growth centers in beautiful and natural settings that offer her opportunities to explore new psychological and spiritual terrain. When I was leading women's wisdom workshops in these places, among the participants there invariably would be wonderful models of late-blossoming Artemis women.

If an Artemis is in an enduring marriage, chances are that it is a companionable, egalitarian, and comfortable one, with each partner also having separate interests and friends. Artemis has an aversion to being fenced in by possessive partners. If she found herself in a traditional, patriarchal marriage, something had to change. Marriage is not an institution that Artemis women have a deep need for, and should she form a new intimate relationship in her crone years, she is likely to prefer maintaining her autonomy as a single woman, and even his-and-her separate residences, if possible.

By the time they are crones, Artemis lesbian women often are a part of an extended family, which includes former partners who are now enduring friends. The heterosexual woman who switches her sexual orientation in the third phase of her life is often an Artemis whose new relationship grows out of her predisposition to explore new territory and to want a relationship with an equal. Thus, if she is strongly attracted to a woman, she will follow this attraction where it leads her.

A crone-aged Artemis with grown children and grandchildren usually has an easy relationship with them. With the mother bear as an appropriate symbol for her maternal style, it is likely that she protected them when they were young, kept them from being abused, and fostered their independence when they grew older. Artemis women may not be as close to their children as some other women are, though they can be, especially if they share mutual interests. As she grows older, an Artemis crone is concerned that she not become dependent on her children and makes every effort to keep her independence and not be a burden.

If she has a passion for her work, an Artemis is unlikely to retire. When this is so, she usually is doing work that keeps challenging her and affords her autonomy. She can work alone, with a team of equals, and even be part of a hierarchical institution as long as she can freely work within her own sphere. She will be eager to retire, however, if her work is repetitious or she has a controlling boss. She chomps at the bit when she has had to rein herself in and eagerly awaits being put out to pasture so that she can immediately jump the fence into her chosen wilderness.

Georgia O'Keeffe had Artemis qualities all her life and was in her crone years for over four decades. She kept her own name when she married, was an artist who weathered self-doubts and art critics as she broke from tradition to create her own art. She was not a mother, which was apparently a choice she agonized over, feeling that she could either be a mother or an artist, not both. Once she fell in love with the stark beauty of New Mexico's deserts and mountains, she kept returning there to paint. That meant months in which she and her husband Alfred Stieglitz would be apart even when his health was beginning to fail. Once her husband died, there was nothing to hold her in the east and she moved to New Mexico, where she would spend the rest of her life. She painted until her eyesight failed, and then worked in clay. She lived where she wanted to live and lived as she wanted to live, all the time creating a body of work that places her among the most famous artists in the world. She once said that she differed from most people in knowing what it is she wanted. Whether it was to create something or acquire it, she had an intense ability to focus her will and her talents on her chosen goals.

LATE-BLOOMING ARTEMIS

In some women, after decades of being cut off from this dismembered aspect of themselves, Artemis reemerges in their crone years. Circumstances that make it possible have changed, and only now is she free to be her Artemis self. Once upon a time this woman knew Artemis as a part of herself: she may have climbed trees, enjoyed summer camp, or practically lived at a stable. She was sure of herself and unself-conscious, until something changed, and Artemis went underground.* Or Artemis may have emerged for a time in early adulthood, when she was in a consciousness-raising group or in college, and then receded. Or she may have lost Artemis after she was raped.

There are many reasons why women become cut off from Artemis. Puberty and attraction to boys may bring Aphrodite into the fore-ground of her psyche, while academic expectations call upon the development of Athena. Social pressure may be brought to bear to inhibit Artemis traits. The more patriarchal the family, religion, or cul-ture, the more this is so. When "feminist" has a negative connotation, then Artemis is suppressed. Sometimes the loss of Artemis can be mostly attributed to the lack of time and energy, due to the demands of family and work. Whatever the cause, the emergence of Artemis in the crone phase is most welcome—there now may be a reclaiming of one's free spirit, a finding of one's true voice, an affinity with nature, or a sense of rekindled purpose.

ARTEMIS LEARNS WISDOM

The lessons that will make an Artemis wiser are those that come with life. In the maiden phase, she may be able to focus her energies on her career or causes, but lessons in reality and humility will come as they do to anyone who thinks they can stay eternally young, or are always right. When she becomes aware of her own vulnerability, she may begin to understand the choices and compromises that others make. When she makes mistakes and feels remorse, she begins to be less

---

*At eight or nine, a girl has definite ideas, trusts her perceptions, speaks up, and is self-confident and unself-conscious, which are Artemis qualities; by adolescence, she has become tentative and self-conscious. (Findings from the Harvard Project on Women's Psychology and Girls' Development, in Lyn Brown and Carol Gilligan, *Meeting at the Crossroads: Women's Psychology and Girls' Development*. Cambridge, Mass.: Harvard University Press, 1992.)

judgmental of others. While she may naturally be quick to act, like the moon itself, she has a capacity for reflection. She can go off by herself and ponder upon matters. When she does, she will likely take what she learns to heart. She goes into nature for solace when she is confused, hurt, or grieving, and is comforted. Through this a wisdom grows about the cycles of life. Nature may also teach her patience, which is one of the lessons most Artemis women need to learn.

Artemis was quick to punish and retaliate and she could be merciless and wrathful; these are shadow elements for a younger Artemis woman as well. When these feelings arise in a wiser Artemis, they may be fleeting, and they are restrained. An evolved Artemis is aware of her shadow, and is not controlled or possessed by such feelings. Lessons learned from inner work contribute to her understanding of herself and of others. While other women in their crone phase may finally say enough is enough, this is not an issue for an Artemis. She is not likely to have endured an oppressive relationship or become a codependent. Instead, she may have left significant relationships rather than worked on them and only later see the consequences and wonder how her life might have turned out otherwise.

WISDOM OF HECATE AND HESTIA

Hecate, the goddess of the crossroad and the waning moon, is the archetype of wisdom with whom Artemis has the most affinity. It is part of her own moon nature to be spiritually affected by the beauty and majesty of the wilderness, to feel a sacred connection to the elements and the great mystery of being part of the universe—especially under the nighttime sky, when Hecate is afoot. Moonlight and firelight (her hearth might be a campfire) draws an Artemis inward to Hecate and to Hestia, the goddess of the hearth and temple. Through reflection and meditation, she may become more inner-directed and spiritual than ever before.

When such is the case, the Artemis woman in the crone phase of her life may decide to put her resources and acquired wisdom and competence to a new use; to "give back" by mentoring individuals and supporting organizations that protect women, children, or wilderness areas. Or she may be most drawn toward finding her own spiritual path.

An Artemis who becomes wise has learned to be at the crossroad with Hecate. If you are an Artemis, you've reacted strongly, taken a stand, come to someone's aid, acted precipitously—and found that there were unexpected facets and consequences to these actions. Regret and remorse have taught you to pause and confer with Hecate before you do something that can change your life or impact others. You have learned that observation and reflection need to precede action. Gaining Hecate's wisdom comes through acquiring her vision: to see three ways at once—how you got here and where the choices may lead.

Athena, the Goddess of Wisdom and Crafts

Strategist, Warrior, Craftswoman

Athena was the Greek goddess of wisdom and crafts, known to the Romans as Minerva. She was a stately, beautiful warrior goddess, protector of her chosen heroes and namesake city, Athens. She was the only Olympian goddess portrayed wearing armor—the visor of her helmet pushed back to reveal her beauty; a shield over her arm and a spear in her hand. Befitting her role as the goddess who presided over battle strategy in wartime and over domestic arts in peacetime, she sometimes held a spear in one hand and a spindle or bowl in the other. Her symbol was the owl. She was the daughter of Zeus and considered him her sole parent. Her mother was Metis but, as we have seen, Athena had no memory of her. When Metis was pregnant with Athena, Zeus tricked her into becoming small and swallowed her, after which Athena was "born" as a full-grown woman out of Zeus's head to became Zeus's favorite child and the only Olympian he trusted with his symbols of power.

Athena's wisdom was pragmatic and practical. She was the protector of cities, patron of military forces, and goddess of weavers, goldsmiths, potters, and dressmakers. The martial and domestic skills associated with Athena involve planning and execution; activities that require purposeful thinking and action. In the contemporary world, corporate executives, computer program and product designers, legal minds, and marketing strategists would be under her protection.

Athena the archetype fosters achievement and ambition, with an astute eye for alliances and a chess mastery of strategic moves in whatever field she is in. Athena is the dominant archetype in logical women who are ruled by their heads rather than their hearts. She predisposes a woman to think clearly, to keep her head in the heat of an emotional situation, and be tactical in the midst of conflict.

Athena is the archetype of "the father's daughter" in women who naturally gravitate toward men in Zeus-like executive positions, or toward men whose psychology is that of the Greek heroes of mythology whom Athena provided with the strategy to win battles, capture the golden fleece, or take the head of Medusa. The women's movement opened opportunities for nonfeminist Athenas to enter the male world of power, where they found male mentors, were at ease among male competitors and colleagues, and could achieve a place in the once all-male hierarchy for themselves. Since the women's movement, individual Athenas have risen to top positions in government, business, academia, and even the military. They are the successful daughters of the patriarchy.

The historical exemplar of a successful Athena was Queen Elizabeth I of England, who was known as the Virgin Queen, the daughter of Henry VIII. With a combination of strategy, diplomacy, and ruthlessness, she forged alliances and outlived her rivals to become queen, and then kept herself and her country out of the clutches of foreign and church powers.

The goddess Athena was a warrior who defended authority and the prerogatives of power, which mortal Athenas are likely to do also—rather than seek truth or justice. Another shadowy aspect of Athena that can also be a problem for some Athenas is the willingness to do whatever it takes to achieve her ends—without considering whether it is unscrupulous or heartless. In the *Iliad*, for example, when Achilles and Hector were engaged in one-on-one combat, Athena deceived Hector, the Trojan hero, into believing his brother was at his side as his spear carrier. After Hector hurled his spear and missed, he then turned to his "brother" to get another, only to find he was alone and unarmed, which made it easy for Achilles to kill him. Athena's support not only gave Achilles an unfair advantage, she used deception to destroy his competitor.

Any woman whose dominant archetype is Athena the warrior and strategist can become too involved in school or work to develop other aspects of her life. She is a competitor who strives to win. The battle-ground can be the marketplace, the political arena, or academia. Success makes it difficult for her to see that it is extracting a high price. By focusing so intently on her career, she may arrest her emotional development and, as a result, she may lack intimates in her personal life, not have much of an inner life, and have few simple pleasures or spontaneous moments—something that she usually does not notice until she does slow down.

CHANGE AND GROWTH

Change and growth come to an Athena if life deals her some blows and they shift her perspective or open her heart. This may be initiated by a painful betrayal and fall from grace as a favored father's daughter, or by other losses strong enough to penetrate her intellectual armor and reach feelings of grief, vulnerability, and loneliness. Painful as this period can be, the introspection and openness to feelings can be transformative. She may see her past actions in a different light. She may remember the cost to others of her previous winning strategies, and feel remorseful, and be able to feel compassion.

Awareness that life is passing by may be the jolt that causes her to retreat inward and become introspective, or become a late-blooming feminist. This can happen to an Athena whose focus on work has been all-absorbing until she approaches midlife, when she realizes that it may be too late to have a family, feels this as a loss and, for the first time, feels lonely around the holidays. This is when she realizes that her male colleagues did not sacrifice having a family for career advancement, which she did. It is also when she may discover that there is a glass ceiling on advancement for women, and that the feminists she disparaged were right about sexism, after all. Or she has the vague discomfort and depression that can accompany achievement and find herself wondering, "Is this all there is?"

Athena the goddess was impervious to love, but Athena women do fall in love and it is this or an unexpected surge of maternal instinct that brings other archetypal energies into her psyche. This is when a once-focused Athena woman finds herself in conflict over priorities and values, and no longer fully identifies with this archetype. Athena women also marry and have children and yet stay focused on work in the same way that men traditionally have done. It is not whether or not she marries and has a family that makes a difference, but how it affects her.

The need to "remember Metis" is a psychological task for every Athena. Remembering Metis has several meanings, all to do with acknowledging and developing a connection to the feminine—to feelings, nature, instinct, the sacred feminine, or an identification with women and feminism. Metaphorically, it is to become a mother's daughter as well as a father's daughter. This potential is being realized by many women who start out as Athenas, become open to emotions, grow in compassion, and then have their consciousness raised about women's issues.

CRONE-AGED ATHENA

Settling into being a post-menopausal crone-aged woman may be remarkably easy for an Athena. Since moderation, sensible behavior, and planning ahead are Athena traits, she is likely to enter the third phase of her life physically and financially in good shape. She has planned for retirement if it is mandatory, or will probably continue working if she is in a profession or has a business of her own—because she likes to be productive. If she retires or was in the traditional role as a full-time wife and is widowed, she will probably create a routine and a schedule of activities that take her to the meetings, classes, or cultural events that interest her. Many Athenas are active and effective volunteers and board members.

A crone-aged Athena craftswoman may be entering the phase in which she receives recognition for her work, mentors others in her craft, or is at her most creative. If she had a craft as an interest or hobby, she may now be able to pursue this interest more seriously. While she may not be attracted to meditation as an idea, her concentration while weaving or throwing a pot on a wheel—the absorption of craftsmanship, whatever its form—is a meditative experience that can also be alchemical in its effect on the psyche of the artisan and the created work.

Most Athenas like the amenities and cultural events that a city provides its residents. She may see people regularly, have season tickets to lectures, or take emeritus college courses, and have a circle of acquaintances of all ages. If she is married, she usually has a companionable marriage. Her attachment to tradition and pragmatic sense of marriage as an alliance also makes it possible for her to stay married for appearances' sake to a man whose infidelity would have caused another woman to file for divorce long before. She can maintain form without emotional substance or a depth of meaning. Church, holiday traditions, or family observances then become persona performances, in which she plays her designated role.

A crone-aged Athena with grown children may have an easy, though not likely an intimate relationship with them, especially if they were enough like her to do well and are leading conventional lives. An Athena mother probably had difficulties with an emotional child, or one who did not do well at school, or reacted negatively to the emphasis she placed on performance, or was a dreamer, or rejected her conventional values. It is not in her Athena nature to be empathic, see herself at fault, or understand why what she says could be upsetting when it was common sense. Learning compassion is her biggest challenge, and one that often comes only through painful confrontations with family members. If her grown children have to give up on her being anything other than the rational and conventional person she is, it is they who either stay resentful or have accepted that this is just who she is.

With a proclivity toward discernment and detachment, if a crone-aged Athena turns inward, she most easily finds a connection with Metis's wisdom or Hestia's centeredness. Keeping busy and productive is usually the main obstacle in the way of developing these two crone archetypes.

Love, suffering, or unexpected emotional or physical vulnerability may strip an Athena of her defensive and intellectual armor. Becoming wide open to feeling, taken over by pain or grief or love, an Athena woman becomes a woman like other women, without protection.

Later, when she is able to grasp the experience with her mind, she may find that her perspective is altered by the compassion of Kuan Yin. She may notice suffering she had not seen before, and feel that enough is enough. Sekhmet's fierceness in a crone-aged Athena is formidable force for change.

MORE TIME TO BE WITH ATHENA

A woman who has not had time to do the reading she has longed to do, or take the courses that she has eyed and circled, or has drawers filled with material for projects she didn't have time for, looks forward to having an empty nest as a time to liberate Athena. A pre–women's movement Athena may have been expected to go to college, but she was not expected to do anything with her education. She was expected to marry well or sensibly, and if she did and had a comfortable and conventional life, the third phase can be a time of rebirth of an academic Athena.

An Athena warrior in the workplace may look forward to the winding down of her career in order to shift into the side of Athena, symbolized by the spindle rather than the spear. In the second phase of her life, she has lacked time to do all of the domestic projects that she has in mind. Martha Stewart with all of her many house, garden, kitchen, and craft projects combined with her business acumen in creating a corporate empire succeeds at both. Most Athenas focus on one during their productive middle phase and look forward to having time for the other when they are older.

LATE-BLOOMING ATHENA

As late as a century ago in the United States and still in parts of the world, most women received little education or none at all. Although this has changed for the most part in America, there are individual situations in which Athena is not allowed much of a place in the first two phases of a woman's life: you may have married young and had many children, or come from a family or be in a marriage in which girls and women are not expected to be smart or independent, or you may have been limited in what you could do by poverty or a disability. A late-blooming Athena can then flourish only after circumstances change—and by then, you may be a crone-aged woman.

For the first time in your life, you may discover the exciting world of the mind and be able to take courses in subjects that fascinate you, or find that you can hold your own in a discussion group, a classroom, or the Internet. Or as a widow, you may discover that you have a head for business or for investments. Or you may take up a craft and find that you have a natural talent for it, and become absorbed in learning and creating. There is a joy in being able to pursue intellectual interests and learn things for the love of it. A late-blooming Athena archetype is then born, full-grown, out of your own head.

Hestia, the Goddess of the Hearth and Temple

Hearthkeeper, Anonymous Woman

Hestia, the Greek goddess of the hearth and temple (and one of the crone archetypes of wisdom), can be the dominant archetype in an introverted child and younger woman who, in former times, might have become the self-effacing spinster in a large family. Hestia was the least known of the original twelve great Olympians, the firstborn and eldest child of Rhea and Cronus, the parents of Zeus, Demeter, Hera, Poseidon, and Hades. She is hardly mentioned in myths, because she, alone of all of the original Olympians, never took part in their disputes or wars, nor in their sexual or romantic affairs. Apollo and Poseidon could have been rival suitors, but she swore eternal virginity, preserved peace among the Olympians, and was granted her wish by Zeus. Hestia was not represented in human form by painters or sculptors—she was the goddess without a persona. Instead, she was present in the sacred fire in the center of a round hearth that was the spiritual center of home, temple, and city.

Neither home nor temple were sanctified until Hestia entered, and she was greatly honored to receive the best offerings made by mortals to the gods. She was a spiritual presence and the sacred fire. Her fire provided illumination and warmth in the temples of all of the divinities, as well as in the home. Sacred hospitality, temple sanctuary, and the inviolateness of Hestia are archetypally related and part of our social and religious heritage. The safety of guests and the sanctuary of the temple (later the church), are deeply-held conventions—to do other than be hospitable desecrated sacred ground that Hestia had made holy. The center of Greek life was the domestic hearth, and Hestia as its goddess represented personal security, happiness, and the sacred duty of hospitality.

In Rome, Hestia was worshiped as the goddess Vesta. There, her sacred fire was the center that united the Romans into one people. In her round temple, the Vestal Virgins were the hearthkeepers who tended her sacred fire. They embodied the virginity and anonymity of Hestia; living images that were symbolic representations of the goddess. The girls were taken into the temple when they were quite young, usually not yet six years old. Dressed alike, their hair shorn as new initiates, there was to be nothing distinct and individual about them. They were set apart from other people, honored, and expected to live like Hestia, as anonymous, chaste, holy women, with dire consequences if they did not remain virginal.

As one of the three virgin goddesses, anonymous Hestia seems to have little in common with Artemis or Athena. Yet the three shared essential intangible qualities, however different their spheres of interest or modes of action. Each had the one-in-herself quality that characterizes the virgin goddess archetype. Each was able to focus on what mattered to her and concentrate on that (in Latin, the word for "hearth" is *focus*). Artemis and Athena were externally oriented, while Hestia's is an inwardly-focused consciousness needed for meditation, contemplation, and prayer. The Hestia archetype is introverted. She looks inward to intuitively sense the essence of a situation or the character of a person. She has a natural detachment and seeks tranquility, which is most easily found in solitude.

These Hestia qualities are those of a wisewoman, and this archetype often develops as a woman becomes older and wiser. However, it can be the dominant archetype in an introverted child who has an "old soul" quality about her, which is not noticed by most people. She is likely to have been a pleasant, easy child, who was able to entertain herself and keep her room neat. A typical American family calls her shy and prods her to go out and play with others. Later, she may be urged to be more competitive, to stand up for herself, and do well in school; or the expectation placed on her may be to do better socially, to fit in with her peers, have a boyfriend, and pay attention to the impression she makes. A Hestia woman, especially in the first half of her life, has a hard time living in extroverted, postfeminist America. Depending upon how successfully she adapts, her self-esteem can suffer. The discrepancy between who she is inside and outer expectations can be very great. Hestia the archetype does not have a shadow, but the woman in whom Hestia is the dominant archetype can develop feelings of inadequacy or see herself as a misfit.

Marriage used to be a haven for most Hestias who, in the traditional role of housewife, could thrive and create a warm and inviting home. This is still the role that provides a place for many Hestia women. Her internal harmony is reflected in the harmony that she creates in the home. There is a beauty and order that does not call attention to itself but is felt.

In the past, a Hestia woman could also find her place in the anonymity of a religious order, especially a cloistered one, or she may have been valued in an extended family household as a maiden aunt. Living alone was formerly not an option for an unmarried woman. Now an introverted contemporary Hestia can have a place of her own. Depending upon her circumstances and the development of other aspects of herself, however, many Hestias appear to others as "centered" rather than introverted. Managing her own life, working, having a circle of friends, and marriage—the usual expectations of an adult— are compatible with being a Hestia in a world that supports women to become whole people.

CRONE-AGED HESTIA

A crone-aged Hestia in good health and with adequate resources to keep her comfortably settled quietly comes into her own in the third phase of her life. With an archetypal talent to be inwardly centered without lessons in how to meditate, and minus the obsessive potential of other archetypes, she doesn't suffer the angst of not having a man in her life—if such is the case—or of not having children. Never persona-driven, she doesn't look into a mirror and note every new wrinkle, and besides, her face probably lacks worry lines. She may retain the same basic and ageless look long into her crone years. Earlier parental and social pressures to conform to expectations are gone. As an older woman in a patriarchy, she is supposed to become invisible—and this suits her just fine.

LATE-BLOOMING HESTIA

Hestia is a crone-age archetype that becomes more important and likely to develop as we grow older and wiser. It is naturally late blooming. Unless Hestia is a dominant archetype—and too often even if it is—there is little time for Hestia until age and circumstance finally provide the opportunity for a woman to be with herself. Everyday life is a juggling act for most women in the first two stages of their lives. Solitude is hard to come by, especially if there are children. Sometimes, the only time a woman has for her own thoughts is when she commutes, and even then she may be focusing on a list of to-dos. Cell phones have turned this island of "alone time" into an extension of work or a time to return personal calls. When this is what life-as-usual is like, Hestia can hardly be present.

However, when life takes an unexpected turn, and you are alone with your thoughts and prayers, finding Hestia will be a comfort. Or, when perimenopausal symptoms keep you from sleep and you are awake in the middle of the night, you may keep company with Hestia. Or, if you separate or divorce, and the children spend time with their father, and for the first time ever you live by yourself, it may also be a first time for you to be with Hestia. Or, it may be the empty nest or widowhood that creates an empty space for Hestia to enter. These are circumstances that may lead us to find the still point inside ourselves, which is Hestia.

Hestia is also developed through taking time out of busy schedules for yoga classes and meditation, for retreats or women's circles that provide a time to "center" and enter a ritual Hestia space. It's my impression that the transition years from the mid-forties to mid-fifties are when the urge for inner focus is taken seriously, and commitments are made to these ways of making time for Hestia and, in turn, lead to a desire for more quality inner time.

When Hestia becomes the major archetype in the third phase of life, it is a significant archetypal shift that is little noticed by others. Only once can I recall that such an event made the newspapers; this was when a very socially prominent woman in San Francisco entered a cloistered order. Hestia remains anonymous unless her presence brings about a noticeable change in outer life. However, once Hestia is the center of a woman's life, she acquires a one-in-herself sense of wholeness that can have consequences for others and can result in major changes in her life. Solitude, meditation, an inner life, a spiritual practice, are too often not compatible with others who want her company.

When Hestia becomes the important archetype in a formerly outer-directed woman, there will be problems between the expectations of others and her own inclinations. She wants to go on a retreat alone. He wants her to keep him company. He wants them to socialize with people that she no longer wants to spend time with. He looks forward to his retirement, and she dreads losing the time alone that she has gotten used to having. Similar issues arise with relatives, friends, and acquaintances who expected her to be available for them. At work, she may turn down a promotion or not take any new clients. Others cannot see the hearth that now warms and illuminates her inner world, or understand that she might prefer to spend time with Hestia instead of with them. Late-blooming Hestias treasure this newfound sanctuary and work toward achieving a balance between their new inner life and the people who are important to them.

Hera, the Goddess of Marriage

Archetype of the Wife

Hera, whom the Romans knew as Juno, was the stately, regal goddess of marriage, the wife of Zeus (Jupiter), the chief god of the Olympians. There were two very contrasting ways to see her. In her worship, she was solemnly revered as the powerful goddess of marriage; in her mythology, she was a vindictive, quarrelsome, and jealous shrew. Revered and reviled, honored and humiliated, she, more than any other Greek goddess, has markedly positive and negative attributes. Her symbols and rituals indicate that before she became Zeus's consort, she was once the great goddess or triple goddess. She was worshiped in the spring as Hera the Virgin; in the summer as Hera the Fulfilled One; and in the winter as Hera the Widow.* These three aspects represented the three stages of a woman's life, and were reenacted symbolically. A statue of Hera was immersed in a bath in the spring, symbolically restoring her virginity; in the summer a ritual sacred marriage took place; and in the winter a dispute and separation from Zeus were enacted, and Hera went into hiding as the widow. In the mythology of the Greeks, the triad that was associated with Hera

---

*Married to the immortal Zeus, Hera was not literally the widow. The winter ritual of Hera the widow was mythically based on those times when she withdrew from Zeus in grief over his behavior, wrapped herself in deepest darkness, and wandered to the ends of the earth and the sea. Hera's rituals honored the phases of women's lives as maiden-wife-widow.

(though very little was said about it) was Hebe the maiden, Hera the matron, and Hecate the crone.

Hera's marriage to an archetypal philanderer and her wrath and humiliation by him was the major theme in her mythology. Time and time again, Zeus would seduce or rape a nymph, mortal, or goddess, and impregnate them, fathering the second-generation Olympians and demigods. Hera typically responded vindictively and destructively against the other woman and her offspring. Zeus repeatedly dishonored marriage that was sacred to her, shamed her further by honoring the children of his liaisons, and, in one story, abused her.

When the Hera archetype is a powerful force in a woman's psyche, her psychological well-being and even her fate is dependent on her marriage and the character of her spouse. This archetype has the inner force of an instinct that propels a woman toward being a couple and makes it very hard for her to be single. In the sacred marriage ritual, Zeus was called "Bringer to Completion" or "Bringer to Perfection," which is the underlying expectation that Heras project upon potential partners. Since marriage is the source of her identity and well-being, a Hera woman is deeply affected by her mate's fidelity and the importance he places on the marriage. Thus, whether she is married and to whom are the key to the state of her fulfillment or misery. She is vulnerable to being overwhelmed by pain and jealous rage toward the other woman if her husband is unfaithful. If he divorces her, the psychological wound can be devastating and the degree of denial can even become delusional.

From the mid-sixties to the present, marriage as an institution has been in sharp decline. Living together out of wedlock, open marriage, communal living, divorce, and blended families are all trends that have been inimical for the Hera archetype, whose yearning to be a wife or at least part of a committed couple remained as strong an inner force as ever, despite societal shifts. Lesbian women differ in their sexual orientation, but the force of the archetype is the same.

Although the women's movement supported the development of other archetypes, if Hera is the dominant archetype and she never married or married and divorced, she will feel deprived, regardless of satisfactions in other aspects of her life. Most troubled marriages tend to dissolve before a woman is of crone age, but a number of husbands do leave their older wives for younger women after decades of marriage. For a Hera woman in this situation, it is a trial by fire for her soul to come through without becoming stuck in rage and bitterness. Recovery is particularly difficult when her former spouse remarries. This can propel her into years of psychotherapy or spirituality in order to heal. To find her way through this dark night of the soul requires that she stop blaming the other woman, fully experience her grief, and accept that her marriage is over—which takes a long time.

A betrayed Hera woman can become possessed by jealousy and stuck in anger and bitterness. Taken over by the negative power of the archetype, she is in a Hera complex. When this is so, she thinks obsessively about the other woman and wants to retaliate. In the grip of her anger, she feels her humiliation rather than her sorrow, and is blind to how destructive this obsessive focus is to her own soul. Introspection does not come easily, and yet it is this that she most needs to do.

The Hera archetype is a bonding force reflected in the words of the marriage vows "for better or worse." The depth of her bond makes it possible for many marriages to last a lifetime and become a sanctuary for both partners, after having weathered the difficulties that couples ordinarily have or a situation that would have been the end of the marriage for most. A lasting marriage can be a growth process, a source of spiritual meaning and emotional sustenance. It also is an accomplishment that fulfills the archetype. The strength of the Hera bond can also prove disastrous to the mental and physical health of a Hera wife whose spouse is abusive or has an addiction. His behavior and the Hera archetype together cause her to become a codependent or a victim. It can also be a disaster for a child when Hera's blind loyalty to her husband is stronger than her concern for the child he abuses.

The archetype of the sacred marriage is the ideal that Hera yearns for. She wants to be in a spiritual, emotional, and physical union in which the intimacy between the couple is experienced by both as sacred. It fulfills the deepest spiritual meaning of a Hera and may be most real and possible in older, loving couples who have discovered this together.

CRONE-AGED HERA

Women who find that their crone years are golden often are content Hera women whose husbands are enjoying retirement, and both are in good health. These may be the best years of her life, a time when as a couple they enjoy recreation and travel, often in the company of other couples. Their children are grown, his work doesn't compete for his time, they may move into a smaller house that requires very little maintenance, or even into a retirement community of other like-minded people, who share similar interests and recreation.

Some of the happiest crone-aged women are Heras who were devastated at an earlier time, and not only survived but learned and made choices that resulted in their now being in good marriages. She may have been unpartnered for a time, or the original marriage was transformed through counseling and mutual efforts to change, so that she is now in a committed relationship with intimacy and trust. Gratitude is a characteristic of such women who have known the dark side of the Hera archetype and who grew in wisdom and compassion. There are also contented Heras who are in enduring, stable marriages, whose lives seem to others to lack substance and be mainly form. For these Heras, being a social couple is enough.

When a Hera is widowed, she is at a major crossroad. Much depends next on her spiritual depth, on whether she developed other archetypes, and if she has friends and interests beyond the world of coupledom. There may be no place for a single woman in her former social world, which can be devastating to her. If being married to her husband was her only identity, and her only relationships were those in which she was half of a couple, she becomes a nobody shortly after the memorial service, and can become deeply embittered.

A widow with a soul connection to her husband is still married to him; she has lost his company but the bond remains. She misses him and may from time to time feel his presence. She may still talk to him and have a conviction that she will be reunited "on the other side." She has bouts of loneliness, but if she becomes a wisewoman, she will be grateful for the years they had together. She knows that she hasn't lost him or her identity.

A widow with other interests or dormant archetypes may find that these now blossom. She may travel, move, return to school, have time for creative pursuits, develop friendships, or find she has a head for business or investments. She may live for decades after his death, consider him her one and only, and have a full but different second life. When this is so, Hera has been fully lived as an archetype, leaving space in her psyche and time in her life to develop in other ways.

LATE-BLOOMING HERA

Sometimes Hera makes an appearance in a woman's psyche in the third phase of her life serendipitously. She is not looking for a new spouse and is not feeling needy. She is not an unconscious Hera, ready to see any new man as Zeus-bringer-to-completion. But then she meets someone who becomes a soul mate first and her husband later. The deepest yearnings of a Hera for a sacred marriage is fulfilled when this happens.

Hera also can be an unfulfilled late-blooming archetype after other archetypes have taken their due and receded. This is when a woman who was identified with the virgin goddesses or with Aphrodite sees the companionship that older couples have and feels regret for the marriage that she ended, or the good men she never married. The emptiness or pangs of envy she feels now is due to a late-blooming Hera stirring in her psyche.

The Hera archetype predisposes women to be half of a couple. This applies to creative work or to projects, not just to marriage. She works best with a partner. The issue for her is her archetypal need to be a couple rather than a one-in-herself person. To maintain initiative and be faithful to the project or even to the creativity in herself, she needs a partner. In the crone phase, many Hera women are often no longer married and find that they flounder on their own, and that their creativity thrives when the work is done with a partner. When they find such a person, a man or another woman, the book can be written or the project can get off the ground, or the new business can thrive— and Hera blossoms, in this new form.

Demeter, the Goddess of Grain

The Mother Archetype

Demeter, the Greek goddess of grain, was known as Ceres to the Romans. She was described as a beautiful woman with golden hair, dressed in a blue robe, and was most commonly portrayed in sculpture as a seated, matronly figure. She was worshiped as a mother goddess, goddess of grain, giver of the Eleusinian Mysteries, and a personification of the mother archetype and maternal instinct. In mythology, she was the grieving mother of abducted Persephone. She was powerless to prevent the rape of her daughter, and was herself raped by Poseidon while she searched fruitlessly for Persephone. In her wanderings among the people of earth disguised as a mortal beyond childbearing years, she became a nursemaid for another woman's child, but this could not substitute for her loss. She persisted in her insistence that Persephone be returned, until finally, when she withdrew her fertility from the earth, Zeus heeded her and sent Hermes to fetch Persephone from the underworld. On Persephone's return, Demeter provided people with her beautiful Mysteries so they need not fear death. She is the only major Olympian who was grief-stricken, with symptoms that fit the diagnosis of a major depression. Persephone, Demeter, and Hecate represent the three phases of women's lives and the three aspects of the triple goddess: maiden, mother, crone.

Demeter is a diminished version of the Great Mother Goddess who was worshiped long before Zeus and the Olympians, and was overpowered and unable to protect her daughters. She disappeared from religion but is a powerful archetype that can determine the course and quality of a woman's life. Like Hera, the Demeter archetype acts from within as a directive to be fulfilled, and can be followed blindly by a woman, even when it is not in her own best interest. Teenage pregnancies are one result. Codependency and burnout are also consequences when she responds maternally to the needs of others and cannot say no (to them or the archetype). Like Hera, fulfilling the archetype as mother and nurturer can be deeply meaningful. Conversely, when she cannot be a mother or if a child is taken from her by death or by circumstance, grieving Demeter can become the center of her inner world. The archetype makes a woman susceptible to depression.

The life of any woman is greatly affected by whether or not she has had children and under what circumstances. It is the central issue for a Demeter woman. The Demeter archetype can be one of several strong elements in a woman's psyche, which helps her to have a balanced inner and outer life. But sometimes, when a woman puts off childbearing until she is well into her thirties and then has an infertility problem, she may find herself "possessed" by Demeter and become single-minded to the point of obsession about becoming pregnant.

CRONE-AGED DEMETER

The transitions from maiden to mother and from mother to crone are most deeply felt by a woman whose primary archetype is Demeter. Just as becoming a mother is a fulfillment of the archetype, the end of childbearing years is felt as a loss, a major one if she was unable to have children. But even if she has had several children and did not plan to have more, the Demeter woman feels a loss at menopause, because it is now impossible to have another child.

Menopause may coincide with an empty nest, which is a double loss for a Demeter. When all women were expected to become full-time mothers, and there were few opportunities to develop other aspects of themselves, serious "empty-nest syndromes" were quite common. Called "involutional depressions," they were responsible for first-time psychiatric hospitalizations of many crone-aged women. Now that women are better educated, in the work force, and have more complex lives, along with the advent of antidepressants, this kind of depression is hardly seen. When a woman's value to society and to herself depended upon being a mother, archetype and culture acted in concert, and the woman felt her life was over when there were no children at home.

Still, it is a sad day for a Demeter when her only or last child leaves home. Besides a tearful good-bye, she may suffer through a period of mourning. If there are other archetypes that took a backseat to Demeter, however, a shift takes place in the inner world of goddess archetypes. Demeter recedes in importance and new energies emerge. The transition can be smooth and welcomed: now there is time to travel, to be a couple, to take up an interest that has been biding its time. Or the transition can have the impact of a revolution; one that begins in the inner world and results in a major upheaval in the outer, when the Demeter archetype held her in an otherwise unhappy situation. A woman who has stayed in a marriage, a neighborhood, or an occupation because she sees it as being in the best interest of her children to do so, may leave when they do.

DEMETER AT THE CROSSROAD

A woman is at a major fork in the road when her last child leaves home, especially if Demeter has been her source of meaning. The two roads lead either to change or depression. If she has ignored a deteriorating marriage, she can do something or nothing about it. With Hecate's crossroad perspective, she knows that she will either change the course of her life or the shape of her marriage.

Another crossroad decision comes when she becomes a grandmother. Holding the newborn in her arms, a woman can reenter the archetypal Demeter configuration of mother and child. If she is a wise grandmother, she knows that she needs to restrain possessive feelings that arise, and not let Demeter take her over and compete with the young mother. The older Demeter woman who hasn't found new sources of meaning and pressures her grown chidren to "give her" grandchildren is projecting a preview of problems to come. In moderation, a Demeter grandmother is wonderful; the role is a joy for her, and her presence in the family enriches everyone. In excess, her unfulfilled needs make her intrusive, critical, and demanding. A Demeter grandmother or a potential one needs to draw upon Hecate's wisdom in order to be patient and wise in what she does and says.

A depressed Demeter whose divine daughter has been taken from her, who is agitated or withdrawn, is not only the picture of a biological mother who has lost her child. It is also a potential fate for a woman who put her maternal energy into work that was taken from her. When such is the case, her maternal juices flowed into an organization or small business that she gave birth to, losing sleep when it was small and survival was at stake, and nurturing it for years as it grew. Or maybe she represented a talented person that she discovered and helped become accomplished. When what or who she raised becomes attractive as an acquisition or a property and is "abducted" and taken from her, it is a Demeter loss that often seems to coincide with the perimenopause. Both circumstance and age then bring her to Hecate's crossroad. Spiritual resources are needed to recover from this loss. She is at a fork in the road and needs to see what her choices are and realize the cost to her body and soul of going in the direction of bitterness.

Hecate, Hestia, and Sekhmet

A Demeter becomes wise through developing Hecate's wisdom. When the chief source of meaning and major role is a maternal one, the vulnerability to loss is great. She often feels a personal loss at each stage of her child's growth, beginning when she stops nursing her infant. And yet, being a good mother requires that she let go of a child's dependency on her in stages, again and again. Hecate helps a Demeter make wise decisions, mostly to do with letting go rather than holding on. Hecate's wisdom tells her that like the goddess herself, she may not be able to protect her children from suffering. This realization and knowing that change is part of the cycle of life, is Hecate's wisdom. Demeters have many opportunities to learn from Hecate, but to do so, they need to be able to be introspective, which is not a Demeter trait.

Often it is only in the troughs of depression, when she feels empty, that she gains Hecate's wisdom.

Hecate urged Demeter to go to the god of the sun to learn of Persephone's fate. Her wisdom counsels us to seek the truth, face reality, know what happened and who was responsible. She also accompanied Demeter and was present when Persephone was returned. Hecate has a significant supportive role as a friend at times of loss and transition. As an inner quality, Hecate is a source of wisdom and patience, enabling us to wait until we have some clarity and can wisely choose the path we will take at significant junctures. A Demeter woman who acquires Hecate's wisdom becomes this kind of friend herself. Wise friends and women's circles provide Hecate support through these transitions.

Besides Hecate, Hestia and Sekhmet are the crone archetypes that a Demeter woman most needs to develop. Hestia, so she can find a center in herself, and Sekhmet, in order to act decisively once she sees the truth of her situation.

LATE-BLOOMING DEMETER

There has been an upward age shift in the childbearing years. When I was delivering babies in the fourth year of medical school and internship, most new mothers were in their twenties or younger. A midthirties first-time pregnancy was the exception, the pregnant woman was referred to as an "elderly primip" (short for "primiparous"), and doctors were concerned that she was too old and would have complications. With women pursuing graduate degrees, entering professions and having careers, using birth control and being able to have abortions, childbearing in the thirties is commonplace, and if there are infertility difficulties, efforts to become pregnant may continue until perimenopause. The achievement focus of Artemis and Athena recedes, and Demeter comes into the foreground when the biological clock is running out of time or after the hormonal shift that accompanies pregnancy or the birth of an infant. A maternal Demeter may become a source of great meaning; in some women it is a momentous discovery that being a mother now matters much more than the profession or career she took so long to achieve. She may want to quit work and be a full-time mother, or want more children. Late-blooming Demeters will often be in their fifties before a child reaches adolescence.

Another group of late-blooming Demeters are childless women who adopt children. Sometimes adoption came about because they were the closest relative, did not plan to have children, and now find the unexpected motherhood deeply rewarding. Or the adoption was the culmination of months or even years of effort until, finally, it was possible. There are numerous women in their forties and fifties who have been going to China to adopt abandoned infant girls. It takes an active Demeter (with the aid of Artemis/Athena) to persevere and commit to such an undertaking, and a joyful Demeter who knows that she has truly rescued her infant Persephone from the underworld when she returns with a baby girl in her arms.

Persephone, the Maiden and Queen of the Underworld

Eternal Girl, Inner Guide

The goddess Persephone, known to the Romans as Proserpina, had a dual nature, as the maiden and as queen of the underworld. Persephone was the only daughter of Demeter. Her father was Zeus. She was gathering flowers in a meadow when her carefree world came to a sudden and terrifying end with her abduction and rape by Hades, the god of the underworld, who had Zeus's permission to make her his bride in this way. Demeter was not consulted and could not protect her, but she did not accept the situation and insisted on Persephone's return. Eventually, Persephone was reunited with her mother, but because she had eaten some pomegranate seeds in the underworld, she would spend a third of each year with Hades in the underworld and two thirds of the year with Demeter on earth.

Persephone was the *kore*, or "nameless maiden," a slender and beautiful goddess, her mother's daughter, and the picture of a young woman untouched by life and unawakened sexually. Persephone the maiden does not know "who she is" because she is as yet unaware of her desires and strengths. Persephone the eternal girl or girlish woman is a familiar archetype. When all that a young woman was expected to be was attractive and charming, Persephone was the model for the role. It is her nature to be receptive, playful, and malleable. As a vulnerable goddess, she doesn't have an innate ability to focus like the virgin goddesses, nor does she have an instinctual inner drive to fulfill which Hera, Demeter, and Aphrodite have. A young Persephone doesn't know what she wants to do with her life and this lack of definition makes her susceptible to "being abducted" by stronger personalities who can impose on her their expectations of whom they want her to be. It is her pattern to be chameleonlike, to unconsciously "try on" whatever others expect of her or project upon her.

Persephone the maiden is a difficult archetype for a woman to have, especially since the women's movement. It was easier to be a Persephone when finding a husband to take care of her, having children, and staying at home was the cultural norm. It didn't matter that she lacked a focus of her own, and her passivity and dependency were appreciated as feminine qualities. Zeus fathers used to give their virgin daughters away, and even if this initially felt like an arranged abduction by Hades, marriage and children was an enviable end in itself that would transform her from maiden to matron and mother. A contemporary Persephone suffers from feelings of inadequacy as she feels herself flailing around undecided about what she wants to do with her life, especially if she is well into her thirties or older.

It is possible for a woman to remain a Persephone all her life, particularly if she is unable to make a commitment or take responsibility for another person or for her own goals. She will stay the eternal maiden or the eternal victim, until she stops withholding herself, denying the truth about her situation, and learns from experience. Only then does she become a woman who has "eaten the pomegranate seeds" and is committed to following her own destiny. If Persephone had not eaten anything in the underworld, she would have been restored to Demeter untransformed by the experience. Eating the pomegranate seeds meant that she would return, but never again as a victim. By eating the seeds, she symbolically integrated (or digested) the experience that now was a part of her. An abducted Persephone can literally be an incest or rape victim, or she may be in a withdrawn depression, or be an addict, or be overwhelmed by the unconscious, and be out of touch with reality. When she recovers and if she integrates the experience and is stronger and wiser because of it, she is then able to be a guide for others, perhaps as an AA sponsor, or therapist, or indirectly through her creative work as a poet, artist, musician, or writer.

When Persephone emerged from her abduction, the experience

had changed her. She was no longer the *kore*, an innocent virgin and a Mother's daughter. From that day forward, Hecate was said to precede and follow Persephone wherever she went. In other words, she acquired Hecate's wisdom and discerning twilight vision, and then became queen of the underworld, ruled the realm of the spirits with her husband Hades, and was a guide for those whose mythic journeys took them into the underworld.

Persephones often come into their own around fifty years old. Without a focused archetype or an instinctually directed role, it takes longer for a Persephone to find her direction. Her route is circuitous rather than a straight line; she has dabbled and gathered experiences. Significant and strong personalities told her who she was and what should make her happy, and now she has lived long enough to know herself and what she values. If she also had to take responsibilities and be a choicemaker, she now has a self-confidence that she earned through experience. Never one to be an "I'll do it all by myself" person, she now has tried and tested people she can count on. She also is likely to have become a sexually responsive woman aware of her own Aphrodite qualities. With the archetype of queen of the underworld, she can draw upon her empathy, imagination, and easy access to the collective unconscious, which are resources for creative work that she may by fifty finally have found. If she has psychic abilities, this may be a time to develop them wisely.

CRONE-AGED PERSEPHONE THE MAIDEN

A woman is able to play and enjoy "picking flowers in the meadow," as long as Persephone the maiden is in her psyche. She has pastimes that are pleasant ways to spend time. She may enjoy leafing through catalogs, visiting museums, gathering seashells on the beach, shopping for nothing in particular, or picking flowers. She can meander through these landscapes, playfully choosing what pleases her, and be totally engaged in these pastimes, which makes her grandchildren delight in her company. She can do this and also be a mature woman, who learned from her descents and is now a guide for others. In this case, she retains the wonder of childhood and has the wisdom of Hecate.

She may have settled into a stable marriage and/or a stable identity after a chaotic underworld period. Her receptive, diffuse consciousness lends itself to receiving psychic impressions, which she needs to learn to trust and use through experience.

The fate of Persephones can also be sad, even tragic. Some remain identified with Persephone the maiden into their crone years. The archetype is eternal but they grow older. These are aging social butterflies or women who continue to alight briefly on one interest and then another, and never settle down or develop their potential. Or Persephone the abducted maiden and the archetype of the victim may be lived out. Some Persephones never recover from abuse, mental illness, or addiction and exist tragically as crone-aged women on the edges of society and continue to be victimized. Then there are others who identify with being a victim even when their circumstances were not particularly difficult, and are forever envying others, blaming parents or someone else for what they lack, and in their self-absorption never grow up.

LATE-BLOOMING PERSEPHONE

Surprisingly, Persephone the maiden is a very common archetype to emerge in full bloom only when a woman is over fifty. For many women, childhood and early adulthood are difficult years. "I never had a childhood," they say. As children, they may have been abducted into the underworld of loss, fear, sickness, or abuse. Poverty or early responsibilities may have made them grow up too soon. As mothers they may have been overburdened. Women work and still do most of the household tasks along with childcare and parental responsibilities, leaving very little time to play.

The ability to be a good mother to yourself, enjoy free time and resources (friends, imagination, enough income) make the crone years a glorious time for many women. Sometimes, Sekhmet/Kali had to emerge first, before it was safe for Persephone to come out and play. Or an abducted Persephone had to emerge from an abusive relationship or an addiction before a playful Persephone was possible. Often it is the laughter and freedom of Baubo/Uzume, found in the company of women friends, that finally liberates the spontaneous girl in every woman.

ABDUCTED PERSEPHONES: THE UNDERWORLD IN OLD AGE

The active crone years are not defined by age so much as by how independent and competent we remain. We know of bright, spry women in their eighth and ninth decades, and of women whose decline began decades before this. The diseases and infirmities of old age mean that any woman can become a dependent and vulnerable Persephone. You may already be a mother to your own mother, and see how poor health and a loss of mental functioning abducted her into this dimly lit (by consciousness) underworld. It is not hard to imagine the possibility of this fate for ourselves. A decline in health and mental functioning spares no archetype. But while we are in the world where the sun is still shining, there are experiences to savor, and we can be playful Persephones and at the same time draw upon the wisdom of Metis, Sophia, Hecate, and Hestia.

Aphrodite, the Goddess of Love and Beauty

Lover, Creative Woman

Aphrodite, the goddess of love and beauty, whom the Romans called Venus, was the most beautiful of Olympian goddesses. She was the favorite subject of sculptors, who portrayed her undressed or in a state of partial undress to reveal her sensual body. Aphrodite's birth from the sea was immortalized in Botticelli's *Birth of Venus* during the Renaissance, with no hint of the underlying violence that preceded her mythological birth. Cronus (the father of Zeus) defeated his father, the sky god Uranus, castrated him, and threw his genitals into the sea, from which Aphrodite was born, emerging from her oceanic conception as a fully-grown goddess. When she came ashore, she was welcomed into the company of the Olympians as one of them. Many of the gods vied for her hand in marriage, and she was free to choose. She selected Hephaestus, the lame god of the forge.

Aphrodite had the awesome power to compel gods and mortals to fall in love. Only the virgin goddesses could resist. She herself had many love affairs which she entered freely. In her worship, she once had been revered, but as the culture changed, she became a reviled goddess of harlots. The madonna-whore split that the church fathers emphasized, made it impossible to revere her or to celebrate women's sensual and sexual nature. Of all the feminine archetypes, Aphrodite has been the most suppressed and exploited: a "good woman" had to renounce this part of herself.

Myths about Aphrodite tell of her many lovers, of whom Ares, the god of war, and Hermes, the messenger god, and the mortals Anchises and Adonis are the most famous. She had children by most of them, many of whom are also noteworthy. She had no children by her cuck-olded husband Hephaestus, but as a symbolic union of beauty and craft (or muse and artisan), it could be said that the beautiful orna-ments and innovative objects that he created were the offspring of this marriage.

Among the Olympian goddesses she was an exception. She was free to follow her own inclinations like Artemis, Athena, and Hestia, but was hardly virginal. She was known through her relationships like Hera, Demeter, and Persephone, but unlike them was not humiliated, raped, or abused. Aphrodite herself was affected by her spell of love; she was irresistible, but it was she who was first attracted to the beauty of Adonis and Anchises. The mutuality of an attraction is the "chem-istry" that happens between lovers; in chemistry, when two substances react, both are transformed in the process.

There is often a similar though nonsexual eros or "chemistry" between the two people in transformative and creative relationships such as mentoring, teaching, directing, editing, doing therapy, or even parenting, in which the potential of one person is brought out by the other through a combination of skill and love. People engaged in these professions, who are good at what they do, put themselves into their work, and their psyches are affected by these relationships. In doing this, they are like the alchemists of medieval Europe, who were believed to be at work trying to transform baser materials into gold, while engaged in an esoteric spiritual quest to transform themselves. Metaphorically, whatever is ordinary and undeveloped is the baser material of everyday life that can be turned into "gold."

An Aphrodite who believes in her beloved's dream of what he could accomplish or become is a "vision carrier."* Vision carriers see and believe in a talent or potential (the beauty of the person or project) before it becomes evident and sustain the dream until it does. While

---

*From Daniel Levinson's study of successful men. Each had a woman who believed in them and in their dream, whom he called a "vision carrier." Cf. references in chapter notes.[1]

one special Aphrodite woman may be the vision carrier or muse for a particular man at a critical time in his life, and be his lover or wife, professionals who see and bring out the potential in others need to be mindful that Aphrodite is activated by this work, and the archetype could draw them into a personal relationship that crosses ethical boundaries. There is a risk of falling in love with your creation; becoming like the mythical sculptor Pygmalion or Professor Higgins in the musical *My Fair Lady*. This is not only a risk for men, but sometimes for women in creative and mentoring professions.

APHRODITE — A DIFFICULT ARCHETYPE

Aphrodite the archetype of the lover is a problematic one for a woman when it is an active part of her psyche. In contrast to the vulnerable goddess archetypes that seek long-term committed relationships, the archetype of Aphrodite seeks intensity. When passion wanes in one relationship, and Aphrodite is drawn to another, there can be severe consequences for the woman. Women's sexual independence is threatening to individual men and to the patriarchy, with the strongest epithets and punishments directed toward unsanctioned sex. Even in a cultural climate such as ours, a single woman who enjoys her sexuality with more than one person knows to keep it hidden in order to avoid condemnation and jealousy. Maintenance of male control (religious or state) over women's bodies is a fundamental issue underlying the opposition to birth control and abortion and the efforts to overturn the *Roe v. Wade* decision by the Supreme Court, which made abortion a private matter between a woman and her doctor.

Fundamentalists define women as either good women or whores. A woman who is desired does not have to feel desire herself in order to be blamed if a man finds her desirable, even if she is raped. In biblical times, an adulterous woman could be stoned to death. Death of the woman is still the penalty for loss of virginity by choice or through rape, as well as adultery in many Islamic fundamentalist societies. Until the last century in the United States, patriarchal custom and law decreed that a woman's body and her sexuality became male property. She was to stay a virgin until she married and, once married, her body belonged to her husband for his sexual pleasure alone and for procreation that assured that her children had been fathered by him and him alone. A husband who caught his wife with another man could murder her and get away with a crime of passion. While laws and customs are changing, expressing the Aphrodite archetype is still fraught with danger for women.

There have been Aphrodites who became renowned as courtesans and celebrated but it has always been a dangerous career. There is a thin line between being treated as a courtesan and used as a prostitute, and one swiftly becomes the other through the loss of beauty or a protector.

CONSCIOUS CHOICES AND CREATIVITY

Falling in love is an archetypal experience, like a force of nature. It happens *to* a woman. What she does next, however, is up to her. This is where wisdom and concern for others, seeing the pattern and being aware of consequences all need to be considered. When they are not, Aphrodite creates chaos for the woman and for those whose lives are connected to hers. A mature woman in whom Aphrodite is evoked often finds herself at a major crossroad in her life. She needs the wisdom of Metis and Hecate, the compassion of Kuan Yin, the ability to know herself and, finally, to be a choicemaker.

Aphrodite is a powerful archetype responsible for the instinctual sexuality arising suddenly in an adolescent and, if unchecked by good judgment, can be disastrous for a young girl. Sexual availability exposes her to being used, to pregnancy, sexually transmitted diseases, rejection, and lowered self-esteem. When Aphrodite is evoked in a woman with other active archetypes—especially Athena and Artemis—it is much easier for her to look out for herself and take other priorities into consideration. Conscious choicemaking is needed again and again when Aphrodite is a strong archetype, especially in a physically attractive woman.

Aphrodite is also the archetype of creativity. The same intensity and total absorption that happens when we fall in love is essential to the creative process. Each new work or new direction has vitality, the creative person is often fascinated and preoccupied with what is emerging in the work. There is skill and spontaneity, disappointments and epiphanies, and then, once a work is completed or the energy for it runs out, the Aphrodite woman moves on to a new canvas or new project. With creativity, the work can evolve. Each effort can add to the depth of experience and range of the artist.

There is an aliveness that Aphrodite brings to the psyche, that imbues life with love and beauty and is enhanced by her ability to be in the present moment. The shadow side of Aphrodite is the other side of this same coin: when only the present moment exists, she can be heedless of consequences to herself or others. From missing appointments to major betrayals of trust and fidelity, the shadow aspects of Aphrodite can disrupt relationships, darken the life of a woman, and provide many hard lessons. As a result, she either has to suppress Aphrodite, which is all too common, or find a place for Aphrodite in her creativity, her work, her imagination, or in her marriage.

CRONE-AGED APHRODITE

An Aphrodite who ages very well does so because she has developed wisdom—as personified by Hecate, Metis, Sophia, or Hestia. She is not driven by the Aphrodite archetype nor has been deserted by it. She retains an ability to be fascinated by the beauty she sees in the world and in people. She savors experience and, hence, enjoys life. Her ability to be in the present, which may have been a problem at a younger age, becomes a positive talent that enhances the quality of life after retirement and on into old age. Regardless of her age, she is a sensual woman. She is truly a juicy crone.

Aphrodite's sensuality is found in women who enjoy good food, good sex, or a good massage. Her aliveness to experience is a facet in women who appreciate the sensory experience of life. Aphrodite sees beauty and loves what she sees, qualities that make us feel good to be alive. The ability to fall in love with people, objects, and places doesn't go away as we grow older, as long as Aphrodite is active, but the intensity lessens and is tempered by wisdom.

Gloria Stuart, the actress who was nominated for an Oscar for her role in *Titanic* as the ninety-year-old survivor, published her autobiography after the movie brought her fame. In it she revealed Aphrodite qualities. She described herself as being a sexual woman all her life, and got press notice by her good-humored advocacy of masturbation in the absence of a sexual partner. Once a woman is old, she may become invisible as a sexual object, but the archetype can still be there, regardless. Sexuality and sensuality are inherent in an Aphrodite woman, whether men respond or not.

Aphrodite women are sensual, and sensuality doesn't disappear with age. I saw this in the hula movements of an "Auntie," or Hawaiian elder, in her seventies, whose natural sensuality belied her seventy-plus years and the excess weight—by our standards—that she gracefully carried.

The crone years also provide time for the creative aspects of Aphrodite that may come only after the juggling roles of wife-mother-job-household recede. Grandma Moses, the painter, or Tillie Olson, the writer, put their creative talent on the back burner while they took care of families, which women often do. To develop her creativity, a woman needs the support of others, which is often not possible until later. Unless her work is marketable, a woman who has an Aphrodite passion to create in the first two phases of her life is discouraged from doing so. To take the time is viewed as indulgent, impractical, or selfish. Not until she is a crone and others think of her passion as a hobby, might the creativity of Aphrodite be liberated.

LATE-BLOOMING APHRODITE

In our culture, women in their crone years are not expected to fall in love or be sexy and sensual. They may not fit the image of Aphrodite the lover in the eyes of others, but nonetheless this archetype does not retire at fifty or sixty-five, it may bloom anew or even bloom for the first time even at seventy, which I have observed. When two people of a certain age fall in love, the magic may be more about beauty that is soul-deep rather than skin-deep, particularly because it is not driven by instinct having to do with the survival of the species. That it happens is all the more magical in its unexpectedness.

What to do with it or about it is another matter. If one or both are already married, she may have to enjoy the glow as a secret wonder; or she may be as much in pain as in love because of the impossibility of being together; or she may be at a moral crossroad over what to do. If both are legally free to be together, the course of true love may still not run free because of the opposition of his or her grown children, or because of the opposition from the virgin goddess archetypes within her—she may cherish her independence more than her beloved.

Later-life passions may turn out to be more unconventional as well as highly personal choices, which, I suspect, is happening. In this case, there will be more May-December relationships between older women and younger men, more first-time late-blooming love between women, lovers with different backgrounds or of a different race. Many older women—especially if they have Aphrodite as an active archetype—become younger in attitude, broader in perspective, and more radical in their outlook as they grow older. They find men from their own background and age boring and "older" than themselves. However unconventional, a crone-aged choicemaker is part of a generation of women who are used to defining themselves. If this is true of her, she will consider the family opposition, her own fear of looking like a foolish old woman or a seduced one, and then decide for herself.

Aphrodite can also imbue a relationship between two people with love and beauty; and unadulterated joy can result, especially in two older people, who know how blessed they are to have found each other at this stage of life and whose friends and relatives are delighted for them.

A late-blooming Aphrodite can also appear unexpectedly in a marriage that has endured for decades. Sometimes Aphrodite is awakened after the last child leaves the house and husband and wife can be a couple again, or the husband retires, or an alcoholic spouse becomes sober, or one or the other has a close call with death. Sometimes menopause itself liberates Aphrodite, who emerges only after there is no risk of becoming pregnant. Changing circumstances, archetypal and hormonal shifts all contribute to the possibility of becoming a late-blooming Aphrodite.

PART 4

SHE IS
A CIRCLE

When the Grandmothers speak, the Earth will be healed
When the Grandmothers pray, Wisdom will be revealed
When the Grandmothers sing, the Earth will be made whole.

—Circle of Grandmothers Newsletter

Circles of Wisewomen

Clan Mothers, Grandmother Circles, Crone Circles

A circle of wisewomen is an archetype in itself. The image that comes to mind is a group of respected elders, grandmothers, or clan mothers meeting together in a circle. Each is equal in importance, none is elevated above the rest, and all are concerned about the well-being of their community. This circle has both a sacred dimension and embodies the collective wisdom of its members. It is the archetype that has the potential to channel women's wisdom into the culture. This archetype is not a goddess. She is a Circle.

When older women meet together in a wisewomen circle, they are reenacting what was lost when indigenous and goddess-worshiping cultures were conquered, and yet each circle is a new creation with unique possibilities. Each circle helps us remember a time when women elders were looked to for wisdom and authority. Whatever once existed and then was not allowed, still exists in the collective unconscious or morphic field, waiting to be brought back into consciousness. It is not about needing to "reinvent the wheel" but about remembering it. The respect for the sacred feminine and its expression through women elders, priestesses, or oracles may be excised from patriarchal history, forbidden, and then forgotten, but once the process of remembering begins, it is like uncovering a blocked spring that once was a holy well.

Each circle of women is its own invention, and yet a common pattern emerges. Wisewomen circles meet as if in a temple space around Hestia's warm hearth. These circles have an energy pattern in the shape of a wheel. Each woman is connected to the others through her connection to the center of the circle and a spiritual center in herself; each has a place on the rim of this wheel of energy. The invisible pattern is felt and strengthened over time, each time the circle meets it's as if another invisible layer is added to the pattern. In such circles, rituals and meditative silences evolve to "center" the circle at the beginning, hold the center during, and dissolve the circle at the end.

Members of wisewomen circles have qualities we associate with the crone goddesses—wisdom, compassion, humor, outrage, decisive action, maturity—but they are also imperfect mortal women in the third phase of their lives, aware that they are aging and vulnerable to all of the feared aspects of growing old and dying. They know that the vitality, creativity, and influence they now have will pass, and they know that their time is limited and precious. Each woman has her lifetime of experiences and lessons to draw from. Individually and collectively, they have more psychological insight and compassion than they did when they were younger. Many will have past group experiences to draw from. They may have known each other most of their lives or met for the first time when the circle was formed.

A wisewomen circle may be comprised of women with something in common; they may be activists, grandmothers, corporate women, psychotherapists, craftswomen, writers or musicians, alumnae of the same institution, cancer survivors, or residents of the same retirement community or neighborhood; they may be of a similar class, background, or race. Or, on the surface, they may appear to have nothing in common. In either case, what shows doesn't matter—for what is valued is the essence of each woman herself, her soul qualities and psychological maturity. Their honesty, trust, healing laughter and compassion makes the circle a sanctuary for authenticity, and a spiritual home base. I think of women who comprise these circles as crones who have been toughened and tenderized in the right places.

PRECURSORS TO CIRCLES OF WISEWOMEN

Consciousness-raising groups proliferated from the mid-1960s through the 1970s. These groups brought the pervasiveness of sexism into our awareness. The members were usually women in their twenties or thirties who met primarily on college campuses and in urban centers. For many, these groups were transformative, and resulted in their members' developing a sense of sisterhood, a shared identification with all women. Many women left their groups when they moved geographically, or moved psychologically into another stage of their lives. Others left hurt and disillusioned, but most had a taste of what it was like to speak freely in a group where they could be strong and vulnerable, angry and tearful. In CR groups, they could talk about their ambitions, relationships, sexuality, and dreams of whom they might become and how they could change the world.

Women told the truth of their own lives to each other in these small groups and what they discovered was communicated widely to others through anthologies, articles, and conferences—generating anger and activism that led to the women's movement and changed assumptions about women. In *The World Split Open: How the Modern Women's Movement Changed America*, Ruth Rosen documents how the women's movement was revolutionary in its impact, forever altering the lives of women and changing American culture. Women learned that when they acted together, they could be a powerful force for change. Sisterhood *was* powerful. In consciousness-raising groups, the essential idea was: *Tell your personal truth, listen to other women's stories, see what themes are shared, and discover that the personal is political—you are not alone.*[2]

The recovery movement was the next major movement in which people met in groups. Addictions to emotion-numbing substances (alcohol, narcotics, food) and the process addictions (workaholism, gambling, shopping, sex, codependency) were the focus of recovery groups in the 1980s and early 1990s. The Alcoholics Anonymous model of meetings, in which people told their own stories, combined with a twelve-step program was widely adapted to all addictive behaviors. Meetings were open to all; confidentiality, the admission of powerlessness over the addiction, and the need for help from a higher power were essential principles. These groups helped many women who are now of crone age change their lives by overcoming addictions and codependency. Insights into codependency and dysfunctional relationships came from examining the characteristics of alcoholic marriages with new consciousness gained from the women's movement. Once more, there was an outpouring of literature, and the result was a proliferation of grass-roots codependency groups. Codependent and abused women learned about denial and saw how they had been enabling their partners to continue addictive behavior. Alcoholic women realized how they had used alcohol to numb feelings they could now express in a recovery group. Ann Wilson Schaef's *Women's Reality, Co-dependence*, and *When Society Becomes an Addict* brought insights from both movements together. Women saw how they were repeating painful family patterns and how church and society expected them to do so.

A grass-roots, little-noted women's spirituality movement also had its beginnings in the 1980s. Its origins were predominately on the west coast and were psychological and apolitical. Symbols, myths, music, meditation, art, and ritual were common elements, along with a reverence for nature, the sanctity of women's bodies and the earth, and a return of goddess spirituality in many forms. Women met in small groups that often had been inspired by attendance at women's spirituality conferences or by participation in women's workshops and retreats. They told their stories, adding a spiritual narrative to the content; made beautiful altar spaces in the center of their circles; and honored the sacred feminine. The first "crone rituals" to mark women's passage into the postmenopausal phase were done in these large and small gatherings.

Cancer support groups were another testimony to the supportive power of being in a circle of women. They became an adjunct to the treatment of cancer, especially breast cancer, in the 1990s. They grew out of the unexpected results of research done at Stanford in the mid-seventies that were not evaluated until 1989. The study involved eighty-six women who had metastatic cancer, half of whom were in support groups, and a control group of matched subjects who received the same standard medical treatment but were not in groups. The study was designed as a short-term project meant to demonstrate that women in support groups might have less anxiety and use less pain medication than the control subjects, which was found to be so. In these groups, women told their stories and shared whatever they found helpful, including visualization. Over a decade later, prompted by his skepticism that such alternative adjuncts could really help, and thinking that this early study could prove this, David Spiegel, M.D.,[3] traced the records of women in the study and was astonished by what he found. Women in the support groups lived almost twice as long (36.6 months vs. 18.9 months) as women who were not in them, and well over a decade later, three women who had been in the support groups were unexpectedly still alive. Cancer support groups are now commonly attended by women coping with a diagnosis of cancer and undergoing treatment. Support groups of all kinds proliferated in the last decade of the twentieth century: people with a myriad of serious physical illnesses including AIDS, incest and rape survivors, parents of children who have died or been murdered are examples. These groups form in the aftermath of a natural disaster, or a terrible accident, or act of violence in which many are affected. The healing and helping potential of circles of people who are surviving whatever they suffered in common is now known.

Consciousness-raising groups, recovery groups, support groups, and women's spirituality groups will have been the precursors of wise-women circles for many individual women in the crone phase because they participated in them. We didn't need to be in one to be affected; these were movements and experiences that changed collective consciousness. If we were in them, however, we had the experience of learning the healing power of being in a circle where women say what they know from their own lives.

ADDING INDIGENOUS WISDOM

The perception of indigenous peoples worldwide is of being in relationship to all living things and the earth, not as owners or dominators, but within a sacred interdependence. The photograph of Earth from outer space taken by *Apollo* astronauts brought an awareness that we are all indigenous people to humanity and fostered an indigenous sensibility in many of us. *Indigenous* means *native,* as in living or growing naturally—at home, here. Indigenous perception and consideration for "all our relations" has influenced environmental and ecological activists in their efforts to save endangered species and preserve wilderness areas and rain forests. Indigenous Native American wisdom includes council meetings that consider the effect a decision would have on seven generations to come. Indigenous practices, such as meeting in a circle where listening as much as talking is enhanced by the use of a talking stick, and decision-making by consensus were adopted by meetings of women's spirituality, New Age, ecological, and environmental groups. These teachings came from numerous Native Americans whose mission was to bring indigenous consciousness to the white culture, often in accordance with a prophecy.

The framers of our Constitution and Bill of Rights were inspired by and liberally took ideas from the Iroquois Great Law of Peace, particularly the system of checks and balances. What they chose not to borrow included the concept of rights and privileges for women, the responsibility for and rights of children, and the unacceptability of slavery.

The governance process in the Great Law of Peace served the Iroquois Confederacy (the six Seneca nations) well, long before the arrival of Western Europeans, and is still operating. The well-being of the tribal community depends upon the perception and discriminating judgment of its elder women, who form the Council of Clan Mothers. The Clan Mothers, chosen by the people, are women old enough to have grown children, yet young enough to still be active. The Council of Clan Mothers, in turn, chooses the members of the Council of Community, which is the men's council. The women's council gathers the concerns of the people and, by consensus, identifies which of these most need attention. They then ask the men's council to take up the problem, and suggest action. What the women elders see as a need, is not to be ignored. When the men's council reaches a consensus about what to do, they report back to the women's council. If the women approve, there is agreement to proceed. If not, the process begins again.[4] This same procedure was followed by the Iroquois Confederacy before the six Seneca nations of the confederacy could go to war. War was a decision that required the consensus of the Clan Mothers whose primary concern was the well-being of the community. When the decision was made, the men's council became a council of war and chose the war chief from among themselves.

WOMEN'S CIRCLES AND THIRD-WAVE FEMINISM

First Wave: the Suffragettes

In 1848, five women friends met around a circular mahogany table to write together a revolutionary document modeled after the Declaration of Independence. It was the *Declaration of Sentiments* that was presented several days later at the First Women's Rights Convention in Seneca Falls, on July 19–20, 1848. The convention produced the *Declaration of Rights of Women*. At the time, women could not own or inherit property and, in fact, were the property of their husbands, as were their children. They did not have a right to their own wages. They were considered incompetent to testify in court. Husbands had the right to physically discipline them and could rule them as they saw fit. The legal position of women was virtually the same as it had been in ancient Greece, except that fathers could not sell their deflowered daughters into slavery. Of course, women could not vote. The legal strides toward democracy that began with the Greeks and led to the formation of the United States of America, and rights guaranteed by the Constitution and the Bill of Rights, applied only to men in 1848. *The Declaration of the Rights of Women* enumerated eighteen legal grievances suffered by women and also called attention to women's limited educational opportunities. Seneca Falls was the starting place for equality for women. This was, geographically, in the midst of the Iroquois Confederacy and these white women were aware of the rights held by indigenous women of the area that they didn't have themselves. The circle of five women friends (Elizabeth Cady Stanton, Lucretia Mott, Martha Coffin Wright, Jane Hunt, and Mary Ann McClintock) who organized that first convention and wrote the first statement together exemplified Margaret Mead's inspiring and pragmatic words: *Never doubt that a small group of committed people can change the world. Indeed it is the only thing that ever has.*

The Seneca Falls circle raised issues of equality and justice for women, which initiated the women's suffrage movement. The right for women to vote was resisted and ridiculed. Suffragettes struggled against arguments that for women to vote went against the divine order and their nature. Suffragettes were harassed on the street and denounced from the pulpit. An amendment to the constitution that would allow women the vote was introduced forty-five times in Congress, before it finally passed and was sent to the states for ratification. There was resistance to overcome in every state. Women went to meetings, discussed the issue among themselves, met together in homes to organize. They formed delegations to speak to legislators. They demonstrated, marched, and were arrested. Finally, after seventy years of effort, the Nineteenth Amendment to the Constitution was ratified. On November 2, 1920, American women finally were able to cast a ballot. Among them was Eleanor Roosevelt, who, at thirty-five, voted for the first time.

Second-Wave Personal and Political Feminism

The suffragettes were the first wave of the American women's movement, and once they achieved the vote, feminism receded. The second wave had its origins in World War II, when women manned the home front, as men went to war. It was a temporary necessity, and women were expected to be independent and competent only "for the duration." In the postwar United States of the late 1940s and 1950s gender roles became stereotypical. Men went to work and women stayed at home. This was when women went to college to get their "MRS. degree," and their "PHT" (putting hubby through). Women had babies—collectively producing the baby boom (from 1946 to 1964)—and the ideal was togetherness in suburbia. Women went from wartime in the forties, when, in the absence of men, they filled every position that they could, to the fifties, when the only acceptable occupation for a woman was "housewife." Almost everyone strove for the appearance of conformity and normalcy; no one wanted to be different.

Women who had had a taste of independence and were not fulfilled—as they were supposed to be—as housewives, were silent. Women who did work, were divorced, childless, or never married, were also silent (and shamed) through the fifties, but a feminist wave was building. The women's movement began with consciousness-raising groups in the mid-sixties and reached a crest in the 1970s, the Decade of the Women's Movement.

The Suffragette Movement had begun with one small group of women friends who met together to draft a statement and plan a conference. This "new" women's movement's momentum came from uncounted numbers of consciousness-raising meetings, where women discussed feminism and told their own stories, which tapped into and unleashed anger and pain that had been buried under the silence of the postwar generation of conforming women. The movement began with protests and publications. It drew from the ranks of intellectual and politically active liberal women in New York and Chicago, and their ability to articulate ideas, organize protests, and publish. Between 1968 and 1973, five hundred publications appeared, reaching women across the country and giving them an awareness of sexism and patriarchy. Revolutionary changes resulted. In *The World Split Open: How the Modern Women's Movement Changed America*, Ruth Rosen describes the events that led to momentous changes in the United States and spread to become a global women's movement. Resistance and backlash followed. There was an initial momentum for passage of the Equal Rights Amendment, and then, as the deadline for ratification approached and met organized resistance, it failed to be ratified by the requisite number of states in 1982.

Third Wave: Spiritual Feminism

The first and second waves of feminism began with women meeting together and talking about their lives, dreams, and issues—as friends do—and then taking action. The third wave of feminism is gathering now in women's psyches. Its first visible sign is the growing number of grass-roots women's circles that have a sacred dimension. The third wave contains within it the essence of the first and second waves. It will be seen once there is sufficient momentum and size. I

188 GODDESSES IN OLDER WOMEN

believe that the third wave has to do with bringing women's wisdom and spirituality into the world.

Might a circle with a spiritual center be a vessel for women to transform themselves and the world? This was the visionary premise of my book *The Millionth Circle*. I had been thinking about the archetype of the circle and women's aptitude to form circles, when "the hundredth monkey" came to mind and inspired the title. *The Hundredth Monkey* was the allegorical tale that sustained the efforts of antinuclear activists who worked to end the nuclear arms race when conventional wisdom said that it was impossible for ordinary citizens to change the inevitable destructive course of the superpowers. *The Hundredth Monkey* told the story of how scientists studied monkey colonies on separated islands by dumping sweet potatoes on a beach, drawing the monkeys out of the trees where they could be studied. They observed a young female monkey washing her sweet potato before she ate it, which was new behavior. Time passed, and first her friends, then their mothers, and finally the male monkeys on this one island adopted this new habit. But what was most remarkable was that this new behavior was now observed on the other islands as well, with no direct communication between them. This became a new norm: this was now what monkeys did. "The hundredth monkey" was the one who—by adopting this new idea—not just tipped the scales on the initial island but brought the new behavior into the consciousness of the entire species. Rupert Sheldrake, a theoretical biologist, postulated the Morphic Resonance Hypothesis, which accounted for such an effect in birds and animals. Applied to people, it means that when a critical number of people change how they think or behave, the culture will also. For there to be a hundredth-monkey effect, there have to be ninety-nine others who make it possible. Nuclear nonproliferation treaties and the intention of the superpowers to disassemble their nuclear arsenals is now a reality. As I put these thoughts together, I made an intuitive leap: what if "the millionth circle" will be the one new women's circle that brings humanity into a postpatriarchal era?

The structure of a circle is inherently egalitarian rather than hierarchal, which is why it can serve as a wonderful model for how honest and caring communication among equals is practiced. This knowledge can have a radically positive effect on relationships outside the circle, when what is learned in the circle is taken as the model into other relationships and groups. In hierarchal relationships, power is the ordering principle. In hierarchies, you must know your place and act accordingly in order to get along or get ahead; and you can be punished overtly or subtly if you do not observe this arrangement. A hierarchy can be as small as two people, when one person is habitually deferred to by the other (this also defines a codependent). When the hierarchal unit is a man and a woman, to transform the relationship into a circle of two requires conscious effort because it goes counter to the unconscious configuration of four thousand years of male superiority that has only recently been examined and questioned in western civilization.

The conventional tasks of the first two phases of a woman's life are personal and the issues that arise are about her rights and relationships. These were also the focus of the first two waves of feminism. The agenda was achieving the vote or having a political voice, equality of opportunity and egalitarian relationships. Each wave of feminism requires consciousness-raising—which is about what women *know* in contrast to what we have been told; it's about women defining for themselves what they want and are capable of.

In a circle with a spiritual center, silent prayer or meditation centers the women and the circle, and allows the sacred feminine to enter. The circle becomes a *temenos,* which means "sanctuary" in Greek. Spiritual consciousness-raising is a thread that has run through both the first and second waves of feminism, but the focus was on changing relationships and circumstances for women in the world. These outer concerns are also the focus of the first and second phases of individual women's lives. When women's groups become circles with a spiritual center, they become vessels for women's spirituality to grow into consciousness.

The sacred feminine and the archetype of the triple goddess disappeared into the collective unconscious under patriarchy, and women's wisdom has been absent from politics and governance. In contrast, the checks and balances provided by the Iroquois model of governance with a women's council and men's council acknowledged the need for both the feminine principle of relatedness, which fosters the care of all members of the community, and the masculine principle of problem-solving and achievement of goals.

A whole person develops both of these aspects of the psyche, *when it is possible*. When stereotypes are enforced, development of the whole person is thwarted. The first two waves of the women's movement have had a profound effect on an individual woman's potential to develop both sides of herself, and on changing the relationships between men and women from male dominance to equality. The culture remained patriarchal and unbalanced, however, with women now also contributing to this when they are focused solely on success. Whether the goal to be won is the bottom line of profitability or the battle that wins a war, when the masculine principle is not balanced by the feminine principle of relatedness, there are noncombatant casualties because individuals and the environment are treated as expendable. Suffering is inevitable when this is so, and the effect will be passed on for generations.

True relatedness has a sacred dimension. Between individuals it is an I-Thou, soul-to-soul acknowledgment, and there is no hierarchy. Deep ecology extends this to all life. Might a third wave of spiritual feminism bring this principle of relatedness into planetary consciousness? Might "grandmother and clan mother" concern for all the world's children be the spiritual foundation of third-wave feminism? On Mother's Day, 2000, I watched the Million Moms March on television and wondered if I were seeing the first demonstration.

Like other feminists of my generation, I have been annoyed at how younger women feel entitled to opportunities that did not exist or were not open to women when we were their age, especially when they also said, "I'm not a feminist." My mental (and sometimes verbal) comeback used to be, "Who do you think opened the doors for you?" Then I observed myself being just as entitled and unappreciative of the suffragettes, about my right to vote. This is what a shift in the morphic field is like: what was once unimaginable and then a struggle to obtain, is taken for granted.

WISEWOMEN CIRCLES

When the members of a circle with a spiritual center are crone-aged women, they form a circle of wisewomen in a culture that no longer recognizes the wisdom of older women, but as we have seen, support can come from archetypal patterns. We have the example of Clan Mothers from the Iroquois Confederacy or Grandmother Lodges from other Native American traditions, and the image of circles of wise-women in our imagination that tells us about the archetype.

In *Buffalo Woman Comes Singing*,[5] Brooke Medicine Eagle noted that "Grandmother" is a title which honors an elder woman, whether or not she has grandchildren. Taking an initiatory tradition into the wider world and adapting it, Brooke created an initiation ritual for contemporary wisewomen. She suggests that each woman decide for herself whether she is ready for this initiation. Besides being post-menopausal (which could be a result of an hysterectomy or chemotherapy), does she have the energy and concern for more than her own goals, her primary relationship, or immediate family? In this initiation, each woman must pledge to a circle of witnesses to use her energy in service of nurturing and renewing of life for All Our Relations. What this means and what form this will take is entirely up to the individual woman. The intention is to use the abilities she has honed, or the knowledge she has gained, or her financial resources, or personal influence to do something that will make a difference.

A circle of wisewomen can be a Grandmother Lodge for its members, each committed to use herself and her resources for her community— from local to global—in different ways. Support and ideas can flow about a project or an obstacle to overcome. The circle can be a place for an activist to retreat and resoul with women who know what she is trying to accomplish and what it will mean if she does. This can be a home base, whose members hold each other in consciousness or prayer.

A wisewoman circle might also be the spiritual and emotional foundation for a project. I saw how this works for the Sacred Grove Women's Forest Sanctuary, a nonprofit organization whose mission is to save a stand of old-growth redwoods by buying the acreage and keeping it from being logged in perpetuity. For five years, using principles from *Wisdom Circles* for guidance, they have met in a circle once a month on a Sunday afternoon. They meet first as a circle—checking in, staying current with each other's lives, observing special times, being silent together, making beauty and ritual—doing what women's circles do that is soul-nourishing, and then they turn their attention to what needs to be done for the trees, which may be about raising money for the next payment, doing a mailing, holding a fund-raiser or a thank-you event for donors, or plan a visit to the forest, or an occasion that will bring others there. A similar circle is also at the heart of Women of Wisdom, another nonprofit organization that sponsors an annual women's spirituality conference in Seattle. In Arizona, women friends began meeting together as the Grandmother Circle. They decided to organize a larger meeting for interested women, which grew into an annual conference-retreat. Their circle was the seed idea that has grown into numerous circles of crone-aged women—helped by their willingness to provide information and facilitate the formation of other grandmother circles.

THE WISEWOMEN'S MOVEMENT:
SPIRITUALITY AND ACTIVISM

Women who have grown older and wiser have "maternal common sense," and can see how much of the origins of the ills of a community as well as nations can be traced to whether its children are wanted, loved, healthy, and safe from abuse; learn impulse control and compassion; and are given opportunities commensurate with their abilities. For us, it is obvious that the well-being of children is related to the well-being of their mothers, which in turn depends on how women are treated. In the latter part of the twentieth century and at the beginning of the twenty-first, this correlation is finally being voiced but not yet heeded.

American women who are now grandmothers began the women's movement. Their daughters were beneficiaries, and now they are passing over the menopausal threshold to be among an estimated forty-five million still-active American women in the crone phase of their lives. With this numerical base to draw from, might wisewomen circles birth the wisewomen's movement? If a generation of clan mothers take on the responsibility to look out for the well-being of the human tribe, might a "wisewomen's movement" come into being in the first decade of the twenty-first century?

Third-phase-of-life women react viscerally on hearing of a twenty-nation survey report that one out of every three women worldwide has been beaten, raped, or somehow mistreated, and concludes that violence against women should be treated as a global health problem.[6] Besides the immediate physical injuries, abuse and abusive relationships are linked to problem pregnancies, substance abuse, gastrointestinal disorders, chronic pain syndromes, miscarriages, infant deaths, and child mortality before the age of five.

Meanwhile, the United States in the year 2000 is the only industrialized country that has refused to ratify the *United Nations Convention on the Elimination of All Forms of Discrimination Against Women*. Twenty years ago, President Jimmy Carter signed the treaty and every year since, the Senate has failed to ratify the convention (along with North Korea, Afganistan, and Iran). Signed by 165 nations, the treaty expands the definition of discrimination to protect women and girls' human rights or fundamental freedoms in the political, economic, social and cultural, civil and legal fields. The agreement also insists that each country provide social services that allow women to combine family responsibilities with their participation in public life, and affirms a woman's right to reproductive choice. The failure to ratify this is consistent with the shameful failure to pass the Equal Rights Amendment.

Older women have learned that women's issues and needs are not important priorities for men in power, and they have experienced how the women's movement brought about major changes. We learned that women together are a force for change and that a movement can originate in circles of women.

WISEWOMEN AT THE CORE OF THE CULTURAL CREATIVES

With simple deductive reasoning, it is likely that the readers of *Goddesses in Older Women*—all the women and the exceptional man who would read a book with this title—are "Cultural Creatives," the designation that began with population studies at Stanford Research Institute, described in *The Cultural Creatives: How Fifty Million People are Changing the World*, by Paul H. Ray and Sherry Ruth Anderson.

The values and concerns of this large segment of the population, comprising 26 percent of the adults in the United States, would likely be those of any wisewoman circle. Ray and Anderson wrote, "What politicians often refer to as "women's issues" are a key to understanding the Cultural Creatives. They see women's ways of knowing as valid: feeling empathy and sympathy for others, taking the viewpoint of the one who speaks, seeing personal experiences and first-person stories as important ways of learning, and embracing an ethic of caring. They are distressed about violence and the abuse of women and children, and they want more good childcare facilities and far more attention on children's needs and education. They have strong concerns about the well-being of families and want to improve caring relationships in all areas of life, private and public."[7]

The Cultural Creatives are more idealistic and altruistic and less cynical than other Americans. They are concerned with personal authenticity, global ecology, and the well-being of all people on the planet. Of the fifty million, 60 percent are women. In addition, Ray and Anderson differentiated a "Core" group of Cultural Creatives based on the intensity of their values and beliefs, and the extent to which they put their values into action. Some twenty-four million people—twice as many women as men—were in the more committed group of Cultural Creatives. The Core group is characterized by their concern for both social justice and their inner life: they found that "strikingly, the stronger their values and beliefs about altruism, self-actualization, and spirituality, the more likely they are to be interested in social action and social transformation."[8]

Circles of women and consciousness-raising are the means through which women bring about change in themselves and change patriarchy. Circles proliferate organically. Circles are like plants: some disseminate seeds of information and inspiration, and new circles grow from them; others send out runners that take root close by—one woman talks about her group to another woman who decides to form a circle herself. However they begin, the essential form is the same. The power of circles to bring about change in the culture is in their numbers and in the archetypes that are active in the women in them.

She Is a Circle

Creating a Wisewoman Circle

To transform a group that you already have
into a wisewoman circle
or create a new one—
the first consideration are the members.
Who will be in this circle?
Are they juicy crones?
Does each woman have wisdom and compassion,
a sense of humor, a great laugh,
spirit, and soul?
Is she outraged at injustice and indifference?
Does she want to make a difference?
Does she have a sense of community,
faith that there is meaning in life and that it matters what we do?
Does she care about the well-being of others beyond her own,
for values that are being lost,
for the survival of a neigborhood or the planet?
Has she grown through her difficult times?
Can you count on her?
Does she have time and energy
to be in this circle
as an activist or contemplative or clan mother?
And will the circle be a sanctuary
for her?
Experiences in past groups
and wisdom gained through life
will help sustain and maintain a circle.
There are also resources, books on the subject of circles
that I recommend.

My own *Millionth Circle* is a poetic and intuitive slender volume.
A Zen and the art of circle maintenance.
A right-brain approach to sacred circles.

Wisdom Circles by Charles Garfield,
Cynthia Spring, and Sedonia Cahill
builds upon Ten Constants,
which are
solid foundation principles for wisdom circles
and guidelines for being in one.

Christina Baldwin's *Calling the Circle*
contains the most specific "how-to" of the three.
There are agreements and procedures,
enumerated principles,
a bibliography and references.
Information and examples that aid this endeavor.

Books help when forming and sustaining a circle.
Are food for thought and ideas to contemplate.
Talk about this with others.
Be visionary together.
Reflect on what you might do,
pray for guidance.

Silent prayer centers a circle of wisewomen,
each praying in her own way
for wisdom, courage, insight, compassion.
May the highest good come into the circle
and go out from it.

CONCLUSION

This Is Act III

Ⅰf you are postmenopausal or on the threshold of this phase, you are in or about to be in Act III of your life. Knowing which archetypes are stirring and strong in you will help you to come into your own third phase with additional consciousness and a means of finding some bearings as you proceed. In the theater, the performance onstage builds toward Act III. For those who think of themselves as spiritual beings on a human path, the third phase of life holds the promise and possibility of coming into wisdom and seeing the purpose and meaning of your life. Whether or not the concept of being on a spiritual path is part of your consciousness, the wisdom of age has to do with seeing life from a broader perspective and acting accordingly.

For some women, the fifth and sixth decades are the culmination of achievements, a time when position and influence are at their height. Until the women's movement, this was an exceedingly rare position for a woman to have, and now it is not. Paradoxically, just as a woman's competitiveness and striving for excellence, success, and recognition bear fruit or are within sight, the crone archetypes begin to stir. She then may question their importance as ends in themselves, and ask: *Why am I doing this?* What was once the goal can then become a means of making a difference and, in the process of this shifting emphasis, wisdom can become the focus of her inner world.

These decades can also be a time of affluence, through earnings, inheritance, retirement funds, or settlements. The question that may then arise is: *What shall I do with this?* In the past, the relatively few women in this position were expected to leave such decisions up to male members of the family or managers, and the premise was to conserve assets and pass them on. When women now come into crone age and have control over such financial assets, they are likely to make their own decisions. The United States is in the midst of the largest transfer of wealth from one generation to the next, and this involves a great number of people whose middle-class parents are leaving sizable estates due to the astronomical appreciation of the value of their homes and investments. Unexpected wealth beyond one's needs can raise the question about the meaning of it: *What do I have it for?*

For women who are fortunate in having a healthy body and mind, the asset in question is time: *What shall I do with the good years I have left?* When this question is not asked or the answer to it is not sought, time will likely be spent without thought about its preciousness or about the choices we have. Time can be frittered away, unless the crone archetypes come into consciousness and affect how we see ourselves and the lifetime we have left.

For women with adult children, their fifth and sixth decades are when grandchildren are often born. Their birth, like the birth of one's own children, can stir deep maternal feelings, which are similar and yet differ. To become a grandmother is a new role that draws from having been a mother. What a woman knows and does as a grandmother can enrich the lives of three generations. The birth of grandchildren can draw a woman who is now a grandmother and her grown children who are now parents into a new appreciation and empathy for each other, and when there is an affinity between a grandchild and a grandparent, which often happens, a new and special bond is created. The experience also brings us a new appreciation of ongoing life, of caring about what will happen to future generations beyond one's own lifetime.

Every active woman of crone age is in a position to make a difference in her own life, and most have the potential to make a difference to others. This can be a "give back" time. Thanks to the efforts of others, we were given opportunities that women did not have until very recently. Now can be a time to express gratitude by doing unto others through mentoring, offering support, or becoming an advocate or an activist.

Taking stock is crucial if we are to be choicemakers whose decisions will affect the quality and meaning of this stage of our lives. It may be the last time you have to face the truth about being in a state of denial about an addiction and its effects upon your health. It may be time to face the truth about a dysfunctional and damaging relationship. A crone-aged woman who still harbors fantasies instead of doing something for herself or with herself while she still can, is in a state of denial that she can ill afford.

This is also a time to enjoy the pleasures of being in this world and being yourself in it, knowing that your body and mind will not last forever. It may be a time for creativity, for play, for work that is play, for travel, or inner exploration; whatever it is that calls to you. It is the time when appreciation can be an accompaniment to the large and small pleasures of life. It is gratitude that makes us connoisseurs of experience, people who realize the specialness or the value of being alive and having this particular moment. This same awareness is shared by people who have been through a life-threatening experience and savor life afterward.

There is also the possibility that demands upon our limited time and energy can deplete us in the third phase unless we find a perspective and a means of holding both ourselves and others in consciousness. Ailing and elderly parents may need us more than before and so may our adolescent or adult children. At this same time, our spouses or friends may retire and have expectations of spending leisure time with us or want us to fill the void that retirement has created. Or they may develop health problems and be increasingly dependent on us for tangible and emotional help. Then there are the patterns we established that once were enjoyable and have become obligations, such as responsibilities for holidays and hospitality. How much of us we willingly give, or others take, will depend on how much we value ourselves and how willing we are to define our own priorities and boundaries.

The tasks of everyday life and the amount of communication—publications, correspondence, calls to return, bills to pay, e-mail—seem to expand and overflow the time and space that we have. It sometimes feels as though these tasks multiply like mushrooms in the dark and we start each day more behind than the night before. Whether in traditional women's roles or in work situations, there are the feelings of others to attend to, the caretaking that goes with everyday life. With friends, family, and the assortment of people who engage us in their lives, it is altogether too easy for women to become functional codependents though not necessarily to anyone in particular.

For Act III to be more than this, you will need to take "time out" to get your bearings and replenish your energy: "time in" might be a more accurate description because inner wisdom is not accessible unless you have the time and solitude to listen. Then the crone archetypes become sources of perspective and action.

It is a project to arrange a true respite and retreat to replenish energy and reconnect with yourself. It takes scheduling and planning. It often requires overcoming your own inertia, or sense of being indispensable, or the resistance of others. You could go to a meditative retreat, or go camping in the wilderness or go to a spa, or to the seashore, perhaps to a workshop or on a pilgrimage. You could meditate every morning, or take a daily walk, or turn off everything that rings and take the time to do whatever you need to do in order to listen to yourself. Since women often discover themselves in talk, it helps many of us to have a listener and to be one. Women's familiarity with each other's experiences and feelings, our ability to actively listen to each other, is then a growth medium for authenticity and a means through which we hear our inner wisdom.

Time away, with or without others, may be what you need. If you choose solitude, then the conversation might be in your journal. The third phase of life needs to be *inner-directed* if it is to be about the evolution of the wisewoman in yourself. To do this, you need to spend time with your inner circle of archetypes.

Just as the rhythm of the heart has a systolic phase, when it sends blood throughout the arterial tree, and a diastolic phase, when it fills, so must we replenish and be filled again. Burnout or brownout times of diminished energy and vision need recreation and relaxation, or rest and recuperation, through which we find our center, tap into sources of spirituality and vision, and collect ourselves.

Many wisewomen have regular pauses in their day or week for soul-satisfying experiences that are "diastolic." These are centering and nourishing experiences, such as regular times to meditate, to be in a women's circle, attend a yoga class, take a morning walk, or spend time in a studio, garden, or kitchen being creative or being with people who bring us joy.

NOT OVER THE HILL

Menopause often coincides with thoughts about retirement, your own or your husband's, sometimes with becoming a widow or a divorced woman, often with the emptying nest. Retirement has connotations of being put out to pasture, but it takes on a positive new meaning if it marks the end of a particular phase of employment and a shift into new activities. These days, most postmenopausal women are not "retiring" as in disappearing into the woodwork and being neither seen nor heard; nor are they "retiring" or metaphorically going to sleep. Quite the contrary. Older women are reinventing themselves, growing in awareness, and saying their piece.

Grandmother is the acceptable traditional role for postmenopausal women but hardly sufficient as a life in itself. In *The Feminine Mystique,* Betty Friedan struck a note of truth when she said that it was not enough for women to live through others, to be someone's wife and someone's mother but not someone in their own right. To be a grandmother may be wonderful but it is not enough for women who have a life of their own. To accompany one's husband to where he wants to retire is also not enough, though many women do try to adapt.

In *Over the Hill*, the actress Olympia Dukakis portrays Alma Harris, a New England widow who rebels when she is expected to retire from life and live in the remodeled basement of her son's house. Getting her spine up, she flies to Australia, presenting a problem for her super-scheduled daughter, the wife of a politican. Dukakis thwarts efforts to be packed up and returned and, instead, drives across Australia in a souped-up car and discovers more and more of herself. Rarely do we see films in which the protagonist is an older woman whose adventure is discovering herself. Dukakis accepts an invitation to be initiated by aboriginal women in the outback, which adds a mystical and earthy dimension to the film. Though she has to decide whether she will accept or reject two very different men, one offering her a replay of her old life, the other a reflection of her new self, this film is not about them or about defining herself through them, but about discovering and developing her authentic self. She becomes an unexpected role model for a daughter who had previously viewed her as an embarrassment.

While this is a movie and not your life, your own third stage may require that you also actively resist the plans others make for you, and instead of fading away or be cast in the supporting role or as a minor character in others' lives, be vividly yourself.

GOING TO SEED

"Going to seed" is yet another good phrase that has become a pejorative for growing older. "Going to seed" is a symbol of the third face of the triple goddess, and for women in the third phase of life. The three phases of our lives were seen reflected in nature, in the waxing, full, and waning moon, and in the flower, fruit, and seed of vegetative life. "Going to seed" is used as a derogatory and dismissive statement. Hidden in its symbology, however, is a beautiful concept for this period of life. The seed is the bearer of information, the concentration of nutrients and essence that ensures the survival of the species. It's the seeds of wisdom that we have and have to pass on. "Going to seed" can also describe the individuation process of getting to one's essence, to the soul and spirit, the Self that animates us.

Every book that I write is an expression of what I have learned so far, the information and intuition that I want to pass on to others on a spiritual and psychological journey. Each life is new territory, and yet the terrain that each illuminates with consciousness has a similar structure. In the collective unconscious, in the human morphic field, in the dream and instinctual realms, in the evolution of our species and our connection to the great mystery of creation and divinity, we each are singular beings and part of a greater whole. The Eastern philosophical mind refers to the invisible connection between us and between us and everything in the universe, as the Tao which fits C. G. Jung's concept of the Self.

When something comes to my mind and heart in the midst of a deep conversation, an analytic session, a creative project such as writing, or in a ceremonial circle of women—and I trust and develop that seed—the subjective experience is of being myself and being connected to a greater source. Each time I have had an *Aha!* experience and passed it along, I held or incubated that insight in my psyche, where it drew ideas and images to it, and translated it into my own words. Then when I take them out into the world through speaking or writing, I am "sowing" these seeds. The metaphor works only this far, because when such an idea encourages or inspires someone else's growth and creativity, the person in whom my words have had an effect is not a passive vessel who receives the seed. Furthermore, seeds of wisdom—even as metaphors—do not obey physical or economic laws.

In the physical and economic world, if I give you something, then I no longer have it. Wisdom and love behave altogether differently: if I give you my love or wisdom, both of us can have it. And even more remarkable, you may pass it on and not only still retain it, but it will grow with each transaction. The more we give away, the more there is and the more we have. Another remarkable quality is that if I give you my wisdom and it rings true in you, what I gave you was really already in you, and you recognized it as your own. The more we bring our wisdom into the world, the more wisdom there will be, and the easier it will be for other women to find it in themselves.

ARCHETYPES AS SEEDS

Archetypes are like seeds that are in all of us from the beginning. Depending upon circumstance and predisposition, some become activated and others remain dormant. The archetypes I have described in this book have existed as potentials in the psyche, and though they may come into their own—if they do at all—in the third phase of our lives, they could have been an active aspect of an individual woman for a long time before. When I write or speak of the goddesses in us, there is a possibility that one or several of them turn out to be familiar, but until named, they remained unacknowledged. Once there is an *Aha!*

of recognition, consciousness brings the possibility of doing something with the energies of the now-acknowledged archetype. To me, naming the goddesses and finding that they are a strong aspect in another's psyche is like naming a talent or gift that is there—and inviting its development. Most of the goddesses in older women have carried a "develop at your own peril" risk, and so have been silent or suppressed. They have been like seeds women have carried through millennia, awaiting a change in climate. At the beginning of the third millennium, the "weather" is changing. There is a receptivity and a growing place for older women to be an influence.

GROUNDWORK

As anyone who has gardened knows, the seasons matter. Just as flowering, fruitbearing, and going to seed occur according to the season, so chronological age and hormonal stage determine the season when a woman comes into her crone phase. For a garden to flourish, the soil has to be tended. For a particular tree or perennial to thrive, special attention may be required. Psychological preparation works in the same way.

To tap into the energies of these archetypes and flourish in the third phase of life requires letting go of the resentments and disappointments of the past to live contentedly in the present. It will take a strong intention to do so, and much work and effort to cease being a victim and a hostage to the past. This exercise of wisdom and will is well worth the psychological and spiritual work it takes.

The good and the bad of the past have shaped you into the person you are now. To accept this and not be filled with resentment, anger, or envy takes maturity and an acceptance that your life is your own, and the spirit in which you live your life is up to you. It's easier for some than others, though this is not necessarily related to the severity of one's difficulties. This was vividly brought home to me by a woman who spoke up at a breast-cancer event. She shocked many in the audience when she said that she was thankful for the beatings she got as a child, thankful for the alcoholism she had overcome, and thankful for the cancer that she had had, "because they all shaped me into the person I am!" This was not Pollyanna speaking, I could hear that in her voice and in her story. She was in her fullness as a woman of wisdom and strength, living in the present and not attached by cords of resentment and pain to the past.

Personal feelings of failure commonly prevent women from entering fully into the third phase of life. You may be tied to the past by what you didn't accomplish, and the person you hold responsible is yourself. The transition between stages of life is a time when most women need to grieve and let go of what did or didn't happen. By forgiving yourself and others, you are freer to move into this third stage without the encumbrances of resentment and guilt. When there are feelings of failure, the premise behind these feelings needs examining. How much do they have to do with failed expectations, as in, you were supposed to have a happy marriage and raise perfect children, you expected yourself to have a successful career, or both? And here you are at fifty-plus, with what you have and who you are. Maybe the life you have is truer to who you are than whom you were supposed to be. Maybe fate or karma plays a part that needs to be acknowledged, even when it is unknown. Maybe what really matters bears little resemblance to what you thought of as success.

The possibility of flourishing in the third phase often depends upon what you choose to do at the threshold, beginning with whether you can accept yourself as you are now and go on, or whether you need to make major changes first. If you cannot forgive, let go, or act wisely at this juncture, the path you are on will inevitably take you through a depressed landscape. This will affect your relationships and your health, as well as your mood and mind. Change takes knowing you must, having the will to do so, and seeking the best way.

The crone archetypes need to be recognized and cultivated to become a conscious part of ourselves. It is Hecate who counsels seeking the truth and provides insight and intuition. To act on what you know will take the "enough is enough" energies of Sekhmet/Kali, tempered by the practical wisdom of Athena/Metis and the spiritual perspective of Sophia's wisdom. Sometimes the major task is forgiving, which requires the compassion of Kuan Yin for yourself and others. Hestia, the centering archetype, warms and illuminates our inner world, and is also the invisible hearthfire around which wisewomen circles gather and become a place for the healing laughter of Uzume/Baubo and of all of the archetypes in older women.

I have been drawn to the phrase *The life of significant soil*, from T. S. Eliot's *Four Quartets*,[1] as a poetic way to describe a meaningful life, one in which archetypal seeds become active and manifest through our inner spiritual and psychological life, sometimes becoming evident in dreams and synchronicities, or expressed outwardly in our actions, creativity, and relationships. A life of significant soil feels authentic, rooted in our own nature and in the seasons of our particular life. The crone archetypes invite us to reflect upon what we know from our own experience. They bring us into the inner realm of meaning, help us to see what matters, to be compassionate, decisive and, if need be, fierce when change is called for. They help us have a life of significant soil.

Love to you.

NOTES

Introduction: How to Be a Juicy Crone

Sources

Bolen, Jean Shinoda. *The Wisewoman Archetype: Menopause as Initiation* audiotape. Boulder: Sounds True, 1991.

———. *Crossing to Avalon: A Woman's Midlife Pilgrimage*. San Francisco: HarperSan-Francisco, 1994.

———. *Goddesses in Everywoman*. San Francisco: Harper & Row, 1984.

Friedan, Betty. *The Feminine Mystique*. New York: Dell, 1964.

George, Demetra. *Mysteries of the Dark Moon: The Healing Power of the Dark Goddess*. San Francisco: HarperSanFrancisco, 1992.

Illuminations of Hildegard of Bingen. Text by Hildegard of Bingen with commentary by Matthew Fox. Santa Fe: Bear & Company, 1985.

Joseph, Jenny. "Warning," in *When I Am an Old Woman, I Shall Wear Purple: An Anthology of Short Stories and Poetry*. Sandra Martz, editor. Manhattan Beach, Calif.: Papier-Mache Press, 1987.

Jung, C. G. *The Archetypes and the Collective Unconscious*. 2nd ed. Vol. 9, 1954. In *The Collected Works of C. G. Jung*, edited by Sir Herbert Read, Michael Fordham, and Gerhard Adler; translated by R. F. C. Hull; executive editor, William McGuire. Princeton, N.J.: Bollingen Series 20, Princeton University Press, 1968.

Sams, Jamie. *The Thirteen Original Clan Mothers*. San Francisco: HarperSanFran-cisco, 1993.

Sheehy, Gail. *The Silent Passage: Menopause*. New York: Random House, 1991.

Shuttle, Penelope, and Peter Redgrove. *The Wise Wound: Myths, Realities, and Meanings of Menstruation*. Revised Edition, New York: Bantam Books, 1990. (Originally published in England by Victor Gollancz Ltd., 1978.)

Walker, Barbara G. *The Crone: Woman of Age, Wisdom, and Power*. San Francisco: HarperSanFrancisco, 1985.

Notes

1. Sams, Jamie, *The Thirteen Original Clan Mothers* (San Francisco: HarperSanFrancisco, 1993), 2.

2. Bolen, Jean Shinoda, *The Wisewoman Archetype: Menopause as Initiation* (audiotape). Boulder: Sounds True, 1991.

3. Bolen, Jean Shinoda, *Goddesses in Everywoman*, San Francisco: HarperSanFrancisco, 1984, chap. 13.

4. Postulated by theoretical biologist Rupert Sheldrake, morphic fields are responsible for both form and behavior, much as iron filings are organized in magnetic fields. With morphic resonance, these fields are broadcast across time and space, which means that the past can influence the present. For Sheldrake references, see Sources, Part 4, She Is a Circle.

PART 1: HER NAME IS WISDOM

1. Jung, C. G. "Wotan," in *Civilization in Transition*. Vol. 10, *The Collected Works of C. G Jung*, edited by Sir Herbert Read, Michael Fordham, and Gerhard Adler; translated by R. F. C. Hull; executive editor, William McGuire (Princeton, N.J.: Bollingen Series 20, Princeton University Press, 1964), 189.

Goddess of Practical and Intellectual Wisdom

Sources

Bateson, Mary Catherine. *Composing a Life*. New York: Dutton / Plume, 1990.

Eisler, Riane. *The Chalice and the Blade*. San Francisco: Harper & Row, 1997.

Eisler, Riane. *Sacred Pleasure: Sex, Myth, and the Politics of the Body*. San Francisco: HarperSanFrancisco, 1995.

Gimbutas, Marija. *The Language of the Goddess*. San Francisco: Harper & Row, 1989.

Gimbutas, Marija. *The Civilization of the Goddess*. San Francisco: HarperSanFrancisco, 1991.

Gimbutas, Marija. *The Goddesses and Gods of Old Europe: 6500–3500 B.C., Myths and Cult Images*. Berkeley and Los Angeles: University of California Press, new and updated edition, 1982. (Originally published in the United States under the title *Gods and Goddesses of Old Europe: 7000–3500 B.C.*, University of California Press, 1974.)

Graves, Robert. "Zeus and Metis," *The Greek Myths: Volume 1*. New York: Penguin (1955, reprint, 1982).

Hesiod. *Theogony*. In *Hesiod*. Translation, introduction, and notes by Apostolos N. Athanassakis. Baltimore: Johns Hopkins University Press, 1983.

Keuls, Eva C. *The Reign of the Phallus: Sexual Politics in Ancient Athens*. Berkeley, Calif.: University of California Press, 1993.

Olson, Tillie. *Silences*. New York: Delacorte, 1978.

Pert, Candace B. "Breaking the Rules," in *Molecules of Emotion: Why You Feel the Way You Feel*. New York: Scribner, 1997.

Stone, Merlin. *When God Was a Woman*. New York: Harvest/HBJ, by arrangement with Dial Press, 1978. (Originally published in Great Britain under the title *The Paradise Papers* by Virago Limited, in association with Quartet Books Limited, 1976.)

Organizations

EMILY's List, 805 15th Street NW, Suite 400, Washington, D.C. 20005, www.emilyslist.org.

Notes

1. Baring, Anne, and Jules Cashford. *The Myth of the Goddess: Evolution of an Image*. London: Viking, 1991.

2. Pert, Candace B. *Molecules of Emotion* (New York: Scribner, 1997), 107–129.

3. Ibid., 111.

4. Stone, Merlin. *When God Was a Woman* (New York: Dial Press, 1976), xxiv.

5. Walker, Barbara G. *The Women's Encyclopedia of Myths and Secrets* (Edison, N.J.: Castle Books, 1999), 629. (Originally published in San Francisco by Harper & Row, 1983.)

Goddess of Spiritual Wisdom

Sources

Anderson, Sherry P., and Patricia Hopkins. *The Feminine Face of God*. New York: Bantam, 1991.

Bancroft, Ann. *Weavers of Wisdom: Women Mystics of the Twentieth Century*. London: Arkana, 1989.

Baring, Anne and Jules Cashford. "The Hidden Goddess in the Old Testament," *The Myth of the Goddess: Evolution of an Image*. London: Viking, 1991.

Bolen, Jean Shinoda. *Close to the Bone*. New York: Scribner, 1996.

Craighead, Meinrad. *The Mother's Songs*. New York: Paulist Press, 1986.

Davies, Steve. "The Canaanite-Hebrew Goddess," in *The Book of the Goddess Past and Present*, edited by Carl Olson. New York: Crossroad, 1985.

Eisler, Riane. *The Chalice and the Blade*. San Francisco: Harper & Row, 1987.

Flinders, Carol Lee. *Enduring Grace: Living Portraits of Seven Women Mystics*. San Francisco: HarperSanFrancisco, 1993.

Flinders, Carol Lee. *At the Root of this Longing*. San Francisco: HarperSanFrancisco, 1998.

Matthews, Caitlin. *Sophia Goddess of Wisdom: The Divine Feminine from Black Goddess to World-Soul*. London: Thorsons, 1992.

Norris, Kathleen. *Amazing Grace: A Vocabulary of Faith*. New York: Riverhead, 1998.

Olson, Carl, editor. *The Book of the Goddess Past and Present: An Introduction to Her Religion*. New York: Crossroad, 1983.

Pagels, Elaine. *The Gnostic Gospels*. New York: Random House, 1979. (Major source of information about early Gnostic Christianity, Gnostic references to Sophia, and opposition from the early church fathers.)

Patai, Raphael and Merlin Stone. *The Hebrew Goddess*. Detroit: Wayne State University Press, 1990.

Perkins, Pheme. "Sophia and the Mother-Father. The Gnostic Goddess," in *The Book of the Goddess Past and Present*, edited by Carl Olson. New York: Crossroad, 1985.

Robinson, James M., general editor, *The Nag Hammadi Library in English*, translated by members of the Coptic Gnostic Library Project of the Institute for Antiquity and Christianity. San Francisco: Harper & Row, 1978.

Shlain, Leonard. *The Alphabet Versus the Goddess*. New York: Viking, 1998.

Walker, Barbara G., "Sophia, Saint," in *The Encyclopedia of Women's Myths and Secrets*. (1983. Reprint, Edison, N.J.: Castle Books, 1996).

Notes

1. Bancroft, Ann. *Weavers of Wisdom* (London: Arkana, 1989), vii.

2. Ibid., viii.

3. Anderson, Sherry R. and Patricia Hopkins. *The Feminine Face of God* (New York: Bantam, 1991), 59.

4. Craighead, Meinrad. "Immanent Mother," in *The Feminist Mystic and Other Essays on Women and Spirituality*, ed. Mary E. Giles (New York: Crossroad Press, 1982), 76.

5. Flinders, Carol. *At the Root of this Longing* (San Francisco: HarperSanFrancisco, 1998), 5.

6. Ibid., 325.

7. Anderson and Hopkins, 131.

8. Ibid., 186–187.

9. Ibid., notes, chapter 8, note 4, 234.

10. Baring and Cashford, 447.

11. From *The Holy Bible*, RSV, Proverbs 8:14, 8:22–31, 9:1.

12. Baring and Cashford, 417.

13. Davies, Steve. "The Canaanite-Hebrew Goddess," in *The Book of the Goddess Past and Present*, edited by Carl Olson (New York: Crossroad, 1985), 72. (Attributes the

periods in which Asherah was a presence in the Jerusalem temple itself to Raphael Patai.)

14. Walker, Barbara G. "Asherah," 66. *Encyclopedia of The Women's Myths: Secrets* (1983; reprint, Edison; N.J.: Castle Books, 1996).

15. Shlain, Leonard. *The Alphabet Versus the Goddess* (New York: Viking, 1998), 82–83.

16. Tertullian, *De Praescr*, 41. Reference from Pagels, Elaine. *The Gnostic Gospels* (New York: Random House, 1979), 60.

17. Tertullian, *De Virginibus Velandis*, 9. Pagels reference, 60.

Goddess of Intuitive and Psychic Wisdom

Sources

Barstow, Anne Llewellyn. *Witchcraze: A New History of the European Witch Hunts*. San Francisco: Pandora/HarperCollins, 1994.

George, Demetra. *Mysteries of the Dark Moon: The Healing Power of the Dark Goddess*. San Francisco: HarperSanFrancisco, 1992. (Most comprehensive Hecate source.)

Graves, Robert. *The Greek Myths*. New York: Penguin, 1955, reprint 1982.

Karagulla, Shafica. *Breakthrough to Creativity: Higher Sense Perception*. Santa Monica, Calif.: DeVorss, 1967.

Kübler-Ross, Elisabeth. *On Death and Dying*. New York: Macmillan, 1970.

Walker, Barbara G. *The Crone*. San Francisco: HarperSanFrancisco, 1985. "4. The Terrible Crone," "5. The Crone and the Cauldron," "6. The Crone Turns Witch."

Walker, Barbara G. *The Women's Encyclopedia of Myths and Secrets*. San Francisco: Harper & Row, 1983. Reprint, Edison, N.J.: Castle Books, 1996. "Hecate," "Witch," "Witchcraft."

Notes

1. "Hymn to Demeter," *The Homeric Hymns*, Charles Boer, translator (University of Dallas, Irving, Tex.: Spring Publications, 1979), 129.

2. Allison, Ralph B. "A New Treatment Approach for Multiple Personalities," *American Journal of Clinical Hypnosis* 17 (1974): 15–32.

3. "Weird" or "wyrd" was a Saxon name for the crone or death goddess. The three witches in Shakespeare's *Macbeth* were called the Weird Sisters after the three Fates or Norns, all of whom were usually portrayed as crones.

4. Walker, Barbara G. *The Women's Encyclopedia of Myths and Secrets*, 1076–1091.

Goddess of Meditative Wisdom

Sources

Bolen, Jean Shinoda. "Hestia: Goddess of the Hearth and Temple," in *Goddesses in Everywoman*. San Francisco: Harper & Row, 1984.

Demetrakopoulos, Stephanie. "Hestia, Goddess of the Hearth." *Spring 1979: An annual of Archetypal Psychology and Jungian Thought.* (Major source for Hestia rituals.)

Graves, Robert. "Hestia's Nature and Deeds," in *The Greek Myths*, Vol. 1. New York: Penguin, 1955.

Harding, M. Esther. "The Virgin Goddess," in *Women's Mysteries*. New York: Bantam, 1973, published by arrangement with Putnam.

Notes

1. Steinem, Gloria. "Doing Sixty," in *Moving Beyond Words* (New York: Simon & Schuster, 1994), 249.

PART 2: SHE IS MORE . . . THAN WISDOM

Goddesses of Transformative Wrath: Her Name Is Outrage

Sources

Brown, C. Mackenzie. "Kali, the Mad Mother," in *The Book of the Goddess Past and Present*, edited by Carl Olson. New York: Crossroad, 1985.

Galland, China. *The Bond Between Women*. New York: Riverhead, 1998.

Harding, Elizabeth U. *Kali: The Black Goddess of Dakshineswar*. York Beach, Me.: Nicolas-Hays, 1993.

Irons, Veronica. *Egyptian Mythology*. New York: Peter Bedrick, 1962.

———. *Indian Mythology*. Revised ed. Middlesex, England: Newnes, 1983.

Kinsley, David R. *The Sword and the Flute: K͞alī and K°r°s°na: Dark Visions of the Terrible and the Sublime in Hindu Mythology*. Berkeley, Calif.: University of California Press, 1975.

Kreilkamp, Ann. "Power & Presence: Meeting Sekhmet," *Crone Chronicles*, Number 31, Summer Solstice, 1997.

Masters, Robert. *The Goddess Sekhmet*. St. Paul, Minn.: Llewellyn, 1988.

Mookerjee, Ajit. *Kali: The Feminine Force*. New York: Destiny Books, 1988.

Secakuku, Alph H. *Following the Sun and Moon*. Flagstaff, Ariz: Northland Publishing in cooperation with the Heard Museum, 1995.

Walker, Barbara G. *The Crone*. San Francisco: HarperSanFrancisco, 1985. "4. The

Terrible Crone," "5. The Crone and the Cauldron," "6. The Crone Turns Witch."

Walker, Barbara G. *The Women's Encyclopedia of Myths and Secrets*. Edison, N.J.: Castle Books, 1996. "Hecate."

Wolkstein, Diane, and Samuel Noah Kramer. "The Descent of Inanna," from *Inanna: Queen of Heaven and Earth*. New York: Harper & Row, 1983. (Tells of Ereshkigal.)

Notes

1. Masters, Robert. *The Goddess Sekhmet* (St. Paul, Minn.: Llewellyn, 1991), 45–46.

2. Harding, Elizabeth U. *Kali: The Black Goddess of Dakshineswar* (York Beach, Me.: Nicolas-Hays, 1993), xix–xxii.

3. Galland, China. *The Bond Between Women: Journey to Fierce Compassion* (New York: Riverhead, 1998), xvii–xx.

4. This is a synopsis of "From the Great Above to the Great Below," from *Inanna: Queen of Heaven and Earth*, translated and told by Diane Wolkstein and Samuel Noah Kramer (New York: Harper & Row, 1983), 52–73.

5. Her Hopi name is *Angwusnasomtaqa*. See Secakuku, Alph H., *Following the Sun and Moon: Hopi Kachina Tradition* (Flagstaff, Ariz.: Northland/Heard Museum, 1995), 17, 20.

6. Galland, China. *The Bond Between Women*, 208–215.

Goddesses of Healing Laughter: Her Name Is Mirth

Sources

Camphausen, Rufus C. *The Yoni: Sacred Symbol of Female Creative Power*. Rochester, Vt.: Inner Traditions, 1996.

Lubell, Winifred Milius. *The Metamorphosis of Baubo: Myths of Woman's Sexual Energy*. Nashville, Tenn.: Vanderbilt University Press, 1994. (The major reference for Baubo.)

Redmond, Layne. *When the Drummers Were Women: A Spiritual History of Rhythm*. New York: Three Rivers Press, 1997.

Stone, Merlin. "Amaterasu Omikami," in *Ancient Mirrors of Womanhood*. Boston: Beacon Press, 1984. (Tells of Ama-No Uzume.)

Notes

1. Gimbutas, Marija, in the foreword to Winifred Milius Lubell, *The Metamorphosis of Baubo* (Nashville, Tenn.: Vanderbilt University Press, 1994), xiii.

2. Lubell, Winifred Milius. *The Metamorphosis of Baubo: Myths of Woman's Sexual Energy* (Nashville, Tenn.: Vanderbilt University Press, 1994), 34.

3. Ibid., 36–40.

4. A retelling of a portion of "The Hymn to Demeter" (re: Iambe/Baubo) from *The*

Homeric Hymns, Charles Boer, translator (Irving, Tex.: Spring Publications, 1979), 105–107, with the inclusion of the *ana-suromai* gesture from statues of Baubo and the report of Clement of Alexandria.

5. Lubell, xix.

6. Ibid., 179–181.

7. Stone, Merlin. *Ancient Mirrors of Womanhood* (New York: New Sibylline Books, 1979), 2: 127–129.

8. Redmond, Layne. *When the Drummers Were Women* (New York: Three Rivers Press, 1997), 152–153.

Goddesses of Compassion: Her Name Is Kindness

Sources

Austen, Hallie Iglehart. *The Heart of the Goddess: Art, Myth and Meditations of the World's Sacred Feminine*. Berkeley, Calif.: Wingbow Press, 1990.

Baring, Anne and Jules Cashford. "Mary, the Return of the Goddess," *The Myth of the Goddess: Evolution of an Image*. London: Viking, 1991.

Blofeld, John. *Bodhisattva of Compassion: The Mystical Tradition of Kuan Yin*. Boston: Shambala, 1988.

Cunneen, Sally. *In Search of Mary: The Woman and the Symbol*. New York: Ballantine, 1996.

Leighton, Taigen Daniel. *Bodhisattva Archetypes: Classic Buddhist Guides to Awakening and Their Modern Expression*. New York: Penguin Arkana, 1998.

Matter, E. Ann. "The Virgin Mary: A Goddess?" In *The Book of the Goddess Past and Present*, edited by Carl Olson. New York: Crossroad, 1985.

Paul, Diana. "Kuan-Yin: Savior and Savioress in Chinese Pure Land Buddhism" in *The Book of the Goddess Past and Present*, edited by Carl Olson. New York: Crossroad, 1985.

Woodward, Kenneth L. "Hail, Mary," *Newsweek*, August 25, 1998.

Notes

1. Blofeld, John. *Bodhisattva of Compassion* (Boston: Shambala, 1988), 24.

2. "Walking a Tightrope: An Interview with Robert Coles," *Parabola* (Spring 1994): 73.

3. Both quotes from Bradley, Marion Zimmer. *Mists of Avalon*, 875.

4. Walker, Barbara G. *The Women's Encyclopedia of Myths and Secrets*, 609.

5. Cunneen, Sally. *In Search of Mary: The Woman and the Symbol*, 31.

PART 3: SHE IS A GODDESS GROWING OLDER:
GODDESSES IN EVERYWOMAN, REVISITED

Bolen, Jean Shinoda. "The Virgin Goddesses: Artemis, Athena, and Hestia," "The Vulnerable Goddesses: Hera, Demeter, and Persephone," "The Alchemical Goddess," in *Goddesses in Everywoman*. San Francisco: Harper & Row, 1984; HarperCollins, 1985.

Artemis, the Goddess of the Hunt and Moon

Sources

Bolen, Jean Shinoda. "Artemis: Goddess of the Hunt and Moon. Competitor and Sister," in *Goddesses in Everywoman*.

Athena, the Goddess of Wisdom and Crafts

Sources

Bolen, Jean Shinoda. "Athena: Goddess of Wisdom and Crafts, Strategist and Father's Daughter," in *Goddesses in Everywoman*.

Hestia, the Goddess of the Hearth and Temple

Sources

Bolen, Jean Shinoda. "Hestia: Goddess of the Hearth and Temple, Wise Woman and Maiden Aunt," in *Goddesses in Everywoman*.

Hera, the Goddess of Marriage

Sources

Bolen, Jean Shinoda. "Hera: Goddess of Marriage, Commitment Maker and Wife," in *Goddesses in Everywoman*.

Demeter, the Goddess of Grain

Sources

Bolen, Jean Shinoda. "Demeter: Goddess of Grain, Nurturer and Mother," in *Goddesses in Everywoman*.

Persephone, the Maiden and Queen of the Underworld

Sources

Bolen, Jean Shinoda. "Persephone: The Maiden and Queen of the Underworld, Receptive Woman and Mother's Daughter," in *Goddesses in Everywoman*.

Aphrodite, the Goddess of Love and Beauty

Sources

Bolen, Jean Shinoda. "Aphrodite: Goddess of Love and Beauty, Creative Woman and Lover," in *Goddess in Everywoman*.

Stuart, Gloria. *Gloria! I Just Kept Hoping*. Boston: Little Brown, 1999.

Notes

1. Levinson, Daniel J. *The Seasons of a Man's Life*. (New York: Ballantine, 1979), 109.

PART 4: SHE IS A CIRCLE

Circles of Wisewomen

Sources

Baldwin, Christina. *Calling the Circle: The First and Future Culture*. New York: Bantam, 1998.

Bolen, Jean Shinoda. *The Millionth Circle: How to Change Ourselves and the World, the Essential Guide to Women's Circles*. Berkeley, Calif.: Conari, 1999.

Cahill, Sedonia and Joshua Halpern. *The Ceremonial Circle: Practice, Ritual, and Renewal for Personal and Community Healing*. San Francisco: HarperSanFrancisco, 1992.

Carnes, Robin Dees, and Sally Craig. *Sacred Circles: A Guide to Creating Your Own Women's Spirituality Group*. San Francisco: HarperSanFrancisco, 1998.

Garfield, Charles, Cynthia Spring, and Sedonia Cahill. *Wisdom Circles: A Guide to Self-Discovery and Community-Building in Small Groups*. New York: Hyperion, 1998.

Keyes Jr., Ken. *The Hundredth Monkey*. Coos Bay, Oreg.: Vision Books, 1982 (o.p.).

Ryan, M. J., editor. *The Fabric of the Future: Women Visionaries of Today Illuminate the Path to Tomorrow*. Berkeley, Calif.: Conari Press, 1998.

Rosen, Ruth. *The World Split Open: How the Modern Women's Movement Changed America*. New York: Viking, 2000.

Sams, Jamie. *The Thirteen Original Clan Mothers*. San Francisco: HarperSanFrancisco, 1993.

Schaef, Anne Wilson. *Women's Reality: An Emerging Female System in a White Male Society*. San Francisco: Harper & Row, 1981, 1985.

―――. *Co-Dependence: Misunderstood—Mistreated*. San Francisco: Harper & Row, 1986.

Schaef, Anne Wilson. *When Society Becomes an Addict*. San Francisco: Harper & Row, 1987.

Sheldrake, Rupert. *A New Science of Life: The Hypothesis of Morphic Resonance*. Rochester, Vt.: Park Street Press, 1995. (Originally published by London: Blond & Briggs, 1981.)

―――. "Part 1. Mind, Memory and Archetype: Morphic Resonance and the Collective Unconscious," in *Psychological Perspectives*, 18:1 (Spring 1987): 9–25. "Part 2. Society, Spirit and Ritual," 18:2 (Fall 1987): 329–331. "Part 3. Extended Mind, Power and Prayer," 19:1 (Spring 1988): 64–78.

Organizations

Crone Chronicles (Crone Counsel Conferences), P.O. Box 81, Kelly, WY 80311–0081 (Ann Kreilkamp).

The Grandmother's Circle. P.O. Box 23, 36th St. Mail, 3728 East Indian School Road, Phoenix, AZ 85016. For information SASE Kit Wilson.

The Sacred Grove Women's Forest Sanctuary. P.O. Box 1692, Ross, CA 94957.

Women of Wisdom Foundation (annual Seattle Women's Spirituality Conferences) P.O. Box 30043, Seattle, WA 98103 (Kris Steinnes), www.womenofwisdom.org

Notes

1. Epigraph: from *The Grandmother's Circle*. P.O. Box 23, 36th St. Mail, 3728 East Indian School Road, Phoenix, AZ 85016.

2. Steinem, Gloria. *Moving Beyond Words* (New York: Simon & Schuster, 1994), 270.

3. Spiegel, David. "A Psychosocial Intervention and Survival Time of Patients with Metastatic Breast Cancer," *Advances: The Journal of Mind-Body Health*, 7:3 (Summer 1991): 12.

4. Underwood, Paula, "Clan Mothers in the Twenty-first Century," in *The Fabric of the Future*, M. J. Ryan, ed. (Berkeley, Calif.: Conari Press, 1998), 158.

5. Medicine Eagle, Brooke. *Buffalo Woman Comes Singing* (New York: Ballantine, 1991), 339–340.

6. Heise, L., Ellsberg, M., and Gottemoeller, M. *Ending Violence Against Women*. Population Reports, Series L, No. 11. Baltimore: Johns Hopkins University School of Public Health, Population Information Program, December 1999.

7. Ray, Paul H., and Sherry Ruth Anderson. *The Cultural Creatives* (New York: Harmony Books, 2000), p.14.

8. Ibid., p. 15.

Conclusion: This Is Act III

Sources

Erikson, Erik H. *The Life Cycle Completed: A Review*. New York: W. W. Norton, 1982.

Over the Hill, with Olympia Dukakis. Screenplay by Robert Caswell, directed by George Miller. New Line Cinema and Village Roadshow Pictures. New Line Home Video, 1993.

Notes

1. Eliot, T. S. "The Dry Salvages," *Four Quartets* (New York: Harcourt Brace Jovanovich, 1943, 1971), 45.

INDEX

academic expectations, and Athena, 137
Achilles, 11, 141
Act III, 195–204
activism and spirituality, 190–91
Adam and Eve, banishment of, 53
addiction: substance, 164, 179; process, 179;
   psychology of, 109
Adonis, 169
adoption, by childless women, 162
aegis, etiology of, 19
Aeschylus, 10, 16
affirmative action, xx
affluence, time of, 195–96
afterlife, questions about, 56
Age of Pericles, 16
aging: and declining faculties, 167;
   denial of, 126
AIDS, 181
Alchemical Goddess, 127, 128, 129–30
alchemists, medieval European, 169
alcoholism, 109
Alcoholics Anonymous, 164, 179–80
Allison, Ralph, 52
Alphabet Versus the Goddess, The, 40
Ama-no-Uzume. *See* Uzume
Amaterasu, myth of, 103–104
Amazing Grace, 34
Amenhotep III, 84
American Psychiatric Association, xx
American Woman, The, xix
Anath, 39
Anchises, 169
Ancient Mirrors of Womanhood, 103
Anderson, Sherry Ruth, 30, 35, 191
anima, xxi n
animus, xxi n
Aphrodite, xxi, xxvii, xxviii, 61, 65, 126, 128,
   129–30, 156, 168–74; alchemical power
   of, 130; as archetype, 170–71; birth of,
   168; as choicemaker, 171; as courtesan,
   171; crone- aged, 172–74; Cypriot
   sanctuaries of, 116; and dove, 117; drive
   for fulfillment in, 163–64; lovers of, 169;
   in marriage, 174; power of, 168; sensuality
   of, 172, 173; shadow side of, 172
"Aphrodite consciousness," 130
Apollo astronauts, 181
Apollo, 10, 61, 63; birth of, 132–33
archetype: of circle, 177; of creativity,
   171–72; of crone, 203; "enough is
   enough," 78, 98, 203; of eternal girl, 163;

of father's daughter, 13, 141, 142; of good
   mother, 117, 157–62; of huntress, xxi; of
   integration and inner wisdom, 68; of
   intuitive and psychic wisdom, 44–66; of
   Kali/Sekhmet, 90–92, 96–98; of lover, xxi;
   of meaning, 61–62; of mother, xxi, 57–62;
   of practical wisdom, 11, 203; of wife,
   152–56, of witch, 57. *See also* goddess
archetypes: activation of, xxi; bodhisattvas as,
   111; categories of, 127–31; as committee,
   xxiv–xxv; contrasexual, xxi n, defined, xxi,
   xxiv; inner conflict among, 125–26;
   qualities of, 127–31; relationship-oriented,
   128; as seeds, 201–202; woman's role and,
   126
Ares, 61, 169
Artemis, xxvii, 126, 132–39, 169;
   achievement focus of, 161; attributes of,
   133; crone-aged, qualities of, 134–35,
   136–37; as goddess of waxing moon, 48,
   132; Hestia as aunt of, 61; the huntress,
   xxi; image of, 134; lesbian, 135; lessons for,
   138; maiden aspect of, 132; and marriage,
   135; realm of, 132; as virgin goddess, 65,
   127, 128
Arthurian legend, 115
Asherah, as Great Goddess, 39–40
Ashtoreth, 39
Assumption of Mary, 118
At the Root of this Longing, 34
Ath-enna, 18
Athena, xxi, xxvii, 116, 126, 140–47, 169;
   achievement focus of, 161; and *aegis*,
   18–19; archetype, identification with,
   19–21; birth of, 8, 11, 140; crone-aged,
   143–46; defense of authority by, 141;
   Hestia as aunt of, 61; identification of with
   patriarchy, 10–12; image of as warrior, 140;
   logical women and, 141; means orientation
   of, 141; practical wisdom of, 203; in pre-
   women's movement era, 145; as urban
   resident, 144; as virgin goddess, 65, 127,
   128; wisdom, as goddess of, 11
authenticity: personal, 192;
   sanctuary for, 178
Avalokiteshvara, 111

Baal, 39
Babd, 95
Babylonian mythology, 38
Baldwin, Christina, 194

◣ HarperSanFrancisco  Quill

Books by Jean Shinoda Bolen:

GODDESSES IN EVERYWOMAN: *Powerful Archetypes in Women's Lives*
ISBN 0-06-057284-1 (paperback)

A classic work of female psychology that uses seven archetypal goddesses as a way of describing behavior patterns and personality traits is being introduced to the next generation of readers with a new introduction by the author.

GODDESSES IN OLDER WOMEN: *Archetypes in Women over Fifty*
ISBN 0-06-092923-5 (paperback)

This much-anticipated sequel to the bestselling classic *Goddesses in Everywoman* provides a new set of positive energies and potentials (known as archetypes in Jungian circles) for women in the third stage of their lives.

GODS IN EVERYMAN: *Archetypes That Shape Men's Lives*
ISBN 0-06-097280-7 (paperback)

Jean Shinoda Bolen turns her attention to the powerful inner patterns that shape men's personalities, careers, and personal relationships, demonstrating how men and women can gain an invaluable sense of wholeness and integration when what they do is consistent with who they are.

THE TAO OF PSYCHOLOGY: *Synchronicity and Self*
ISBN 0-06-250081-3 (paperback)

An exploration of the interrelationship between "meaningful coincidences" and the intuitive sense that we are part of some deep oneness with the universe, revealing important links between psychology and mysticism, right brain and left, the individual and the external world.

CROSSING TO AVALON: *A Woman's Midlife Pilgrimage*
ISBN 0-06-250272-7 (paperback)

Dr. Jean Shinoda Bolen's extraordinary memoir celebrates the pilgrimage that heralded her spiritual awakening and leads readers down the path of self-discovery. In this account of her journey to Europe in search of the sacred feminine, she reveals the mythological significance of the midlife search for meaning and renewal.